THE MEDIA HANDBOOK

The Media Handbook provides a practical introduction to the advertising media planning and buying processes. Emphasizing basic calculations and the practical realities of offering alternatives and evaluating the plan, this sixth edition reflects the critical changes in how advertising in various media is planned, bought, and sold by today's industry professionals.

Author Helen Katz looks at the larger marketing, advertising, and media objectives, and follows with an exploration of major media categories, covering paid, owned, and earned media forms, including digital media. She provides a comprehensive analysis of planning and buying, with a continued focus on how those tactical elements tie back to the strategic aims of the brand and the client.

Also available is a Companion Website that expands *The Media Handbook*'s content in an online forum. Here, students and instructors can find tools to enhance course studies such as flashcards, test questions, and PowerPoint slides.

With its emphasis on real-world industry practice, *The Media Handbook* provides an essential introduction to students in advertising, media planning, communication, and marketing. It serves as an indispensable reference for anyone pursuing a career in media planning, buying, and research.

Helen Katz is Senior Vice President and Global Research Director for Publicis Media. She has an extensive professional background in media research and has taught advertising and media planning at Michigan State University and the University of Illinois.

Routledge Communication Series

Jennings Bryant/Dolf Zillmann, Series Editors

Selected titles include:

Fearn-Banks
Crisis Communications: A Casebook Approach, Fifth Edition

Powell/Powell
Classroom Communication and Diversity: Enhancing Instructional Practice, Third Edition

Hollifield/Wicks/Sylvie/Lowrey
Media Management: A Casebook Approach, Fifth Edition

The Media Handbook

A Complete Guide to Advertising Media Selection, Planning, Research, and Buying

6TH EDITION

HELEN KATZ

Routledge
Taylor & Francis Group

NEW YORK AND LONDON

Please visit the companion website at
www.Routledge.com/cw/katz

Sixth edition published 2017
by Routledge
711 Third Avenue, New York, NY 10017

and by Routledge
2 Park Square, Milton Park, Abingdon, Oxon, OX14 4RN

Routledge is an imprint of the Taylor & Francis Group, an informa business

© 2017 Taylor & Francis

First edition published by NTC Business Book 1995

Fifth edition published by Routledge 2014

Library of Congress Cataloging-in-Publication Data
Names: Katz, Helen E. author.
Title: The media handbook : a complete guide to advertising media
    selection, planning, research, and buying / Helen Katz.
Description: Sixth edition. | New York : Routledge, 2017. | Series: Routledge
    Communication Series | Includes bibliographical references and index.
Identifiers: LCCN 2016015193 (print) | LCCN 2016019566 (ebook) |
    ISBN 9781138689152 (hardback) | ISBN 9781138689169 (pbk.) |
    ISBN 9781315537870 (ebook)
Subjects: LCSH: Advertising media planning. | Mass media and business. |
    Marketing channels.
Classification: LCC HF5826.5 .K38 2016 (print) | LCC HF5826.5 (ebook) |
    DDC 659—dc23

ISBN: 978-1-138-68915-2 (hbk)
ISBN: 978-1-138-68916-9 (pbk)
ISBN: 978-1-315-53787-0 (ebk)

Typeset in Minion
by Apex CoVantage, LLC

CONTENTS

DETAILED CONTENTS

FOREWORD

What you have in your hands is not just a text book on media, but rather a powerful lens into culture and change.

When I began a job in the media research department of Leo Burnett nearly 35 years ago (two decades later it would become Starcom), my assignment was to understand and build a case for a "new media" called cable television.

Today the headlines are filled with warnings about the death of the cable television model due to unbundling and streaming made possible by the Internet and new viewing behaviors enabled by mobile devices.

Google, a company that is less than 20 years old, has greater revenue than all the newspaper companies in the United States; and newspapers' existence, especially in the print medium, is being questioned. An idea called Facebook will soon reach 1.5 billion users, with more than 1 billion of them logging in daily. And another idea called Twitter has gone from being "the future" to being discussed as to whether it has a future.

Much as a goldfish lives in water, most of us are immersed in a world of media—we live amidst it. And just like water, it swirls and changes and flows around us and it impacts us and our behaviors impact it.

Media has intrinsically been linked to technology change. The printing press brought the newspaper and wireless brought radio. Today we live in a world of seismic and constant technology change and media are in flux. Also, in the old days, one could separate audio and image and word and video, but today when the *New York Times* sends virtual reality headsets to its print subscribers so they can experience the news and their CEO calls "native" advertising, where brands are incorporated into editorial content, "limitless," you know you are no longer in Kansas anymore!

Helen Katz is uniquely qualified to put together this unique document, which is both a testament to change in media and an illuminating guide to how to navigate it. She has the depth of experience and the knowledge of the science behind the field, and she also has the keen observation of an artist and the organizational mindset of a curator to truly reveal and educate.

This is the sixth edition of this pioneering and essential guide to anyone in the media industry or learning about the media industry. In time there may be no physical books (I really hope that day does not come), and the idea of an edition will be laughed at in a world of real-time updates, but I can assure you Helen Katz and her work will still guide the way.

Rishad Tobaccowala

Chief Strategist and Member of the Directoire+

Publicis Groupe

PREFACE

Welcome to the sixth edition of *The Media Handbook*. Yet again, the industry has changed since the fifth edition was published. Everything could be considered "digital media" now, with TV programs streamed to a tablet, music listened to via smartphone, print media consumed online, and billboards that change their messages every ten seconds. Brands have to work harder to gain consumers' attention amid the clutter of messages out there. They do so, increasingly, by owning or sponsoring the content in which they appear and through earning likes or shares or other types of socially derived responses. Advertisers and agencies spend more and more of their time analyzing the reams of data signals created from individuals' interactions with—and responses to—the brand messages, to the point where they can pinpoint with greater precision than ever before how advertising is, or is not, working.

But people are not machines. And advertising and media are not pure science. There is still a valuable art involved in understanding how media can best be used to communicate a brand's value and how and why people are using those media.

Even as the advertising and media worlds in which we live have changed, the purpose of *The Media Handbook* has not. This book is designed to provide a basic introduction to the media planning and buying process and to help today's college student understand how today's advertising media operate. For those already working in the advertising or media industries, whose responsibilities sometimes overlap with the media function, this book explains the role of media in total brand communications.

This edition starts out with a high-level view of advertising and media, moving from there to discussing the importance of the overall marketing and advertising objectives, including some key concepts and terms that are common in the industry. The next three chapters explore in detail each of the major platforms that brands can use to convey their messages to consumers, whether those are paid, owned, or earned. With each one, we look at the landscape for the medium, consumer usage and trends, and strategic ways it can be used to deliver effective advertising. The chapters that follow explain specific important media terms used in planning and buying, together with an outline of the buying process, audience measurement, and plan evaluation.

Media terms are defined when they are introduced so that, in the jargon-filled world of media acronyms, the reader will start to feel more comfortable in subsequent discussion of GRPs, DMAs, or BDIs. This book also includes numerous examples, both real and fictitious, in order to provide a better sense of how media planning and buying work in the real world for large and small companies. Examples of research studies, from both the industry and the academic world, are noted to give readers additional resources to go to for more in-depth information. At the end of the book, a selection of key resources is offered in the appendices for those who wish to find out more about a particular service or system.

While the advertising media world continues to change at seemingly exponential rates and brands have to try harder to connect with consumers, the life of the media planner, buyer, seller, or researcher is really as exciting as it has ever been. The opportunities to create new ways to reach audiences are infinite, and data and technology are liberating us from the more mundane tasks to devote more time and energy to developing insights and enhancing our understanding of how media work. *The Media Handbook* will act as your guide to the fundamentals of media planning and buying, providing a strong and practical foundation for whatever area of marketing and communications you are, or wish to be, in.

ACKNOWLEDGMENTS

My debt of gratitude to those who taught me what I know remains strong. On the industry side, my media research education began in 1989 at DDB Needham Worldwide, under the guidance of Kevin Killion, my first boss and ongoing friend and mentor. At Zenith Media in New York, I learned more about the nuts and bolts of media planning and buying from Wendy Marquardt and Peggy Green; at GM Planworks, I was hugely inspired by Jana O'Brien, as well as my clients at General Motors, Michael Browner, and Betsy Lazar. And since 2005, in a global research role at Starcom Mediavest Group, and now Publicis Media, both Kate Sirkin and Tracey Scheppach have enabled me to continue to learn more and challenge the status quo, making my work as rewarding and enjoyable as it could possibly be. Thanks are also due to my many colleagues who help me understand the ever-changing media business.

My academic mentors were equally key to my success: Kim Rotzoll, Steve Helle, Kent Lancaster, and Bruce Vanden Bergh always made me think harder, even as they taught me the fundamentals of research, while my colleagues Wei-Na Lee and T. Bettina Cornwell have supported me both personally and professionally throughout my career. My Routledge editor, Linda Bathgate, has made the task of writing and updating this book one of sheer pleasure, while my former intern and Starcom research colleague, Brock Wright, continues to do an outstanding job of creating the content on the *Handbook*'s website.

Since the time I wrote the first edition of this book, I have not only witnessed the dramatic changes in the media industry, but I have also been privileged to see how my own family has grown up. My three daughters, Stephanie, Caroline, and Vanessa, are the most inspirational people in my life, so I happily dedicate this book to them.

INTRODUCTION

This book is deliberately designed as a media handbook. It will not tell you every last detail about each individual medium, nor will it go into great depth on nonmedia advertising elements, such as the creative message or the consumer research that goes on behind the scenes, though it will show you how the consumer must remain at the center of all you do in media. What you will get by the end of the book is a complete picture of how media planning, buying, and research work. You will see what each function entails and how they fit together with each other and within the framework of the marketing mix. You will know enough by the end of this book to be able to create your own media plan or undertake a TV or digital buy. Even if you are not directly responsible for either of those tasks, a greater understanding of how media fit into the marketing picture will help you communicate with those who do such work. Each chapter builds on and works off the preceding ones, although once you have been through them all, it is designed to be very easy for you to refer to specific tasks or concepts at a later date. At the end of each chapter, you will see a checklist of questions that you should ask yourself if you actually have to fulfill the objective of that particular chapter (such as setting objectives or evaluating the plan). At the end of the book, you will find a list of additional resources you can turn to for help in media planning, buying, and research.

CHAPTER 1

WHAT IS MEDIA?

It's 7:30 a.m. You wake up and check texts, Twitter, Facebook, and Instagram. You look at the latest news and weather on your phone apps. At breakfast (while possibly still engaged in those activities), you might watch some of the morning news on TV or ESPN sports highlights on your tablet, which are "brought to you" by Budweiser. On the way to work or class, you watch clips from last night's talk shows on your mobile phone, with branded video ads preceding each one.

In that brief time span, you have been immersed in today's world of media. That world includes various media platforms for which advertisers *pay*: radio, Internet, television, mobile, newspapers, magazines, and outdoor billboards. Then there are segments of those media in which advertisers insert their brands less overtly, to *own* the content. Last, there are social media forms such as Facebook and Twitter where advertisers try to *earn* the trust and attention of the consumer. In all of these instances, when you listen to music on the radio, go online to update your Facebook status, watch a TV show, or read your favorite magazine, you also receive information through a means of communication or a *medium*. Given this broad definition, you can see that there are in fact hundreds of different media available, such as direct mail, TVs at the health club, coupons, stadium signs, tray liners in airport security bins, and samples handed out at the doctor's office. All of these, and many other media, offer us ways of communicating information to an audience. As advertising media professionals, we are interested in looking at media as means of conveying a specific kind of information—an *advertising message*—about a product or service to consumers.

Media play a very important roles in our lives. Media help fulfill two basic needs: They *inform* and they *entertain*. We turn to media when we want to hear the latest world news or what happened in financial markets, for instance. We also look to media to fill our evenings and weekends with escapist fare to get us out of our everyday, humdrum routines. Television entertains us with movies, dramas, comedies, reality shows, and sports. Radio offers us a wide variety of music, talk, and entertainment. We turn to magazines to find out more about our favorite hobbies and interests. Newspapers, whether in print or digital form, help us keep up with the world around us. And digital media, in all its varied forms, provides limitless information and a means of shared entertainment and communication.

The informational role of the media is perhaps best illustrated by considering what happens during an international crisis, such as the Paris terrorist attacks in 2015 or national disasters such as mass shootings in Aurora, Colorado, or San Bernadino, California. On each occasion, millions of people turned to their computers or mobile devices to get breaking news updates, turned to social media to hear that friends or relatives were all safe, or turned on their TVs and radios for ongoing news coverage. Then, they likely followed up the next day or week with newspapers and magazines for more in-depth coverage and follow-up stories.

Media also affect our lives through their entertainment function. Television situation comedies such as *All in the Family* and *Mary Tyler Moore* not only reflected what was happening in U.S. society in the 1970s, but also helped influence attitudes and behaviors concerning the issues of race and equality. Stories appearing in magazines such as *People* or *InStyle* let us know what is happening in other people's lives, both famous and ordinary. And we take our mobile devices with us everywhere so that we can receive the latest sports scores or watch a video while we relax.

A third primary function of media is to socialize. While the informational and entertainment aspects offer "one to many" disseminations of content, the various forms of social media bring people together in a "one to one" way, whether that is you sharing pictures or videos through Snapchat and Vine or putting a favorite recipe on a Pinterest board.

WHAT MEDIA ARE OUT THERE?

Historically, the world of media was broadly divided into two types: print and electronic. Print media included magazines and newspapers, while electronic media covered radio, television, and the Internet. Other media types were not quite so easily categorized. Thus, outdoor billboards were generally defined as a *print* medium, while out-of-home

Exhibit 1.1 Old Definitions of Media: Print versus Electronic

Print Media	Electronic Media
Magazines: consumer, farm, business	Television: broadcast, cable, syndication, spot
Newspapers: national, local	Radio: network, local
Outdoor billboards	Internet
Direct mail	Mobile
Yellow pages	

Exhibit 1.2 New Media Classification: Paid, Owned, and Earned

Paid	Owned	Earned
TV	Product placement	Facebook "Likes"
Radio	Brand website	Twitter mentions
Newspapers	Custom events	Brand conversations
Magazines	Sponsorship	Organic search
Outdoor	Brand integration	Public relations
Display		
Paid search		
Online video		

options such as transit ads or stadium signage have been variously classified as nontraditional, alternative, or ambient media. Exhibit 1.1 provides a list of each type.

In today's shifting media world, however, these distinctions are fast becoming obsolete. Is a newspaper that is read digitally in the print or electronic column? Where does one place mobile phones or word of mouth or brands that are integrated into TV shows? The distinctions that advertisers are now making are in the ways that their messages are delivered. That is, is the message *paid for* or does the advertiser *own* it or is the brand *earning* its impact? These are the distinctions that will be used here and are shown in Exhibit 1.2.

THE ROLE OF MEDIA IN BUSINESS

It is important to emphasize here that the focus of this book is commercial media. The communications media we will be talking about are not there simply to beautify the landscape or fill up the pages of a newspaper; they are designed to sell products to customers. Of course, there are also media that convey information but are not commercial in intent. *Consumer Reports* is a magazine that does not carry any advertising. Neither do public television and radio (except for sponsorships, which we'll talk about later). Google Maps and airline safety instructions are informative, but they are not advertisements in and of themselves (even if they can carry advertisements within or near them). And books certainly communicate information to their readers. Here, however, we will concentrate on those media that currently accept advertising messages. It is worth emphasizing the word *currently*. Twenty-five years ago, you did not find commercial messages at supermarkets, schools, doctors' offices, or ski slopes. Today, advertisers can reach people in all of these places. Even novels are not immune. A popular British author wrote Bulgari Jewelers into her fictional story in 2000, for which the company paid her. People are paid to cover their vehicles, or sometimes even parts of their bodies, in sponsored ads. Companies are routinely paying bloggers to write about their products without the authors publicly acknowledging the payment. While these ventures have been criticized by the public, that does not mean other similar attempts will not be made again in the future. What is true today may very well change by tomorrow. The generic term *media* (or *medium* in the singular) means different things to different people. To Joe, who is sitting at home on a Friday evening, *media* means whatever TV shows he watches or magazines he leafs through or games he plays on his phone. For the local Honda car dealer, *media* provide ways to advertise this week's deals on CRVs and Civics. And the Podunk Electric Utility Company uses *media* to remind its customers that they can get free replacement light bulbs.

Strictly speaking, a *medium* may be defined as a means by which something is accomplished, conveyed, or transferred. This deliberately broad definition means that consumer media would cover everything from handbills passed out in parking lots, to "for sale" signs taped to lampposts, to the 10-page advertising supplement that fell out of the last copy of *Money* magazine you read, to digital billboards flashing in Times Square, to the Toyota vehicles that contestants drive around in on Lifetime's *Project Runway*.

How the Media Business Has Changed

The media business can be thought of as an ocean. Each media type starts out as a few drops of water (e.g., individual newspapers or radio stations). They flourish and grow, and as more drops form, they start to combine together, creating ponds that turn into streams, rivers, and oceans. That has a certain kind of predictability to it. It starts out small, then grows as more and more companies enter the field. Over time, a handful of these companies begin buying out their competitors, and the industry consolidates to the point where only a few extremely large players remain. This cycle occurs in all media at some point. One of the largest media-related consolidations in recent years was the 2011 purchase of NBCUniversal (itself a merger of TV networks and movie studios) by Comcast, the cable company, bringing together content creators and distributors under one roof.

But what does media industry consolidation have to do with advertising? Why does it matter that the TV network NBC also owns the Bravo and USA Network, and Fandango movie site/app, and the Spanish-language network Telemundo? How is a media plan or buy affected by the fact that the Tribune Company owns WGN TV and radio stations and the *Chicago Tribune* newspaper? Well, what happens is that, while consumers are being offered more and more media choices (more radio stations streaming online, more magazine apps, more TV shows they want to watch on their mobile devices), the advertisers trying to reach them find that they must negotiate with fewer and fewer companies selling advertising space or time. This paradox is something we shall return to throughout this book.

MEDIA VERSUS COMMUNICATIONS

In the business world, we think of a medium as a way to transfer and convey information about goods or services from the producer to the consumer, who is a potential buyer of that item. There are various ways to accomplish that in business besides using radio, television, or magazines. Product or company publicity, sales brochures, or exhibits can all be useful ways of conveying information to potential buyers. You should note that throughout this book, we will refer to all potential buyers as *consumers*, but we should really think of them as *us*. One of the biggest dangers in media planning or buying is, as we shall learn in Chapter 3, categorizing viewers or listeners or web users into broad consumer groups (such as "adults 18–49") that make it all too easy to forget that, in the infamous words of one of the founders of the advertising industry, David Ogilvy, "that person is your wife." And, as we shall also learn in subsequent chapters, technology has enabled advertisers to use mass media in an individualized way to reach their "true targets" (e.g., sending dog food company advertising only to homes with dogs) in ways that bring television full circle to a more personalized, one-to-one form of media. Today there are ways, which are sometimes considered controversial, to deliver ads based on the products purchased or programs watched.

Although this book is titled *The MEDIA Handbook,* it is important to think of media in the broadest terms—as communications that may be paid for directly by the advertiser, owned by integrating the brand into the content, or earned by giving people the opportunity to make a direct connection with the brand. Today, most agencies look for integrated ways to make contact with consumers across all these media, whether that is paying to display their brand of soft drink in *The Voice*, sponsoring a blimp flying over a popular baseball field in the summer, or encouraging consumers to "like" Starbucks on Facebook. The goal of these disparate efforts is to surround the target audience with a holistic campaign that presents them with the same message about the brand in various creative ways.

THE ROLE OF MEDIA IN CONSUMERS' LIVES

As our lives grow increasingly busy and demanding, and as technology moves ahead with ever-more sophisticated ways to improve our lives, it seems that media are playing a more and more important role in what we do, where we go, or how we behave. As the example at the opening of this chapter suggested, many of us are constantly connected to some form of media from the minute we wake up in the morning, whether that is paid media (radio, TV, digital) or earned media (social). The number of interactions with media during the day becomes staggering when you stop to think about it. Most likely, within the past 24 hours, you have used several of the following types of media: radio, newspapers, television, magazines, digital, mobile, out of home, or social.

When you sit down to watch TV and see a commercial for a brand that then appears in the magazine you are looking through and on the app you are browsing, and it is mentioned again in that night's evening newscast because the brand is a major sponsor of a sporting event, you generally don't think about the effort that went into coordinating all of those elements. In fact, if the seams between them are too obvious, then something probably isn't working right! While you, as a member of the reading or listening or viewing audience, are interested primarily in the particular program or app or publication, the medium is interested in you as a potential buyer, offering you up to advertisers who wish to talk to you.

The role of media in conveying information through advertising messages is not something consumers generally consider. Indeed, when they do think about it, they are likely to complain about being inundated by commercial messages! Yet despite the fact that no one has yet proven definitively and conclusively quite "how advertising works," businesses continue to believe in its power, as evidenced by the estimated $141 billion spent in the U.S. on advertising in 2014.

HOW MEDIA WORK WITH ADVERTISING

Advertising in the media performs the roles of informing, connecting, and entertaining. It informs us of the goods and services that are available for us to purchase and use. And, along the way, it often entertains us with some humorous, witty, or clever use of words and pictures. Then it can connect us with friends and strangers. For example, let's say you have created a new carbonated fruit juice that you want to introduce to the marketplace. Friends and neighbors have tasted it, and they think it's original and tasty. You have talked to several distributors and manufacturers, and they have some interest in producing it. Now, however, the question arises of what to do next. How do you inform people you don't know personally about this wonderful new product?

This is where the media can help. You could place an advertisement on TV announcing this brand new drink, which you've named Fruitola. Perhaps you'd take out magazine ads in cooking and nutrition magazines that show the product and explain its health benefits over soda. You might create a long-form commercial message, or infomercial, that appears when consumers watch video on demand on TV. You'd want a website for your new product that allows people to purchase online directly from the site or tells them where they can find it. Your Facebook page and Twitter hashtag could generate social awareness and enhance familiarity with the new product. Your message, that "Fruitola refreshes with fruit," would then be disseminated to an audience of hundreds, or possibly thousands, depending on your location. You might also generate additional publicity by persuading a national or local celebrity to endorse the product. Or perhaps you would decide to solicit help from influential media bloggers, offering them a free sample in exchange for their online discussion of the new drink. Whatever form of communication you use, all involve sending a message through a medium of one kind or another.

Again, it is important to keep in mind that we are talking of media in the broadest sense. So in trying to promote your Fruitola drink, your TV, print, and digital presence can show people what the product looks like and give more details on its health benefits. Then, you might sponsor a local food festival as a public relations effort to heighten awareness of the product and let people sample it. You could send out press releases in advance to notify the media of the event and thereby generate additional publicity both for the event and for your drink. You could offer retailers a special deal, such as contributing funds to the ads that they run (an advertising allowance), if they will promote the product in their weekly newspaper or radio ads. You might also arrange for samples to be handed out on college campuses or in health clubs so that people can learn more about Fruitola. Each medium fulfills a slightly different role, but by advertising the product in a wide variety of media, your overall message—that "Fruitola refreshes with fruit"—is conveyed clearly and consistently.

Media advertising also performs another vital function. It helps offset the cost of the media communication itself to consumers. If we did not

Exhibit 1.3 Top Global Advertisers in 2014

	Millions of Dollars	*Percentage of Top Ten Total*
Procter & Gamble	$10,125	23.4%
Unilever	$7,394	17.1%
L'Oreal	$5,264	12.2%
Coca-Cola Co.	$3,279	7.6%
Toyota Motor Corp.	$3,185	7.4%
Volkswagen	$3,171	7.3%
Nestle	$2,930	6.8%
General Motors Co.	$2,849	6.6%
Mars Inc.	$2,569	5.9%
McDonald's Corp.	$2,494	5.8%
	$43,260	

Source: Advertising Age, Global Marketers 2014, December 7, 2015, 24.

have commercials on television or radio or in digital media, the cost of the informational or educational or social content would have to come through sponsorships, taxes, or government monies. Public broadcasting in the U.S. derives most of its income through semi-annual pledge drives, during which viewers and listeners are asked to give money to pay for the services. Government funding provides additional revenues. But even here, more and more public broadcasting radio and television stations are accepting restricted forms of paid commercials as long as they are image-oriented and not hard-sell.

To give you a sense of how much companies spend to advertise, Exhibit 1.3 shows who the top global advertisers were in 2014.

TASKS IN MEDIA

The broad field of advertising media can be broken down into four primary tasks:

1. Planning how best to use media to convey the advertising message to the target consumer (the *media planner*)
2. Buying media space and time for the message (the *media buyer*)
3. Selling that space or time to the advertiser (the *media seller*)
4. Analyzing the relationship between consumers, media, and the brands that advertise to them in those media (the *media researcher*).

Most large companies handle the media planning and buying functions through an advertising agency. Smaller firms will usually handle this task themselves, through their marketing director or public relations coordinator. As the roles of each person have expanded and/or changed in recent years, so have the titles. The planner is sometimes called an *integrated communications specialist*. The buyer may be referred to now as an *activation expert*. Media research now involves more data analytics (statistical evaluation of vast quantities of data) while also managing both primary and secondary research on media audiences. But regardless of title, the fundamental role of the planner is to decide where and when the message should be placed, how often, and at what cost. The plan is then implemented by the media buyer, who negotiates with the media providers themselves to agree on the space and time needed and to determine or confirm where the ad will appear. That buyer will, of course, be dealing with the salesperson at the media company, whose job it is to sell as much advertising space or time as possible (or, in the case of branded entertainment, co-develop the content that the brand can own). Throughout this process, the researcher offers insights into how to make media have the greatest impact on the consumer's brand decisions and measures how well it worked.

SUMMARY

The focus of *The Media Handbook* is the role of media in communicating and conveying information about products and services to potential consumers. It is designed to explore this media world in detail, looking at the changing structure of the industry itself and the various types of communication that are available (paid, owned, earned) and how to use these forms in day-to-day business. The aim here is to provide a better understanding of what media are and how they can best be used to enhance the advertising message. Consumers choose from a wide array of media in their daily lives, turning to them for information, entertainment, and connection. Advertising in the media also helps to offset the costs of production and distribution. Any company that advertises in the media must deal either directly or indirectly with the planning and buying of advertising space or airtime. This handbook will show you how to do this efficiently and successfully.

CHAPTER 2

MEDIA IN THE MARKETING CONTEXT

Although this book is designed to take the media specialist through the planning and buying of media, those functions do not occur in a vacuum. Both media and advertising are part of the bigger picture of the world of marketing. The primary goal of marketing is to increase sales and profits. To return to our earlier example where we were wondering how to market our fruit-based carbonated drink, Fruitola, we considered many elements beyond which media to use. To market any product effectively involves not simply advertising it, but also figuring out how much to charge for it, where to distribute it, and how to manufacture it. In marketing jargon, these four critical elements are known as the four Ps: product, price, place (distribution), and promotion. Although your job as a media specialist does not necessarily involve making the decisions on all of these criteria, it is critical that you have a clear understanding of how they work and, more importantly, how they can impact your media decisions and strategy. This chapter will guide you through these four marketing basics.

In order to sell anything, you must first have a product or service. You have to decide how much you need to charge for it (the price) so that you can make a profit. You must also figure out how and where the product will be made available to people (place, or distribution). And last, but not least, you must consider how you will let potential buyers know what you are offering (promotion). Within that last category, there are several key channels of communication: advertising, personal selling, sales promotion, direct marketing, event marketing, and publicity. All can be thought of as media, or ways of conveying information to potential buyers. You can see how these elements work in Exhibit 2.1.

One of the most important things to remember here is that the arrows move in many directions. Almost any decision you make concerning media will have an impact on something else in the marketing mix. For example, if you decided to advertise on network television, you would have to ensure that your product was in fact available throughout the country. Or if you chose to concentrate your advertising efforts during holiday periods (Memorial Day, Independence Day, and so on), you might consider lowering your price at that time to boost sales even further.

The task of the media planner is to consider all of the marketing information available on the product and to use that information to determine how best to reach the target audience with the brand message through advertising media. In this way, the media plan can be thought of as the pivot point, or hub, of the overall marketing plan (Exhibit 2.2).

Exhibit 2.1 The Marketing Mix

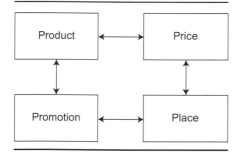

Exhibit 2.2 Moving toward the Media Plan

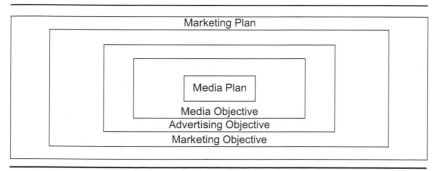

GETTING TO KNOW THE CONSUMER

There are two critical pieces of information that a media specialist needs to know in order to successfully market a product. The first is an understanding of how your consumers view and use your product or service. The second is how they view and use different media types. While much of the former has been developed over many years and is considered fairly traditional market research, the latter is a relatively new phenomenon within the media world, applying market or consumer research principles and processes to enhance the understanding of how and why people use media. First, this chapter will delve into the consumer–brand relationship, and then we will begin to explore the consumer–media relationship.

Consumers and Brands

First, you must know more about the brand and the product category. A *brand* is the individual product or service that you are trying to sell. It can be thought of as the name on the label. So Campbell's tomato soup is a brand, as is their chicken noodle soup or their clam chowder variety. The *product category* could either be defined as all brands of tomato soup or all kinds of soup. In the case of a service, such as insurance, the product category could be one type of insurance, such as life or home or auto, or all types. The brand would be one particular company such as Allstate, State Farm, or Geico.

One way to think about brands is to consider your own behavior. When you go to the grocery store, you are usually not thinking in terms of product categories or brands. More likely, you are thinking about buying a container of Minute Maid orange juice, three boxes of Kraft macaroni and cheese dinners, or a box of Kellogg's Frosted Flakes cereal. Similarly, when you have to decide which restaurant to go to, you will not categorize them the way marketers do, into quick service, family style, or steakhouses, but will instead think in terms of the types of food—Chinese, Mexican, Indian, and so forth. And within those groups, you will probably categorize them by geography, thinking of the specific restaurants by area.

What we need to know as marketers and media specialists, however, is how the consumer decides *which* brands and products to buy, as well as the process he or she goes through when purchasing an item. This will vary depending on the type of product. While a consumer might pick up any brand of floor cleaner, the decision process she goes through to select the car she drives will take far longer because there are more elements to consider and often a higher price involved. Understanding these decision processes will help you decide which media might best be used both to reach your target and to convey the desired message at the right time. For selling your carbonated fruit drink, you could probably use a traditional medium such as magazines to increase awareness of your product along with a digital effort, such as paid search when people are looking for nutritional or diet and fitness information. A company trying to sell a more complex product, however, such as a car or OLED television, will use a wide variety of communication forms to sell its product.

Here, we will take a general look at how consumers view and use brands. From there, we can establish some foundations for the media plan. We will start this by going back into the past and looking at what has happened in the marketplace both to the brand and to the product category in which we are interested.

In looking at how consumers use brands, we must answer several key questions. How much do consumers already know about the brand (brand and advertising awareness)? When, where, and how often do they buy it (purchase dynamics)?

What Do People Know about the Brand?

People have the opportunity to be exposed to at least 5,000 ads every week, so it isn't surprising that they don't remember many of them. Studies routinely show that the percentage of people who can accurately remember the name of the brand they last saw advertised on television is astoundingly low (typically less than 10 percent). Indeed, TV tuning data in homes with DVRs indicate that at least half of the ads that appear in prime time are fast-forwarded because people look to avoid them altogether. And although we talk about "great" ads that we saw on television last night or saw online, we are probably unlikely to remember the brand that was being advertised. Is Jennifer Garner the spokeswoman for Capital One or Bank of America? Does Jennifer Aniston promote Aveeno or Garnier beauty products? In today's increasingly competitive marketing climate, consumers are also likely to be exposed to more than one brand name in an ad. This *comparison advertising* is extremely common in categories such as pain relievers, automobiles, and detergents. But while your brand, Brand A, emphasizes how much better it is than Brand B, will your target audience remember A or B?

How the Media Specialist Gets to Know Consumers and Brands

Finding out how aware your consumers are of your brand and its advertising is quite straightforward, though it is not without pitfalls. The easiest way to do this is through a survey (mail, telephone, online, or in person) in which you simply ask people what they remember about certain ads. You can do this in one of two ways: either *unaided*, where no prompts or assistance are provided, or *aided*, where you offer some kind of memory aid, such as mentioning something from the advertisement or giving an actual list of brand names and asking for further information on the advertising. The unaided method demands more from consumers, asking them to tap deeper into their memories to recall the information you are seeking. With the aided method, you are basically asking people to recognize a brand and/or advertisement when it is placed before them and then prompting them for additional information about it.[1]

There are other issues to keep in mind with brand-awareness research. The most important is that you cannot expect complete accuracy. That is, there is always the danger with any kind of memory check that you will not get full information from the people you survey. Obviously, the longer the time between when people see an ad and when they are questioned about it, the less they will remember about it. Human memory is highly fallible. They may attribute pieces of one ad to another ad or recite a list of brand attributes from Brand A that really belong to Brand B. So if you do test consumer awareness of your ads, be sure that you keep in mind the possibility of inaccuracies in the responses.

In addition, you must remember that all of these responses are what consumers *claim* to recognize or recall. Even if you give people a questionnaire to fill out on their own, they may not respond with their real feelings or thoughts. They might not want to offend the interviewer or admit how they really feel, or for whatever reason they may not want to tell the truth. For instance, they may have only a vague recollection of your brand's name, but they write down that they are very familiar with it.

Having said that, awareness checks do play a vital role in letting you know more about how your consumers interact with the brand and its advertising. If no one can recall your brand name after it has been advertised on television every day for the past year, then you have a problem. It could be the message isn't convincing at all, or it could be you are advertising it in the wrong medium. Perhaps people can recall the brand name very easily, but nothing about the advertising has stuck in their minds. Many companies conduct brand *tracking research* where they conduct consumer surveys on a regular (weekly, monthly, or quarterly) basis to see to what degree people are aware of their brand and its advertising. This kind of data becomes very useful for monitoring not only the health of the brand over time, but also for building statistical models that show the relationship between the media dollars spent and the results obtained. We will cover this in more detail in Chapter 7.

The goal of increasing brand awareness should not be understated. It is commonly accepted that without consumer awareness of your brand, even the most spectacular media plan will be unlikely to generate many sales. People are far more likely to purchase a brand whose name they have heard before than one about which they have no information. There are many companies that conduct this kind of research. Some of the larger ones are listed in Appendix B.

If you want to probe further into people's responses, you can find out more through focus groups, which are groups of five to ten people who are interviewed together by a moderator. They are probed for their beliefs, attitudes, or feelings toward a given brand or product category and its advertising to help in the development of the creative message as well as the marketing and media strategies.

Another more in-depth technique for understanding consumers is the use of ethnography. Developed in sociology and anthropology, the technique involves close observation of what consumers are doing. This may include visiting their homes to watch them prepare a meal (for a brand such as Kraft salad dressing) or spending a few hours with them in the gym (for a brand such as Nike sports shoes). The idea is to see up close how the brand or product category really fits into people's lives.

The Consumer Decision Process

Many research studies have been conducted over the years to demonstrate the decision process that a consumer typically goes through when buying a routine product. In its simplest form, this process has three steps:

1. Think.
2. Feel.
3. Do.

The belief here is that people must first *think* about the item (i.e., be aware of it and know it exists). Then they must then develop some kind of attitude or *feeling* toward it (i.e., like it and prefer it to others), and finally, they must take some action with regard to it (decide on it and actually buy it—the *do* part of the model).

The process is in fact far more involved than this. We can break these three stages down further, coming up with eight stages the consumer goes through in buying a product or service. These are:

1. Need
2. Awareness
3. Preference
4. Search

5. Selection
6. Purchase
7. Use
8. Satisfaction.

To begin with, the consumer must first have a *need* to fulfill. He or she then becomes *aware* of the brands available to satisfy that need. After that, several brands are considered acceptable, and a *preference* is developed for one or more of them. The consumer will then *search* for the brand(s) desired and make a *selection* of one over the others. A specific brand is *purchased* and *used*. Finally, the level of *satisfaction* with that purchase helps determine whether that brand is bought on a future occasion. This is discussed in detail in the next chapter.

Of course, in reality, life isn't always as simple. There are occasions (and products) where people think about a product, buy it, and only at that point do they develop attitudes toward it. This is especially true for new product launches, where consumers have not had a chance to develop emotional bearings for the brand or category. Another point to keep in mind is that the decision process can sometimes get stalled at a point before purchase. In our Fruitola example, your target may be made aware of the brand, decide that they'd like to buy it but be unable to find it in their grocery store, and give up. Or they could try it and decide they actually prefer to stick with Coca-Cola's Sprite product.

A more recent theory of decision making, called *behavioral economics*, posits that consumers do not behave as rationally as we would like to think they do. Moreover, they cannot fully explain why they take certain actions or hold particular beliefs related to brands or services. Therefore, marketers should pay more attention to the actions taken (the *behavior* part) and ask questions in ways that they can be accurately answered.[2]

How the Consumer Buys Products

One of the main drawbacks to using surveys or holding discussions with consumers about how they buy is that they are telling you what they *think* they do, which may be very different from what they actually do in real life. Moreover, measuring brand awareness and advertising recall often ends up being a poor predictor of sales. So in addition to looking at awareness, or the top of the decision tree, you should also pay attention to what is happening at the bottom of the tree with the purchase cycle. When are people buying your product? How much is bought? Is there some kind of seasonality to their purchases? All of this information will prove to be critical in planning and buying your media and will have a major impact on how and when you schedule your ads.

When Do People Buy?

The answer to this question is more complex than it seems at first. You might say "Well, they buy my product all the time." But, if you look more closely at purchase behavior, you will probably detect some kind of pattern. While people are buying houses "all the time," they are more likely to do so when interest rates are low and prices are depressed. People buy cars "all the time," but sales typically increase when the new models come into the showrooms in the fall, and more sales occur in the second half of the month than in the first. There is even a timing component to the purchase of everyday items. Sales of cheese are higher on the weekends and around paydays because that is when people have more money to go shopping. Moving companies are busiest between May and October because that is when most people change their residence. Greeting card sales go up before every holiday (whether traditional, such as Christmas, or "Hallmark holidays," such as Grandparents' Day and Boss's Day).

If you know when consumers are most likely to buy your product, you can time your media advertising to take advantage of that purchase cycle. For major purchases in particular, you might also want to consider when people are *thinking about* buying. This might occur several weeks or even months before they make the actual purchase. Mr. and Mrs. Fleischmann might buy a new Toro lawnmower in May, but they will probably start to think about which one to get several months prior to that. This provides you with a valuable opportunity to get your brand's message to the Fleischmanns early in their decision-making process.

How Much Do They Buy?

The size of consumer purchases is another important element of the purchase cycle for the media specialist to know. That is, what proportion of your brand's sales comes from each size of the product? Coca-Cola offers numerous sizes of its sodas, such as 12-ounce cans, 2-liter bottles, and six packs of glass bottles. The company needs to know which one is most popular. Do most people buy their soda in plastic bottles, glass bottles, or cans? Does Coke sell three times as many cans as bottles, perhaps suggesting that this is where the majority of messages should focus? It turns out that, according to GfK MRI, nearly 50 percent of Coca-Cola, among those who drink regular cola, is consumed in plastic bottles, with around 8 percent from glass bottles and the remainder from cans. This kind of information is not only important for production and distribution purposes, but it can also play a key role in media planning; the users of each size are likely to be different kinds of people with different media habits. The casual drinker who picks up the individual can is more likely to be young, married with

Exhibit 2.3 Profile of Regular Coca-Cola Glass Bottle Buyer

Ethnic minority
Aged 18–34 years
Large markets (A county)
Cell phone only
Young children
Lower household income
Watch *Family Guy* (syndication)
Watch *Vampire Diaries*
Listen to urban radio
Listen to soft adult contemporary radio
Read *US Weekly* magazine
Read *Outside* magazine

Source: GfK MRI, Doublebase 2015.

children, and live in the West, while those who purchase the plastic bottles are fairly similar demographically but are more likely to be female and living along the East Coast. A profile of the Coca-Cola glass-bottle buyer is shown in Exhibit 2.3. This group prefers to watch programs such as *Family Guy* and *Vampire Diaries*, listen to soft contemporary or urban radio formats, and read *US Weekly* or *Outside* magazine. Based on these media preferences, your plan for the glass buyer may well differ from that for the can or plastic bottle purchaser.

LOOKING AT THE MARKETPLACE

Once you know how consumers view and use your brand, the next step for the media specialist is to examine what has been happening to that brand in the marketplace in recent times. Given this information on past efforts to sell your product, you can decide whether to continue along the same path or try something different in terms of your media planning and buying. Examining the marketplace involves doing an analysis of historical data on both the brand and the product category. As the famous philosopher George Santayana said, those who do not learn from the past are condemned to repeat it.

Some of the basic questions the media specialist might ask include the following:

- How long has this brand been available?
- How successful has it been throughout its history?
- How has it been positioned in the past?
- What do you know about the company that makes this brand?

You can think of this as genealogical work—trying to dig up as much "family background" on the brand as possible. You may find that the company has been in business for 150 years, suggesting possible leverage to be gained by emphasizing in the message the long heritage the brand possesses and even placing it in media vehicles that have also been around for a long time. Or perhaps the company has been around forever but is now moving in a different direction and is starting to explore new opportunities, suggesting the use of new or different media. Altoids, for example, for many years just made mints. It then started expanding its product line: first, it created sour candy; then, it began moving into the highly competitive chewing gum arena. Despite the fierce competition, the brand captured several market share points because it responded to the underlying consumer desire for stronger-tasting foods to eat between meals. But the new product was targeted toward different groups of consumers, which, in turn, resulted in a need for more diverse and/or more selective media. While its traditional mint brand continued to have a strong outdoor billboard and print presence, reaching a broad audience, the gum had more appeal to teens and young adults who might not have seen the ads before. The company developed its digital and social media presence to appeal to the teen/young adult user base for its gum, with a Facebook page to encourage comments and brand interactions.

WHAT ARE THE COMPETITORS UP TO?

In doing an historical analysis of the brand, you must also deal with competitive issues. That is, you should not only explore and uncover as much marketing and media information as possible about your *own* brand, but you should also to do the same for *all* the brands against which you compete or plan to compete. The marketing part of these issues may be divided into three main areas:

1. Product category trends
2. Brand trends and share of market
3. Brand's share of requirements.

Product Category Trends

Whether your brand has been available for half a century, two years, or is about to be launched, one of the most important preplanning considerations for the media specialist is what is happening in your product category. If you are creating a media plan for the manufacturer of a Cannondale mountain bike, you would want to know whether sales of bicycles are increasing, decreasing, or flat. That will immediately influence your media budget and who you choose to target and how you will go about trying to reach them. In some instances, in order to determine how the category has fared, you will have to decide what your "category" really is. If you are selling a granola bar, then it might seem obvious that it belongs in the cookie category. But perhaps this is a protein-filled bar designed for endurance athletes that belongs more appropriately in the diet and health food classification. Does a yogurt drink fit better into yogurt products or milk drinks? And what about flash drives? Do they belong with software or in the office supplies section, along with pens and paper?

How you define your product category will determine not only your assessment of the strengths or weaknesses of that category, but also the direction and potential marketing and media strategies you employ for your particular brand. To take the yogurt drink example, if you decide it is part of the health foods category, you might want to advertise in health magazines and sponsor local races where you can offer free samples. As a milk drink, however, you may prefer to advertise in *Parenting* magazine. You could create a product integration in a parent-oriented program on TLC (The Learning Channel). Or, you might choose to advertise the product to both target groups using a combination of those media.

There are numerous stories in advertising lore of how the redefinition of a product category gave new life to a moribund product or service. Perhaps the most renowned case of redefinition is that of Arm and Hammer baking soda. By finding a new use for an established product (keeping refrigerators smelling fresh), the brand in effect positioned itself in two completely distinct categories: baking products and home fresheners. Today, it has a huge market share in the latter category, and it has expanded into numerous other cleaning-related areas, such as carpet freshener and deodorant.

Once you have determined to which product category your brand rightfully belongs (or the category to which you want it to belong), you are then in a position to examine trends in that category. You can do this in one of several ways. You may have access to product category sales from a trade association or manufacturers' group of some kind (such as the Juvenile Products Manufacturers Association, if you are marketing children's toys, or the Electronics Industries Alliance, if you are marketing electronics items). You can often find such data in trade journals in your particular field (such as *Supermarket News* for supermarket food sales or *Chemical Week* for sales of liquid nitrogen). One invaluable source for this type of information is the journal *Sales and Marketing Management*, which comes out several times a year with overall category sales (see Exhibit 2.4). *Advertising Age* also reports an advertising-to-sales ratio in all major product categories periodically that shows spending on advertising relative to sales.

Exhibit 2.4 Example Ad-to-Sales Ratio

Industry	Standard Industrial Classification (SIC) Code	Advertising as Percentage of Sales
Motion pictures, videotape production	7,812	25.1
Transportation services	4,700	24.6
Mailing, reproduction, commercial art services	7,330	21.6
Perfume, cosmetic, toilet preparations	2,844	20.0
Distilled and blended liquor	2,085	14.3
Soap, detergent, toiletry preparations	2,840	12.1
Photofinishing laboratories	7,384	11.1
Educational services	8,200	10.7
Rubber and plastics footwear	3,021	10.6
Dolls and stuffed toys	3,942	10.4
Special cleaners, polishes preparations	2,842	10.1
Furniture stores	5,712	9.5
Games, toys, child vehicles, excluding dolls	3,944	9.5
Television broadcast stations	4,833	9.4
Food and kindred products	2,000	9.2

In many larger companies, these data are routinely collected, usually within the marketing department.

In looking at category trends, be careful to look back beyond the past year. In fact, if you can find five to ten years of data, you'll be in a much stronger position to see what the real trends are. Another important point to remember is that there will be many factors to explain the rise or fall of product sales. These trends do not occur in a vacuum. Sales for construction products fell from 2008 to 2014, but this is not because people stopped building houses; rather, due to the recession, the rate of new home construction was lower than it was before 2008 because home loans were much harder to get. It is worth noting, however, that sometimes marketers can *benefit* from a recession because changes in consumer habits work to their advantage. For example, the most recent economic downturn created a boom in people growing their own fruits and vegetables. This turned out to be good news for Scott's Miracle-Gro, which invested more in advertising, particularly digital media, to make the most of the increased interest in its products.[3]

Interpreting Sales Trends

Four factors that help explain sales trends are economic, social, political, and cultural trends. And each will, in turn, influence your media choices.

For instance, if you are selling the latest smartphone, the overall health of the economy is going to have a large impact on whether people feel they can afford to spend the money to purchase a new version of a device they probably already own. If you decide that, despite the economic downturn, you want to emphasize a sophisticated image for your product, aiming it at innovators who always want to buy the latest equipment, then you might use social media ads targeted to electronics aficionados. If, on the other hand, you choose to emphasize how the new phone has enhanced ways to keep you connected to friends and family, you might look to a broader audience and use programmatic display ads that appear on a broader array of websites.

Politics can play an important role in the marketing of goods and services. For satellite TV services trying to promote themselves to rival cable subscribers, what happens in Washington at the Federal Communication Commission or in state or local politics will affect what they are allowed to sell and whether consumers are likely to buy the service. In 2015, several satellite and smaller cable companies protested the proposed merger of Comcast and Time Warner, claiming that the resulting mega cable company would be anticompetitive. In the end, Comcast withdrew its bid to buy its competitor. Meanwhile, AT&T purchased satellite TV company DirecTV and rebranded it as AT&T. Since the buyer already had an Internet-based TV service (U-verse), there is now one fewer brand name out there from which consumers can choose.

Cultural changes, while slower to occur, can also explain movements in product sales that have implications for media planning and buying. This is seen in the growth of ethnic foods, such as Mexican or Chinese dishes. The increasing popularity of different ethnic food products can be attributed in part to the enormous growth of the Hispanic and other immigrant populations in the U.S., leading to a greater diversity of cultures that are gradually intermingling and changing tastes and preferences. People of Asian ethnicity are 43 percent more likely than the total population to consume soy sauce and 12 percent less likely to eat ketchup. The marketers of these foods will introduce new flavors or adjust the ingredients in existing brands to accommodate the changing tastes of consumers. This is the approach Campbell's soup has taken with its soups to ensure that cultural shifts are accounted for.[4] Marketers may also try different ways of reaching their target audiences, such as through product sampling in stores or sponsorship of community events or location-based digital campaigns.

Finally, social changes, which also tend to happen slowly, can ultimately have a major impact on media activities. While phone companies market the text capabilities that their products offer, they also are actively involved in outdoor billboard campaigns to teach teens (and others) not to text and drive; similarly, alcoholic beverage companies spend a proportion of their ad dollars to remind their product users to "drink responsibly."

So while you as a media specialist may not have to pinpoint all the reasons behind category trends, it is important for you to gain a broad understanding of what is really happening in the category and not simply limit yourself to whether sales are up or down. Having this additional background information will help you decide which media you can or should be using in your plan.

What Should You Measure?

Another important issue when looking at category trends is deciding which trends you should be measuring. Sales? Units? Volume? The answer to this may ultimately depend on the types of data you are able to obtain, but you need to keep in mind that what seems to be a trend when examining one number may disappear or be reversed if you turn to another. For example, while sales of your fitness tracker devices could be going up in dollar terms, you may actually be selling fewer units if sales are rising primarily due to price increases (i.e., you make more money on each unit sold, but sell fewer units as result). When looking at category trends in dollar terms, always remember to factor in the effects of inflation. What may seem to be a 7 percent annual growth rate could turn out to be a 2 to 3 percent rate once inflation has been accounted for. Perhaps the category trend line shows that the number of units of shampoo sold is declining, but volume is holding steady. This might occur if the unit size has been enlarged, so the same total volume is being sold but in larger bottles. Again, ideally, you want to look at several trend lines using diverse measurements so that you can get an overall picture of what is going on in the category.

Brand Trends

When you turn your attention to individual brands, you perform similar analyses to those done at the category level. This time, however, you focus your attention on specific brand names. The use of the plural here is critical: You are not just looking at how *your* brand has been doing over the past several years, but, even more importantly, you need to track how your brand's *competitors* have been faring during that same period. This requires finding the answers to the following questions:

- How many competitors are there?
- How many of these are major, and how many are minor?

In some categories, where there are just a few players, such as the airline industry, you should probably consider all of them, but in larger categories, such as fast-food restaurants, where myriad companies have offerings, you will do better to pay attention to the ones you believe are your most serious threats. In certain instances, it is a good idea to look at all of the competitors regardless of their size; you may find that the fourth-tier player of three years ago has gradually been gaining market share and is now a far bigger concern. HP computers were for several years largely ignored by the likes of IBM or Dell because they were seen primarily as a printer company (its heritage). Today, however, HP is the number-one seller of personal computers in the U.S. and number two worldwide.

- How is the category characterized? Is it an oligopoly, where three or four brands define the category, or are there 20 or 30 brands each shouting to be heard?
- How aggressively do the brands in this category compete against one another? For example, is the category advertising driven or promotion driven? Does everyone rely heavily on digital display ads or search? Do they all have a large presence in social media? You can answer these questions either from your own experience in the category or by looking at any available syndicated data on competitive media expenditures.

For each competitor (or at least for the major ones), you must also find out the following:

- What is the company's financial position? This can be found by looking at stock market information or Standard & Poor's reports, where available, or by obtaining a recent issue of the company's annual report.
- How does the competitor position its brand? To determine this, you will have to use your own judgment. Examine the advertising for the brand and see what is being emphasized. Is it similar to your own current efforts or not? If it is dissimilar, is that because there is an actual difference between the two brands, or do consumers just perceive a distinction between them? And who has the more favorable position?
- How does the competitor promote its brand? Which media are used? How much does the competitor spend to promote its brand? Where and when does it spend its money? The answers to these questions may come from several sources. Many large companies and/or their agencies subscribe to syndicated competitive spending data from either Kantar Media or Nielsen. Both show, on weekly, monthly, quarterly, and annual bases, how much money was spent by a brand in each major media category (see Exhibit 2.5). Smaller businesses may simply try to keep track of where their competitors' ads are appearing.

Exhibit 2.5 Example Competitive Reporting Data

Year	Product	Industry	Category	Sub-Category	Business-to-Business	Cable TV	Internet Display	Local Radio	Magazines	National Spot Radio	Network Radio	Network TV	Outdoor	Spanish-Language TV	Spot TV	Syndication	Grand Total
2015	Coke Zero: Soft Drink	F400 Beverages	F441 Regular Carbonated Soft Drinks	F441.1 Regular Carbonated Soft Drinks	$11,501	$32,097,427	$181,445	$1,305,282	$404,606	$7,928,665	$906,813	$52,658,800	$66,916	$21,118,700	$180,073	$79,200	$116,939,844
2015	Coca-Cola Zero: Soft Drink	F400 Beverages	F442 Dietary Carbonated Soft Drinks	F442.1 Dietary Carbonated Soft Drinks		$9,794,505	$370,383	$205,140		$873,989		$15,103,500	$108,896		$470,787		$26,927,200
2015	Diet Coke: Soft Drink	F400 Beverages	F442 Dietary Carbonated Soft Drinks	F442.1 Dietary Carbonated Soft Drinks		$18,107,127	$1,224	$245,714	$5,550,990	$387,598		$20,412,000	$623,175		$4,058		$45,331,886

Source: Kantar Media January–December 2015.

This is not too difficult if you are dealing with a local product, but it gets more complicated the wider the area that you or your competitors try to cover. You can also subscribe to a clipping service which will do the tracking for you.

Share of Market

Once you have looked at the trends for your brand and its competitors, you must then put that information together and see how your brand is faring in the marketplace. The percentage of total category sales that your brand enjoys is known as the *market share*. You should try to examine how this figure has changed over time. Have you been gaining or losing market share in the past few years? Again, be careful to avoid oversimplifying the picture. It could be that you have been losing market share, but so have your major competitors, because of the entry of several new brands into the category. We can see this in the media arena in television. Whereas ten years ago the broadcast networks commanded about half of the prime-time viewing audience, today one in four people tune in to the broadcast affiliates (such as ABC, CBS, FOX, or NBC) at that time and the remainder watch cable networks. Their share of total viewing is even lower in other parts of the day.

Share of Requirements

One of the most useful pieces of information you can examine is the source of your brand's sales. This is known as the *share of requirements*. It is calculated by taking the percentage of total category volume accounted for by a particular brand's users. Quite simply, it tells you whether your brand is being bought primarily by your customers or by your various competitors' customers. And, conversely, how much of your competitors' sales are coming from your brand users. Looking at this figure, you will be able to determine what percentage of the volume you sell is accounted for by your users as opposed to people who usually buy another brand.

Let's say you are a manufacturer of a local brand of pretzels (Pioneer Pretzels), and you are competing with other regional brands as well as a major national brand. As you can see in Table 2.1, Pioneer Pretzels buyers account for 27 percent of all the pretzels sold in the last 30 days. Of all the pretzels purchased, 15 percent are Pioneer and 12 percent are other brands. This means that 55 percent (15 percent/27 percent) of the total category volume is given to your brand, which gives Pioneer a 55 percent share of requirements. This is the lowest figure among all pretzel types, suggesting that Pioneer's users are not especially brand loyal, which could harm sales and future market share.

Table 2.1 Example of Share of Requirements

	Total Category Volume	Brand Share of Volume	Brand Share of Requirements
National pretzels	38%	25%	65%
Regional pretzels	42%	29%	69%
Pioneer Pretzels	27%	15%	55%
Other brands	9%	5%	65%

WHERE IS YOUR BRAND SOLD?

Once you have found out as much as possible about how your brand stacks up against the competition, you need to think about geographic and distribution considerations. Specifically, you must look at where your brand is selling well and where it is doing poorly in terms of markets, regions, or states and in terms of type of retail outlet. This holds true whether your brand is available nationally, regionally, or locally. Unless your product is sold in just one store or location, there are likely to be some differences in sales according to geography and distribution outlets. What you discover by looking at the sales for your brand in these ways may lead you to develop a media plan with regional or local differences.

Indeed, more and more marketers have adopted a regional approach to selling, realizing that people in Boise have different tastes, customs, and buying habits than people in Boston or Baton Rouge. So marketers are customizing their marketing and media plans (and, in some cases, their products) to meet the needs of specific areas of the country. While some regional differences are obvious, such as higher snow blower sales in Maine than in Arizona, others might seem surprising (such as the fact that insecticides sell most heavily in the South). These types of differences occur not just at the product category level but also for individual brands. Dannon yogurt sells far better on the East Coast than does Yoplait, which has traditionally been stronger out west.

To understand geographic skews, the media specialist can turn to two pieces of information: development indices and market share.

Development Indices

You could, in theory, obtain sales data from every region or store in the country and look through them to find out your brand's sales picture. But a more efficient method for analyzing geographic strengths and weaknesses is to look at how the product category is doing across the U.S. and then to look at how the brand is developing over time. Both of these are calculated by using *development indices*.

Category Development Index

The category development index, or CDI, looks at product category sales in each potential region or market. A norm, or average, is calculated at 100, and then each area is assigned a value relative to that, expressed as a percentage. Numbers below 100 indicate the category has lower than average sales in a given region, whereas those above 100 suggest sales of the category are greater than the national average in a certain part of the country. If, on average, 32,500 tractors are sold per month per region across the U.S., that might mean 25,000 units are sold in the East, 45,000 in the West, 28,000 in the North, and 32,000 in the South. Eastern sales would index at 77 (25,000/32,500), meaning that sales in that area are 23 percent below the national norm, while sales in the West would have a CDI of 138 (45,000/32,500), indicating that that region's sales are 38 percent higher than average. Those in the South have a CDI of 98 (32,000/32,500), which shows that southern sales are 2 percent lower than the norm, whereas in the North, the CDI would be 86 (28,000/32,500), or 14 percent lower than the average. Based on such information, a company might decide to concentrate its marketing and media efforts in the region with the higher CDI, as that is where there is greater potential for all tractor sales.

Brand Development Index

You should not rely solely on the CDI in making geographic media decisions, however. You also need to look at how your brand stacks up against other brands in the category. One tool for this job is the brand development index, or BDI. The calculation is very similar to that of the CDI. You calculate a norm, or average, for all brands (or chief competitors) in the category, which is again set at 100, and then you see how your own brand is doing in comparison. The John Deere tractor company might find its BDI for tractor sales is 10 percent above average in the eastern region and 5 percent below the norm in the West, suggesting that it is doing better than other brands in the category in the East but slightly less well in comparison in the West.

When you look at the BDI, you need to keep the CDI in mind, too. Once you have these two sets of data, you should compare your BDI to your CDI. In that way, you will be able to find those markets where your brand is doing better than the category overall and, conversely, where your brand appears to be underperforming in the category (see Exhibit 2.6). For John Deere, its eastern BDI is greater than the CDI, so the brand is doing better than the category in that region. In the West, however, its BDI is below the CDI, so there is room for improvement here.

Exhibit 2.6 BDI versus CDI

		Category Index	
		High	Low
Brand Index	High	Both brand and category growing	Brand growing and category declining
	Low	Brand declining and category growing	Both brand and category declining

Armed with this information, you may choose to adopt one of three possible marketing and media strategies. You can focus your attention on those areas of the country where your brand is doing better than the category, playing to your strengths. Or you might choose to give more attention (and money) to the weaker markets where the category is doing well but your brand isn't, to try to bolster your sales there. Alternately, you might decide to play it safe and concentrate on markets where both category and brand are successful. The one strategy you should probably avoid is pouring money into areas where both brand and category are doing poorly, as that suggests there is something about all the brands that is not liked or does not meet the needs of those consumers. To try to rectify that situation single-handedly is probably going to be more trouble (and cost) than it is worth.

Market Share

When looking at the development indices, you can also find out how your competition is doing in each territory and calculate their BDIs. It is common to see that where your brand is doing well, your competitors are having a harder time, and vice versa. The exception here would be for a new or relaunched category where all brands are selling well, such as smartphones.

One way of investigating sales further in geographic terms is to look at your share of the market by region or locality. Is your brand number one in sales in the central region but in third place in the South? Are you neck and neck in New York but a distant second in Florida? Faced with these different scenarios, you should explore some of the possible reasons behind the distinctions. And here you should go back to the other Ps of the marketing process. Perhaps you have place (i.e., distribution) problems in Florida that are harming sales. Maybe your brand is being undercut in price in the South by a local manufacturer. Or it could be that your chief competitor is flooding the local airwaves with promotional messages in New York and drowning out yours. By putting together the information you gather from the development indices with your market share figures, you will start to create a picture of how your brand is doing across the country. That will help you decide what marketing and media tactics might be needed in each situation.

One last scenario to consider is a deliberate geographic restriction on product sales. This may be taken for several reasons. You might choose to test launch a new product in only one market or one region of the country to see how it fares there first. This is what Comcast did with its more advanced set-top box, known as X1, before expanding it nationally. Or you might "create" demand by making your product restricted, as movie studios effectively do when they open a new film only in New York and Los Angeles before the rest of the country to assess consumer response there first, which can then help guide their marketing strategies. In either scenario, the advertising required to support these tactics is going to be far smaller than for products available more broadly.

The media plan will not be the miracle solution to all of the problems you might encounter, and you should not expect it to turn a floundering brand into a superstar. But, as we shall see in subsequent chapters, the better your understanding of the marketing situation your brand is in, the more likely you are to come up with creative solutions to the problems. For example, if your problem is distribution, you might want to include extra trade promotions or incentives in your plan to encourage retailers or distributors to push your brand further. Pricing discrepancies might be alleviated by offering a coupon or on-pack premium to offset the lower-priced competitors. And if your consumers are being faced with a barrage of competitive messages in one medium, it might be wise to consider placing your own advertising in completely different media or perhaps move to more owned and earned media to raise your own voice elsewhere. There is also an increasing array of possibilities with geographically targeted ads, such as cable zone advertising on TV or mobile ads that are only sent to phones in specific geographic areas. More will be said in later chapters.

Finally, if possible, you should try to look at your brand's geographic strengths and weaknesses over time to see where the trends are going. Have you always been weaker in the Southwest, or does this seem to have started only in the past year? Is the overall CDI flattening out across the country or moving to different areas? This is especially likely to be true for new product categories when they are first introduced, as was the case when flavored carbonated water was first introduced. As always, looking at several years of data will help you to avoid acting on "blips" in the numbers that might have disappeared without cause within a few months.

CONSUMERS AND MEDIA

Although a successful marketing plan requires a thorough understanding of consumers' relationships with the brand, it is understood that a similarly thorough knowledge is needed to learn the relationships of consumers and media. In subsequent chapters, we will explore in greater detail the characteristics of each major media form, but here we will introduce the notion of the value of media *context*, or environment.

As you start to learn more about the way consumers use and think about your brand, you can also begin to investigate how they use and think about media. Do your tractor owners, for example, rely on the early morning farming report on the radio? How much do they rely on digital media to check on crop prices? With the Fruitola brand, are the people you want to reach with your message about its fresh taste interested in health and fitness magazines? If so, are they reading digital or printed versions, and what do they think about them? And in both cases, how do they respond to ads placed in those key media contexts compared to seeing the same message placed elsewhere?

The impact of context has long been explored by the academic community, primarily by looking at the effects of consumer involvement with the media in which ads appear.[5]

The advertising industry has been exploring media context also. Agencies such as Starcom, with its human experience focus, or MEC, with its engagement planning approach, each recognized that media should be thought of more from the consumers' viewpoints and that it is no longer enough to know basic media usage figures (how often a program is watched or a website visited). Rather, consumers' relationships with the media can be critical to the way they respond to the brand message. One reason that financial services companies advertise in the *Wall Street Journal*, for example, is because its readers place considerable trust in that newspaper's financial coverage. Advertisers, such as Citibank or Charles Schwab, hope that that trust will rub off on their brand messages.

We shall return to the topic of context in later discussions of media in this book.

A WORD ABOUT BUDGETS

One of the most important preplanning issues to look at is how much money you are likely to have to spend for media for the coming year. You may be given a specific amount upfront, or you may have a range within which to work. In many situations, the media specialist is likely to come up with two or three alternative media plans at different spending levels, showing what could be achieved with $500,000 versus $1,000,000 versus $2,000,000, for example. If possible, you should try to be flexible on the budget at this point, keeping in mind that if you lock yourself into a set figure from the very beginning, you may limit your creativity later on when you put the plan together. There has been some research on how much is an ideal amount to spend to be both efficient with the funds and effective with the message impact.[6]

TIMING AND OTHER ISSUES

The last major area to explore in the preplanning phase is that of timing. This may include the month of the year, the week of the month, the day of the week, or the hour of the day. While some timing considerations can be rationalized and justified, others may be out of your control. Some companies skew their messages toward pay periods, such as the 15th and 30th of the month, knowing that people are more likely to spend money when they have just been paid. Packaged-goods marketers may choose an end-of-week schedule to reflect the increase in grocery store shopping from Wednesday through Friday. Other considerations may be out of your control. The CEO of the company that makes your brand of sports drink may demand that you purchase television time during the U.S. Open Golf tournament. He not only likes golf, but he also wants to get tickets to the event. The marketing manager may refuse to have the brand advertised in any magazine that accepts liquor advertisements. Perhaps your candy company has been a sponsor of a local parade for the past 50 years and you cannot break with that tradition.

There might also be key timing opportunities that you should consider. If you are going into a Summer or Winter Olympics year, you might want to look for some way to tie your brand into that. While this sounds out of the league of any but the largest national advertisers, there may be an Olympic swim team member in your own town whom your brand of swim goggles could support in some way. Or if your city is celebrating its 200th anniversary and your tool factory has been around for almost as long, you could get involved in the preparations for related events. Or maybe next year has been designated the Year of the Child, so you can look for opportunities to promote your diaper brand. Be alert and open to new ideas and opportunities such as these that might come along infrequently and sporadically but could greatly enhance your brand's profile and help sales locally, regionally, or even nationally.

SUMMARY

Before getting down to this year's plan, it is important to know as much as possible about what has happened in the past. Find out everything you can on how your company has operated in previous years, how your brand has performed, and what the competitors have done. Think about your brand within the broader advertising and marketing context, especially the four Ps of price, place, product, and promotion. Looking at trends in the product category is not only helpful, but it might lead to new ways to define or position what you have to sell. Be aware of cultural, social, political, and economic forces that might impact your performance. As you examine your brand, consider who its real competitors are and learn about their past and present marketing plans. Determine your brand's share of market and share of requirements, too.

Preplanning should include an analysis of geographic variations in sales through category and brand development indices. Think about how consumers purchase and use your brand, how aware they are of it and its advertising, and when and how much they actually buy.

As you learn more about consumers' relationships with your brand and its competitors, also consider how they respond to the media that are important to their lives. Examining the context, or environment, of your brand's messages can provide you with critical information early on in the planning process that will be helpful as you develop your plans. Finally, keep in mind any budgeting or timing constraints that will affect your media plan.

CHECKLIST: MEDIA IN THE MARKETING CONTEXT

1. Have you considered all elements of the marketing mix (price, place, product, and promotions)?
2. How much do consumers know about your brand?
3. Do you need to conduct research on your consumer through focus groups, surveys, or analysis of syndicated data?
4. When do consumers buy your product? Which time of year, month, day of week, or time of day?
5. How much do consumers buy? Is there a difference by product size or flavor?
6. Have you analyzed the history of your brand (how long it has been available, how successful it has been in the past, how it has been positioned in the past)? Include the company's history here, too.
7. What are your brand's chief competitors doing?
8. What are the product category trends?

9. How is your brand faring compared to competitors in terms of market share and share of requirements?
10. How does each major competitor position its brand and promote it?
11. Have you calculated the category and brand development indices for your brand?
12. Are there regional differences for your brand's sales and market share?
13. Do your consumers have any special relationships with particular media that might affect their responses to brand messages?
14. Are there any contextually relevant media that might be appropriate to link your target consumers with the media they consume and your brand?
15. Have you considered any timing issues for the brand?

Notes

1. "Recall and Recognition: A Very Close Relationship," Jan Stapel, *Journal of Advertising Research*, vol. 38, no. 4, July/August 1998, 41–46.
2. "Behavioral Economics for Market Insights Professionals," Gina Sverdlov, Forrester Research, September 6, 2012.
3. "Recession Proves Fertile Ground for Scotts," Jack Neff, *Advertising Age*, April 2, 2012, 3/18.
4. "Back to the Kitchen," Stephanie Strom, *New York Times*, November 10, 2015, Business Section 1/8.
5. "Editorial Environment and Advertising Effectiveness," Valentine Appel, *Journal of Advertising Research*, vol. 27, no. 4, August/September 1987, 11–16. "A Cross-Media Study of Audience Choice: The Influence of Media Attitudes on Individual Selection of 'Media Repertoires,'" Elizabeth Gigi Taylor and Wei-Na Lee, *Proceedings* of the 2004 Conference of the American Academy of Advertising, 39–48. "Magazine Reader Involvement Improves ROI," Britta C. Ware, ESOMAR, Print Audience Measurement, June 2003. "The Medium Is Part of the Message," Maria Christina Moya Schilling, Karin Wood, and Alan Branthwaite, ESOMAR, Reinventing Advertising, November 2000, 207–229.
6. "Advertising Spending Efficiency Among Top U.S. Advertisers from 1985 to 2012: Overspending or Smart Managing?" Yunjae Cheong, Federico de Gregorio, and Kihan Kim, *Journal of Advertising*, vol. 43, no. 4, November–December 2014, 344–358.

CHAPTER 3

Developing Optimal Media Objectives and Strategies

Setting objectives is something we are all familiar with in our day-to-day lives: "I will get an A on this test," "I'll lose ten pounds by Christmas," "My goal is to become the CEO of the company by the time I reach 35." Whatever the objective may be, if you didn't have one, it would be difficult to know what you've achieved!

In the media planning context, you need to establish firm objectives for your plan in order to demonstrate how it will help your brand achieve its marketing goals. Although you may feel that in order to execute a media plan you must keep returning to your starting point, moving one step back for every two you go forward, it cannot be overemphasized that *everything* you do on the media planning side must be coordinated with the overall marketing strategy. Therefore, in order to establish your media objectives—what you intend the media plan to achieve—you must first reaffirm and clarify the goals of your complete advertising program to ensure that your media objectives fit in with the goals set in your brand's marketing objectives.

Then, once you have determined what your objectives are, you must develop the strategies to achieve those objectives. Again, to put this in a more personal context, if you want to ace a test, your strategies might include setting aside time every day to study, talking to the professor or person administering the test to get guidance, or taking practice tests beforehand. In the media world, your strategies should guide you on how you are going to achieve your objectives not in a tactical way (I'm going to use TV ads for 12 weeks at 50 ratings per week), but at the higher level. With our Fruitola example, if the broad objective is to make consumers see this new carbonated fruit juice as a healthy alternative to regular soda, then your strategy could focus on finding health-oriented paid, owned, and earned opportunities to communicate that idea.

How the Marketing Objective Leads to the Media Objective

The media specialist is likely to be presented with the marketing objective rather than having to develop it on his or her own. It is usually stated in some quantifiable form, such as "sell x thousand more widgets in 2017 than in 2016" or "increase awareness of Brand X to 75 percent within calendar year 2017." It may relate to any of the major marketing functions, such as increasing shelf space in the store or increasing the number of distribution channels for your product. And frequently it is expressed in terms of specific volume and share goals, such as "within calendar year 2017, bring Brand Z's total volume sold to 25 percent of the total category, raising its market share from 35 percent to 38 percent."

If the marketing objective is vague or ill-defined, simply "increasing awareness" or "improving distribution," then at the end of the year (or whatever time period has been set to achieve the goal), there is likely to be considerable debate over whether the plan was successful. It is going to be more difficult for the media specialist to devise the strategies to achieve those objectives. Even if awareness does improve, how much higher must it go in order for the media plan to be considered a success?

Along with understanding the marketing objective, the media specialist should also look at *how* that objective will be achieved, or what strategy to take, because that will affect what the media plan is supposed to do. Examples might be to increase product penetration among potential users by taking sales away from competitors or bringing new users into the marketplace. Alternately, the strategy might be to encourage people to use your brand more frequently, perhaps offering new uses for it. In order to increase the sales of Kraft Singles cheese, the marketing objective might be to get current users to buy additional packs of the product for use in new and different ways besides just for sandwiches. For the media plan, this could lead to an objective of increasing the frequency with which target users are exposed to the message to remind them of the various ways they can use the product by demonstrating the uses in recipes. Your strategy would then focus on looking at media (paid for or created specifically for the brand) that could provide recipes, including the cheese slices.

For a hospital with the marketing objective of introducing a new children's critical care unit and encouraging more people in the community to choose that facility for their pediatric medical needs, the media objective could be to reach 75 percent of people who live within a ten-mile radius to inform them of the expertise available at the new unit. The strategy would focus on how best to achieve that objective (geo-targeted media or social platforms, for example). Clearly, the marketing objective has a major impact on how the media plan develops, affecting the target audience, communications used, and media selected.

MEDIA AND THE ADVERTISING OBJECTIVE

As we noted earlier, the marketing objective may relate to any of the four major areas of the marketing mix (product, promotion, distribution, or price). Therefore, before establishing specific media objectives, it is also essential to focus on how media affect your advertising goals. While your ultimate *marketing* goal for most goods is to sell more product (or services or image), unless your audience finds out about the product through the media that you use, that goal is unlikely to be reached. You need to be aware, at the same time, of the other marketing mix elements. If the product is weak, your media advertising will have little impact. Similarly, if you advertise your product heavily but it isn't available in major stores, sales will likely not improve.

Frequently, the objective of your advertising is tied in to the stage at which the target audience is in the decision-making process. As we noted earlier, this process breaks down into three very broad areas: think, feel, and do (or, in research-speak, the *cognitive, affective,* and *conative* stages). Once you have decided that you need a new smartphone, you will *think* about what brands are available. Then, you will consider how you *feel* about each one of them. And finally, you will select a particular brand and take action (*do*) and buy it.

This process can be better understood by revisiting the eight main stages of the consumer decision-making process introduced in Chapter 2:

1. Need
2. Awareness
3. Preference
4. Search
5. Selection
6. Purchase
7. Use
8. Satisfaction.

Need

Before you can hope to sell any more widgets, people have to have a reason to buy them. Contrary to what many advertising critics maintain, advertising cannot persuade people to buy something they do not want. Indeed, it is often easier to think of this first stage in the decision process as reflecting people's *wants*, for in today's industrial society most people are able to satisfy their basic needs, such as food and shelter.

Even when people buy products that seem pointless or silly, such as Chia Pets or Hula-Hoops, they may feel they have a *need* to indulge in it just for fun. And while you might argue that no one really has a *need* for a $200,000 Tesla vehicle, the person who chooses to purchase one clearly feels that he or she deserves this luxury automobile. Defining what the need might be for the product helps the marketer understand the motivations behind why people might buy it, which in turn may provide some clues as to ways of reaching those people through the media. Though everyone buys shampoo, if you can segment the target into different groups according to their motivation for use, you could reach each one through a variety of media forms. People who are most concerned with how their hair looks may be reached in fashion and beauty magazines. Those who want a shampoo with built-in conditioner to help in their busy lives may respond to ads in women's magazines that offer advice on juggling multiple roles. For the ones who are looking for the most natural ingredients in their shampoo, then print ads in titles that are eco-friendly might be most appropriate. And all of that is just within magazines. Research conducted directly with target consumers may reveal that different segments actually have different relationships with their shampoo, leading you, as a planner, to determine what ways media can help your shampoo brands best fit in consumers' lives, such as a Pinterest board on time-saving tips, content integration in a fashion-oriented reality show, a YouTube channel focused on fashion, or an app featuring natural products. These and other media options are covered in greater details in subsequent chapters, but you should understand how different consumer needs can often lead to different media choices.

Awareness

Once the consumer has determined that he or she needs a particular product, it is the job of marketing to make the consumer aware of the choices that are available. For the media specialist, this means reaching that consumer in the right place and often enough so that your brand's message is the most relevant and convincing. And it is not enough to simply make people aware of your *brand*; the real goal here is to make them aware of your brand's *message*. You might well be able to reach 95 percent of all cat owners to make them aware of the new cat food that you sell, but unless they also learn that your product provides 100 percent of a cat's daily nutritional requirement, which is more than any other competitor, your advertising is unlikely to increase sales. Of course, keep in mind that your message will likely get lost in the clutter of other cat food messages unless you ensure that the message is delivered in a meaningful way that fits in with your target's life, instead of being unwanted advertising bombardment.

Preference

Based on the various choices the consumer sees and hears, he or she will then develop specific brand preferences. Ideally, the marketer would like that consumer to develop *brand loyalty* so that every time Isabella needs to buy a new pair of running shoes, for example, she always chooses Saucony. A media plan to enhance preference might include a co-promotional program with Avon to provide that brand's running shoes to breast cancer survivors participating in Avon's annual walka-thons or a sponsorship of local races where Saucony representatives let you try on their shoes.

Search

Once the target audience decides it might prefer your brand over others, the audience's next task is to find out where to purchase the item. Here, media advertising can be a big help by notifying people of the places that sell your product. The fastest way most consumers search today is on Google (or Bing), simply typing in the brand name or checking on a store's website. Advertisers can buy keyword searches online or in mobile so that when consumers are searching for the brand (or category), it is yours that comes up first. But other media offer search-assisting opportunities, too, such as listing local area stores or dealers that stock the brand in a TV or radio ad or on a billboard. If your audience cannot find the product when it's time to buy it, then not even the best advertising placed in the most appropriate media will help increase sales.

Selection

Brand selection may seem like an easy stage for the consumer. If she has decided already that she prefers Cover Girl nail polish over others, and she has learned that it is sold in Walmart stores, then isn't it obvious that she will buy it? Not necessarily. Today's consumer is faced with so many differ-ent brands that, once in the store and standing in front of the shelf, she may decide to go with Revlon instead, because it is on sale, or it is packaged more attractively, or it comes in larger bottles. So the selection process is a crucial stage for the marketer and the media specialist to consider. From a media perspective, the nail-polish user may be encouraged by in-store vehicles such as in-pack premiums or point-of-purchase radio or a mobile coupon she carries on her phone. Personal experience can also be very important at this stage. Someone who has come into the store to buy a mid-range laptop may be encouraged to select your more expensive model by being offered one year of free parts and service by the dealer.

Purchase and Use

Clearly, the ultimate goal of marketing and media plans is to persuade consumers to purchase the product. But if they buy it and never use it, then there is no reason for them to ever buy another one. No marketer can remain successful by continually targeting new product users; the cost of securing new users is much higher than retaining current ones. Often, one marketing and media objective is that of encouraging consumers to *use* the brand. In media planning terms, this might involve increasing the message frequency so that users are reminded of the different ways in which the brand can be used. A good example of this, in past years, has been Campbell's soup, which often places recipes in its print ads and on its website to encourage people to use more of the product and hence purchase it more frequently.

Sometimes a simple conversation with current users can provide important information on how best to market to them. Whether through focus groups, online communities, or social media, marketers can learn a lot just by listening. That, in turn, can suggest ways that the media message could help solve a problem or offer information. If you are marketing a chocolate bar to kids, then hearing the nutritional concerns of mothers might steer you toward putting some of your media dollars where they are consuming media, with messages of reassurance about the nutritional quality of that product.

Satisfaction

The final stage in the consumer decision process is really a feedback loop into the earlier ones. If people come to your restaurant but are dissatisfied with the quality of the food or friendliness of the staff, then their dissatisfaction will likely mean they won't return to your venue again. What is worse, they may tell their friends about their bad experience and decrease your potential sales even further. And in a world of Facebook, Twitter, and other social media, it is easier than ever to spread the (bad) word. So customer satisfaction is extremely important for future success. *Satisfaction* is generally not listed as the primary marketing or media objective of a plan, but it should nonetheless be kept in mind when deciding where and when to place your advertising message. Social media can be used by the marketer to offer reassurance or an outlet to respond. And social conversations, whether online or offline, can be readily monitored to keep abreast of consumer satisfaction. When the Mexican food chain, Chipotle, faced an outbreak of E. coli in its stores in several western states, it used its pages on Twitter and Facebook to offer messages of reassurance and to ensure that it was responsive to consumer sentiment and satisfaction in how it handled the concerns over food safety.

ADVERTISING OBJECTIVES AND THE CONSUMER DECISION PROCESS

To see how advertising objectives might fit in with each stage of the consumer decision process, let's look at an example. If your client is the city's professional soccer team, the Stars, and they are trying to increase the number of people who attend home games, you may not have to create a "need" for your offering, since anyone who likes sports feels the "need" to attend live games. It is very likely, however, that you would want to increase awareness of your team. So your advertising objective might be to boost awareness of the Stars from a baseline measure of 40 percent to 70 percent among young people under the age of 25 within a 50-mile radius of the city.

It could be that many people have heard about the team, but they are still choosing to attend baseball games instead. Here, your advertising objective would be to improve *preference*, so that instead of two out of ten people under 25 choosing to go to a soccer game over baseball, three out of ten do so. Setting advertising objectives for the subsequent stages in the decision process is somewhat less common, because it is believed that advertising has a less direct role to play here. But you still want to encourage your target to *use* your team by attending games, setting your advertising objective to boost visits to your games from an average of one time per year to four, perhaps by offering promotional tickets in social media or hosting special events at the stadium.

MEDIA AND THE CONSUMER DECISION PROCESS

The advertising media will also affect each of these stages in the consumer decision process. To continue with the soccer team example, you might boost *awareness* of the team through widespread local TV and radio ads or outdoor billboards or digital ads in the communities where you believe there are high concentrations of young adults. Consumer *preference* could be encouraged by sending direct mail or emails to potential visitors offering them two tickets for the price of one. They could be helped in the *search* process by putting ads that provide maps to your stadium in local newspapers or by buying search keywords on local or regional tourist websites. *Selection* might be helped by bringing some of the bigger soccer stars in from out of town and offering the opportunity for fans to meet them, which you promote via social media. These special events could then earn you publicity in local media. Finally, to get current team supporters to *use* the team and attend more games, you could have some of the soccer players send tweets to those supporters to encourage them to come to future games.

Let's take another example. Say you are in the market for a new automobile. That puts you in the initial stages of *needing* a new car. You see some TV ads for various makes and models, which increases your awareness of what is available. Three of the cars that interest you are the Toyota Yaris, the Honda Civic, and the Chevy Sonic. You read several automotive magazines, check out their resale values on Edmunds.com, and pick up the *Consumer Reports* issue on new cars and decide that these models fit your needs. Now you have developed a *preference* for these particular models out of the hundreds that are available. Your next step would be to visit some car dealerships to *search* out the cars themselves. Here, your interaction with the salespeople is likely to play a major role in influencing your decision. You will also probably talk to friends and colleagues, check out what people say on social media about the different vehicles, and look more closely online at each car's specifications. Faced with all of the information you have gathered, you *select* the Civic. You negotiate a deal and drive the car home; now you can *use* it and, based on your experiences, you will develop a degree of *satisfaction* with your new purchase. If you are happy with the car, you may well buy another Honda the next time you are in the car market.

The media's role is important at several points in the process. Television advertising is frequently used to create or enhance *awareness*, informing people of the qualities of the brand and what it has to offer. Both TV and magazines can help develop consumer *preference*. Here, you might see ads that compare the Honda Civic to other cars in the same class or that cite the awards and rankings the car has received in automotive competitions. And, as we noted previously, personal contacts and social media may be critical, too. Local ads on spot radio and television and outdoor billboards, along with keyword searches online and in mobile, help reach consumers who are *searching* for your brand.

To encourage people to *select* your offering, the media may emphasize special discounts or added features, such as a 60,000 mile warranty or $1,000 cash back. Getting people to *use* the product is also important. While this is not an issue in the case of an automobile, it can be for other consumer products. Nestle, for instance, uses print ads that feature recipes for foods made with its Toll House chocolate chips in order to encourage people to take the product off the shelf. Having people talk positively about their post-purchase experiences in social media has become increasingly important for brands and for other potential customers.

As with the marketing objective, the more measurable the advertising objective is, the easier it will be to determine whether it has been achieved. This can be done either through specific testing after the ads have run for a while or by setting up some kind of market test and determining the effect of advertising on sales.

CONSUMERS, BRANDS, AND MEDIA

Both advertising and media objectives require a clear understanding of how consumers connect with brands and with media. This relationship can be thought of as a Venn diagram, or a series of connecting circles. That is, consumers relate to certain brands and are more likely to be receptive to those brands' advertisements when they appear in the media forms that the consumer likes and/or responds to. Exhibit 3.1 displays this relationship.

What some advertisers and agencies have realized in recent years is that the advertising industry has typically focused on just two of the three circles at any one time. That is, the media department has zoomed in on the relationship of consumers to media, while the agency account planning and client brand management departments have concentrated efforts on exploring consumers' relationships with brands. To truly fulfill advertising and media objectives, however, those three elements must be examined together.

As noted in Chapter 2, this practice—known most often as *communications planning*—involves in-depth research (qualitative and/or quantitative) to understand in greater detail who the target audience is and how they relate to both the brands they use and the media they consume. The approach has been embraced by large marketers such as General Motors and Procter & Gamble, each of which invests in learning about that relationship of brand–media–consumer for their products, whether that is the Cadillac luxury vehicle or Pantene shampoo. The concept will be examined more closely as we go through the rest of the media planning process.

Exhibit 3.1 Relationship of Brands, Media, and Consumers

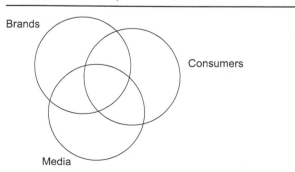

MEDIA OBJECTIVES AND ROI

Another important consideration before you develop any media objectives is that of ROI, which stands for return on investment. This financially oriented term is used to help those at the top of the company (chief executive officer, chief financial officer, etc.) understand how the money being spent on media is helping generate profits. That is, for every dollar spent in media, how much is *returned* to the company in terms of sales or awareness or customer goodwill? As the media specialty has grown increasingly sophisticated and more measurable (with more digital distribution), marketers have put greater pressure on those working in media to prove that their dollars are well spent.

One of the ways this is done is through econometric modeling (described further in Chapter 7). This combines an analysis of economics with the use of statistical metrics or models. The idea here is that statistical models can be created to explain, mathematically, the value of each dollar spent in media by comparing the amounts invested in each media form to the results achieved. These results may be in terms of product sales or consumer awareness or brand preferences.

This is not an easy process, in part because not everything is easily quantifiable. How can Mary Kay "prove" that its product integration into the popular TV program *Project Runway* is what causes sales of its mascara or eyeliner to go up? Perhaps it was the concurrent TV or print advertising that caused it. Or possibly it was the absence of its competitor, Revlon, on the air during the same time period. Or maybe it was the efforts of all the independent beauty consultants that helped sales. These econometric models attempt to parse out all the causes of changes in sales. When sales are increasing, everyone wants to take credit for it. The harder challenge is explaining what is *not* working—what causes sales to decline? Often it may be far broader economic trends, from the recession of 2008 to drastic weather patterns. An unusually warm (or wet or cold) period is often cited as the reason for sales of products to go down. A colder-than-normal summer can cause havoc on sales of suntan lotion, while a sudden freeze will cause a rapid halt to Starbucks' chilled coffee drinks. While the media specialist cannot be held responsible for all these external events, he or she may be required to help demonstrate the accountability of the media included in the plan.

ESTABLISHING MEDIA OBJECTIVES

Armed with clear and concise marketing and advertising objectives that are in sync with how your brand's consumers think about and respond to the brand and to media, you are now ready for the most important part of the media planning process: setting media objectives. As with the other goals, once you have a clearly defined course set for you, it becomes much easier to figure out how to get there. There are three main elements involved in the media objectives:

1. Defining the target audience
2. Setting broad communication objectives
3. Considering creative requirements.

Defining the Target Audience

Although you haven't yet started to put a plan together, you are probably beginning to realize that much of the most important work needs to be done beforehand to establish the media objectives. Defining the target audience is one key step you must take in the objective-setting process, for only by knowing who you wish to reach through the media will you be able to put together a schedule that will convey your brand's message to the right people.

Ideally, the target audience for your media plan should be identical to the audience for the overall marketing plan. Since most of a brand's sales are typically generated by its current users, the target audience definition is likely to include some product usage qualification. A marketing plan that is intended to increase sales of Pantene shampoo–conditioner combinations might have as its target audience women 25 to 54 years old who currently use shampoo–conditioners, with an annual household income of more than $50,000. Life stage can be a crucial factor, too. A plan geared toward increasing awareness of your new Motorola wireless video baby monitor might have as its target adults 25 to 49 years old who have had a child in the past year. Often, however, you will find that the media target may be both more and less precise than the marketing target. This is largely because the media themselves have traditionally been bought and sold on the basis of fairly basic demographics, such as age, sex, income, education, or race. For example, while your brand of Terra sweet potato chips may be aiming to sell 20,000 more packets this year by expanding its user base and capturing more sales from young adult gourmet lovers who enjoy entertaining and eating out, when it comes to creating your media objectives, your target may be adults 18 to 34 who are college educated and have an annual household income of more than $30,000. This is a more precise definition in that it specifies a particular age category as well as particular income and education levels, but it does not take into account (at least definitionally) the lifestyle variables (like eating out, entertaining, and fine foods).

As technology improves and media becomes more data-driven, however, we are seeing the development of more precise and lifestyle/product-usage-based targeting. Much of this is being driven by what has happened in digital media. While traditional media such as television focused solely on age/sex targets, digital media flourished by using household-level information from data companies such as Experian or Acxiom to deliver ads to those homes who are known to have certain characteristics or product habits. For example, Purina could send its dog food ads only to homes known to have a dog. This practice has moved to television, too, through what is referred to as *addressable advertising*. The approach is similar to digital, whereby TV distribution companies such as AT&T and Dish can deliver ads solely to the households of interest. It has been found to deliver significantly more in terms of the message impact (by linking addressable ad exposure to actual sales) and media efficiency (money saved by only paying to reach homes the advertiser wants, thereby reducing waste).

One element that will be as true tomorrow as it is today is that the media target should be identical to the creative target. While this may seem blatantly obvious, occasionally the research and account teams will develop a complex and precise target audience but the creative team will march forward with their own ideas of who the message should speak to. That leaves the media department in confusion. So just as the media specialists should have seen and understood the marketing objectives, they should also be familiar with the creative brief, a document that lays out for the copywriter and art director the fundamental information about who or what the brand is, what the communication goals are for the campaign, and, importantly, who the message is directed at. Ideally, all of the target definitions will match!

As far as media definitions of targets are concerned, the syndicated data sources of audience information are usually the first port of call. Depending on the target, these resources may provide armloads of information, or they may offer up next to nothing. In particular, if you are dealing with a nonconsumer target, such as retailers or dealers, you may find yourself without much syndicated information at all, relying more on your experience and judgment. You can assume, for example, that if you are trying to promote your refrigeration equipment to restaurants, one place to put your message would be RestaurantNews.com.

One important consideration for defining your media target is whether it should be broad or narrow. Because everyone in the country uses laundry detergent, does that mean your media plan should be aimed at all adults in the U.S. who use laundry detergent? Increasingly, the answer will be no. Today's brands are becoming more and more segmented. So we don't just have one box of Tide on the store shelf, but 57 of them, including liquid Tide or PODS, Tide HE Turbo Clean Liquid, Tide plus Febreze Sport, or Tide Simply Clean and Fresh. There are six different sizes of liquid Tide Plus Bleach Alternative and four in powder form, aiming to suit the needs of diverse groups, from singles living alone to large families. Each of these groups is likely to have different media habits and preferences, and trying to create a media plan that would reach everyone would ignore the needs of different population groups in terms of both product benefits and media usage. There might be one plan aimed at mothers with young children, another for those with large families, another with an environmental slant, and a fourth promoting the smaller size for urban apartment dwellers. Each plan has a different target audience.

There is also the opposite danger, however. That is, you might define your target audience so narrowly that it would be almost impossible to reach them. You might, from previous research into who posts on a blog, find that they are most likely to be aged 18 to 34 years, work in professional or managerial jobs, have household incomes of $150,000+, read the Sunday *New York Times* digitally, listen to public radio, use online gaming, and have written articles that have been published (Exhibit 3.2). But there may only be a few hundred of them!

There are two major problems to note here. First, most traditional media will not only present your message to *your* target, but also to many others for whom the product is probably irrelevant. This is a problem that currently can only be alleviated by careful consideration of exactly who your target should be and which media will best reach that audience. As noted previously, addressable advertising is starting to allow marketers to send

Exhibit 3.2 Profile of Blog Poster

People who post on blogs are more likely to	People who post on blogs are less likely to
Be aged 18–34 years	Be aged 45+ years
Be college educated	Have only a high school diploma
Have household incomes of $150,000+	Have household incomes less than $50,000
Live in the Pacific region	Live in the East Central region
Be African America or Asian	Be Hispanic
Contact a politician	Read the daily newspaper
Play online games	Ready the Sunday newspaper in hard copy
Read magazines on	**Read magazines on**
Entertainment	Women's general interest
News and information	Automobiles
Listen to	**Listen to**
Public radio	All news
Watch	**Watch**
Sunday morning news shows	Weekday prime

Source: GfK MRI, Doublebase 2015.

TV messages to a more selective and relevant group of households. This is something that digital advertising already does, delivering ads dynamically based on where the user has been online. But for now, thinking of all three parts of the connecting circles—consumer–brand–media—will help you here, for with a thorough understanding of how your target relates not just to your brand but also to the media they consume, your media plan is not only more likely to reach that target but also do so more effectively.

A second consideration in establishing media objectives is the cost effectiveness of the plan. It may be the chief concern of you or of the top executives of your company. You could come up with an extremely elaborate and highly targeted media plan with a clearly defined target audience and appropriate communication objectives, but if it is going to cost twice as much as is in the marketing budget, you are unlikely to be able to execute it. When defining the target audience, you must be sure that the audience will be reachable at an affordable cost. As the maker of Oral B toothbrushes, you cannot hope to reach everyone who brushes their teeth on a budget of $10 million.

Having defined your target audience, your next step should be to find out as much as possible about the individuals who make up that audience. Ideally, you should not only know their basic demographic characteristics (age, sex, education level, income, profession, etc.), but also learn more about the kinds of products they use and the media they tend to hear or see. Again, depending on the target, you can often obtain this information from syndicated data services. Or you may have to rely on your own judgment and experience. So if your target for your streaming music service is young adults ages 18 to 34, you should also know that they are more likely to have smartphones and take part in online gaming.

Communication Objectives

When it comes to writing down what you expect the advertising message to do for your brand, you will start to find that all of a sudden you are dealing with the art, rather than the science, of media planning. These objectives are measurable to some degree through communications tests with the target audience that find out what information the audience is taking away from the message. In addition, media calculations can be made to estimate what the plan should achieve in terms of how many of the target will be reached and how often (with what frequency). But many of the criteria you need to use to establish what the goals should be are more evaluative and rely on your judgment and subjective responses to everything that you know about the brand, its advertising, and the marketplace. These objectives must also be in line with the overall marketing strategy for the brand. If you are trying to increase your market share in the athletic shoe category by two percentage points by increasing distribution into mass merchandise outlets, then your communication objective might involve increasing awareness of your brand among your target audience by 15 percent within the first three months of the campaign.

Communication objectives will vary depending upon the kind of product you are promoting. For launching a new brand of cat litter, you probably want your advertising to generate awareness of the product. If you are advertising Charmin toilet paper, however, which has been around for decades, your message will more likely serve as a reminder to consumers of the qualities of the product such as its softness or strength. These differing objectives will also affect your reach and frequency goals. For a new product, you would want to establish some broad reach to drive the awareness, whereas for the well-established brand, a higher-frequency reminder message will be more effective.

Don't forget to consider your competition, too. You might set as your objective that within the first six months of your new campaign, awareness levels for your Trek mountain bike will be equal to or greater than those of your closest competitor. Geography is another factor. If your bike is the number-one brand in the category with the highest awareness levels in the Northeast and the Pacific Northwest, but falls to number two or three in the South, then you might set different objectives in different parts of the country, broadening your reach in areas where awareness levels are currently lower.

There are three main factors to consider when developing communication objectives: campaign timing, category and brand dynamics, and media reach and frequency.

Campaign Timing

Here you should consider what stage your campaign is at—are you launching a new product or changing the strategy for selling it, or is this the third or fourth or twentieth year of an ongoing campaign? Also think about the specific timing of the campaign. Are you trying to communicate a seasonal message to warn young adults about drinking and driving during the holidays? Or maybe it's April and people are starting to think about summer vacation, so it's the perfect time to begin promoting your park district's swimming pool. Thinking of your communications objectives within a specific time frame will help to ensure that your media plan stays focused on that period.

Category and Brand Dynamics

If you study the trends for your brand in particular, as well as trends within the category overall, your communication objectives will be firmly fixed in reality. That is, if research shows that users of lawn-care products are extremely brand loyal, it makes little sense to say the objective for Scott's weed killer is to gain 15 market-share points from their competitors in the next 12 months. Related to loyalty, you should think also about what degree of consumer involvement with the category can be reasonably expected. It's hard to get people excited about staplers or canned tomatoes, no matter how wonderful your creative message or media plan. Try to be objective about your brand's positioning, too. Is your advertising message really very different from competitors', or is it in fact just another version of the same idea? If you look at the advertising for most products, you'll see that the latter is far more common than the former. Almost all banks tout their low financing rates, while beers companies talk about great taste, and garbage bags makers emphasize their strength. None of this should be too surprising; you wouldn't want to buy a beer that didn't taste good or a garbage bag that wasn't strong.

Reach and Frequency

Having stated earlier that communication objectives tend to be more subjective than objective, more art than science, there is still a role for some numbers here. But they should only be included if you will have some way of measuring them. The two key concepts to consider here are *reach* and *frequency*. These are the two most commonly used media terms in the whole planning process. The *reach* of the plan refers to the number (or percentage) of the target audience that will be reached by the brand's advertising in the media. As we shall learn in Chapter 7, that number is determined by calculating what percentage of the target audience will be exposed to the media in which your ad appears. Along with knowing how many people will have the opportunity to see or hear your ad, you also need to state how many times they need to do so in order for the message to have some effect. This is the concept of *effective frequency*. You should identify some reach and frequency goals as a way of measuring whether your communication objectives were achieved. If the communication goal is to increase awareness of the brand by 10 percent among the key consumer target, then that can be measured by establishing what percentage of the target was actually reached with the message, how many times they saw or heard it, and whether brand awareness levels did in fact go up. More will be said on this topic in Chapter 7.

Creative Requirements

The last area that should be considered in preplanning discussions is any special creative requirement that will affect the media selected. As noted previously, this should be made evident in the creative brief, and it provides another reason why it is critical for media specialists to be exposed to that document. If, for example, you are introducing a new hybrid car and want to talk about its advanced engineering and environmental benefits in detail, you will have to think in terms of the media that can allow you to do that. Or, if your task is to promote the Florida Keys as a vacation destination for families, then the creative aspect requires media that convey the desired image by depicting many different sights or sounds from that area, such as print or digital, TV, or radio. The message will, in part, determine where you choose to place it. Yet another example might be introducing a new Pillsbury pie crust. Your ads will showcase the delicious results of using the product, so the visual element is going to be particularly important. Immediately, this leads you in a certain direction when starting to consider your media plan strategies and tactics.

SUMMARY

In order for a media plan to be successful, it must be tied directly to the broad marketing objectives for the brand, usually defined in terms of sales and market share. The goals for media should also be derived from the advertising objectives, which show where the advertising fits in to the consumer's decision process, such as increasing awareness or improving customer satisfaction or generating additional use of the product. Both marketing and advertising objectives are tied to the media objectives by considering the relationship that exists between consumers, brands, and media. Media objectives should be developed with a consideration of how they might tie to the brand or company's return on investment (ROI), demonstrating how each media dollar spent contributes to sales. The media objectives state to whom the message will be delivered (the target audience), when it will be distributed (timing specifics), and how many times a given proportion of the target will, ideally, be exposed (media reach and frequency). Special creative requirements for the brand's communications should also be taken into account, in part by ensuring that media specialists are able to review the creative brief.

CHECKLIST: DEVELOPING OPTIMAL MEDIA OBJECTIVES AND STRATEGIES

1. Do you know your brand's marketing objectives?
2. Are they clearly and explicitly stated in an actionable way?
3. What is the advertising objective for the brand?
4. Have you considered where the advertising might fit in with the eight stages of the consumer decision process: need, awareness, preference, search, selection, purchase, use, and satisfaction?

5. What have you learned about how consumers relate to your brand and the media they consume?
6. In which stage of the consumer decision process does your advertising objective fit?
7. Have you clearly defined your target audience or audiences?
8. Are your target definitions in line with those developed by the marketing team and the creative team?
9. What are your communication objectives in terms of a specific time frame, given the competitive situation?
10. What are your media reach and frequency goals?
11. Are there any specific creative requirements for the brand's message?
12. Have you seen the creative brief?

CHAPTER 4

EXPLORING THE MEDIA, PART 1
Paid

We are all familiar with television, radio, digital, newspapers, or magazines from the consumer's standpoint. That is, we don't think twice about check-ing Facebook every morning, listening to the radio on the way to work, going online during the day to catch up on the news, watching TV when we get home at night, and reading a magazine on a tablet in bed before going to sleep. For advertisers, each of those points of contact we make with the medium represents a paid opportunity to communicate with a potential target for their product or service. So, for example, the local car dealer will buy a video ad on Facebook for a Toyota Camry in the hope that you will see it in the morning and stop in at the dealership on the way home from work or on the weekend. The First National Bank might purchase an ad on the radio in the morning hours to reach commuters on their way to work to alert them to the bank's favorable interest rates on savings accounts. And an organic foods company that offers delivery of fresh local foods might buy a keyword so that if someone searches for "organic" and lives in the zip codes served, the company's ad will appear. When you sit back and relax in the evening to watch television, a wide range of advertisers will pay the TV networks to remind you of their brands of beer, cookies, pet food, or coffee. They do so in the hope that when you next visit the grocery store, theirs is the brand you will select. And finally, advertisers that pay to be in the print or digital magazines you look at before you go to sleep will try to persuade you that their credit card company will be there when you need it. In this chapter, we will focus on the paid media forms of TV, radio, newspaper, magazines, out of home, and digital. The next chapters discuss advertising opportunities that can be "owned" through brand websites, integrations, or sponsorships or "earned" via word of mouth, social media, and organic search.

MEDIA VERSUS COMMUNICATIONS

The task of today's media planners has become much broader than in times past. Instead of just considering the traditional media that they pay to put ads in (TV, radio, magazines, newspapers, outdoor), the planner must think more closely about how to use media to deliver brand experiences to consumers in numerous ways. Should Kraft macaroni and cheese sponsor the local Little League teams? Could Tide detergent create an online forum to share stain removal tips? Could Gatorade use its website to help provide tips to athletes? Should the characters in *Modern Family* be seen to be eating Kellogg's cereals? Or could Campbell's soup ads appear on weather.com when the temperature falls below freezing in the location being viewed? The key with all of these different types of communications is that they are designed to provide the target consumers with a brand experience through media. At the same time, they all need to be part of a coordinated effort we call the *media plan*. That is, the message that Kraft conveys in its TV ads about providing moms and kids with healthy, fun meals should be consistent in its sponsorship, in all digital formats, or on TV. And as with all media planning elements, the communications platforms that are used should all relate to and work toward the brand's marketing and media objectives.

MEDIA CATEGORIES

Once you have clearly defined media objectives and strategies for attaining those objectives, the next step will be to decide which media types, and vehicles within those types, will best help you achieve your goals. Before exploring that further, we need to think about what the different media can offer you as an advertiser conveying an advertising message. Here, we will consider the seven major paid media categories: television, radio, magazines, newspapers, out-of-home, digital, and mobile. The many forms of owned and earned media will be covered in the next two chapters.

There are various ways of categorizing the media. It used to be enough to distinguish between print and electronic forms. But in today's consumer-controlled media world, where there are so many ways that advertisers' messages can be delivered, the separation into paid, owned, and earned helps show how each of these communications can deliver the brand experience effectively. Here, we will start by looking at the major characteristics of each paid media form. As a point of reference, Exhibit 4.1 shows how much was spent in advertising in each major media form in 2014.

Exhibit 4.1 Adspend by Medium in 2014

Medium	Amount (Millions of Dollars)
Consumer, Sunday, business, and local magazines	$22,420
National and local newspapers	$16,689
Network TV	$28,315
Spot TV	$16,791
Syndicated TV	$5,191
Cable TV network	$27,833
Network, national spot, and local radio	$6,744
Outdoor	$4,397
Internet display	$12,791
Total paid media	**$141,171**

Source: Kantar Media, 2015.

A TELEVISION IN EVERY HOME

Almost every household in America has a television set, and eight in ten (85 percent) have two or more. The average household owns three TV sets. More than half (58 percent) have three or more sets. Television is the largest mass medium available for advertisers. In 2014, about $78 billion was spent promoting goods and services this way. Households in the U.S. have their TV sets on, on average, 8.6 hours each day, which is one of the highest viewing figures of anywhere in the world. Eight in ten homes have a high definition set, although not all are watching in high definition.

Broadcast television programming is traditionally divided up in two ways: by daypart and by format. *Daypart* refers to the time of day the program airs. There are nine standard dayparts, which are shown in Exhibit 4.2. Program formats are also standardized into 12 main types, which are shown in Exhibit 4.3. It is worth emphasizing that these breakdowns are really only the concern of the programmers and advertisers; you don't choose to watch situation comedies or reality-based programs; rather, you decide to watch *Dancing with the Stars* on ABC on Tuesday nights.

The cost to create a program genre directly affects how much an advertiser will pay to appear in it. Dramas and sitcoms are more expensive to make, in contrast to the less expensive reality shows. Today, the reality genre is a staple of the prime-time TV lineup, although general drama still accounts for about 40 percent of prime-time hours.

The challenge for media specialists is to predict which shows will be popular several months or even one year from now, buying them at lower costs and enjoying higher-than-predicted ratings. We will explore this further in Chapter 9.

Exhibit 4.2 Television Dayparts

Early morning	M–F	7:00–9:00 a.m.
Daytime	M–F	9:00 a.m.–4:30 p.m.
Early fringe	M–F	4:30–7:30 p.m.
Prime access	M–F	7:30–8:00 p.m.
Prime time	M–Sat	8:00–11:00 p.m.
	Sun	7:00–11:00 p.m.
Late news	M–Sun	11:00–11:30 p.m.
Late night	M–Sun	11:30 p.m.–1:00 a.m.
Saturday morning	Sat	8:00 a.m.–1:00 p.m.
Weekend afternoons	Sat–Sun	1:00–7:00 p.m.

Source: Nielsen, 2002.

Exhibit 4.3 Television Program Formats

Animation/children
Daytime serials
Drama/adventure
Game shows
Late-night talk
Movies
News
News magazines
Reality-based
Sitcoms
Specials
Sports

Source: Nielsen, 2002.

How people watch TV has changed; many viewers have digital video recorders (DVRs) that allow them, in effect, to become their own program schedulers. By making it easy to record favorite shows and fast forward or pause both live and recorded programming, DVR providers (such as TiVo and the cable or satellite companies) have helped turn television from a passive medium where viewers watch what is shown when it appears to a much more active experience where people can watch whatever they want whenever they wish to do so. Currently, almost half (47 percent) of U.S. households have a DVR, and people aged 18 and older watch about three and a half hours of time-shifted television per week. The consequences for advertising will be explored further in this chapter.

What people watch is also impacted by who owns the various TV networks. For example, Disney's ownership of ABC, ESPN networks, Freeform, and Disney Theme Parks is seen in ESPN announcers on ABC sports programming or creating a Phineas and Ferb attraction at Disney World. Exhibit 4.4 shows some of what each of the major networks owns.

Exhibit 4.4 Media Company Ownership

Network	Owner	TV	Print	Cable/Satellite	Digital	Radio	Outdoor	Cinema	Other
ABC	Walt Disney Company	ABC, 8 ABC-owned stations	ESPN the Magazine	Disney networks, ABC cable networks, ESPN networks	Disney Interactive Media Group, Babble, Club Penguin	ESPN Radio Network, Radio Disney Network, radio stations	—	Walt Disney Studios, Pixar, Touchstone Pictures, Marvel	Disney Stores, Disney Theme Parks, Disney Cruise Lines
CBS	Viacom	CBS, 16 CBS-owned stations	Watch! Magazine	CBS Sports Network, Showtime, The Movie Channel, Smithsonian Channel	Cnet, CBS.com, CBSSports.com. GameSpot, TV.com, tvguide.com, Last.fm	117 radio stations	CBS Outdoor	CBS Films	Simon & Schuster
Fox	21st Century Fox	Fox, 28 Fox-owned stations, MyNetwork TV, MundoFox	—	Fox News, FX Networks, National Geographic Channel, Fox Sports, Fox Business Network, Fox Movie Channel, Big Ten Network, Fox Deportes	—	—	—	Twentieth Century Fox, Fox Searchlight Pictures	Twentieth Century Fox Home Entertainment, Fox Television Studios, Sky TV
NBC	Comcast NBC Universal	NBC, Telemundo, 10 NBC-owned stations	Time Inc. magazines, Southern Progress Corp., Time4Media	Comcast Cable, USA, CNBC, Syfy, Bravo, E! Entertainment, MSNBC, Golf Channel, Oxygen, NBC Sports, Style, Comcast SportsNet	iVillage, DailyCandy, Fandango, Xfinity	—	—	Universal Pictures, Focus Features	Universal Parks and Resorts; Comcast home technology management; Xfinity TV, Internet, Voice

There are four main types of television to consider: network, syndication, spot (local), and cable. Beginning in the mid-1990s, the ownership of these various entities became more and more consolidated, so that today just a handful of large media companies have majority control of all four types of TV, squeezing out the independents or mom-and-pop operations that flourished in the first 50 years of television. The viewer is not really aware of who owns what, and does not differentiate, for the most part, between network or cable or syndication. He or she chooses to watch a certain program regardless of how or where it airs or who created it or owns it. The distinctions we draw here are purely for media purposes, particularly when it comes to negotiations and media buys.

Network Television

Network television consists of four major broadcast networks: ABC, CBS, NBC, and FOX. There is also one smaller network: The CW, owned jointly by CBS and Warner Brothers. A "network" is actually made up of hundreds of local stations that become "affiliates" of the national organization. A small proportion of them are owned outright by the parent network; these are called the *owned and operated stations,* or O&Os. There are a total of 1,120 network-owned or -affiliated stations, about one-third of all commercial or low-power TV stations on air (3,308). Each station receives a set amount of money every year from the network in return for which they agree to air national programs for a given number of hours every week, though as the networks have looked for ways to cut their costs in recent years, they have attempted to cut or eliminate these payments. Network programs air at the same time in every market within a given time zone. So CBS's *60 Minutes* appears at 7:00 p.m. on Sunday night in the eastern zone, 6:00 p.m. in central markets, and 5:00 p.m. in the mountain zone. Programs in the Pacific time zone are shown at the same time locally as in the East (i.e., *60 Minutes* airs at 7:00 p.m. Pacific time).

Network shows come with several minutes of commercial time both within and between programs that are sold by the network. The local station is then able to sell an additional one to three minutes of commercial time in the hour to local or regional advertisers, depending on the daypart. Historically, local commercials always had to appear between programs, but today local or regional advertising occurs within the program, too. The research findings have been mixed on the relative effectiveness of ads appearing between or within programs. The local station also decides what to air when it is not showing network programs. This might include locally produced shows, such as local news or current affairs programs, or programs purchased from independent producers, known as syndicated programming (discussed next).

Stations not affiliated with a network are known as *independents*. Today, there are a dwindling number of stations in the U.S. that are not affiliated with any broadcast network. Several hundred others are noncommercial or are broadcasting on locally based UHF signals. Each one decides which programs to air throughout the broadcast day and is responsible for selling its own commercial time.

Syndication

One of the major sources of programs for independent stations is syndicated programming. Here, an individual program (or a package of several programs) is sold on a station-by-station basis, regardless of that station's affiliation. The programs may be of any type or length. There are two main types—original shows and off-network fare. The former are filled with game shows, such as *Wheel of Fortune*, and talk shows such as *Dr. Oz* or *Ellen*. They are sold either by the program's producers or by syndication companies, such as Viacom's King World, that put together packages of properties. The distinction between syndication and network shows is that syndicated programs can air at different times in different markets as well as on different networks. This leads to syndicated shows having to be "cleared" by each local station that chooses to buy them. The clearance figure refers to the percentage of markets across the country that can view that particular show. So, for example, if a syndicated talk show is "cleared" in 70 percent of the U.S., it means that broadcast TV stations seen by 70 percent of all TV viewers have purchased that program. Syndication clearances generally range anywhere from 70 percent to 99 percent. It is worth noting, too, that some network programs do not have total (100 percent) clearance because an affiliate station may refuse to air them or will put them on at a different time than the rest of the network. For example, an NBC-affiliated station in Salt Lake City, Utah, refused to air the network's drama *Hannibal* starting in 2013 because they considered it too graphic for that market.

The goal of many network programs is to produce enough episodes to go into the syndicated marketplace (usually 85 or more episodes). This is known as *off-network programming*, and it helps fill up the hours of airtime that stations have when network shows aren't running. Programs that have been popular on the networks can continue to air for many years in syndication. Hits from the 1970s, 1980s, and 1990s, such as *MASH, Seinfeld,* and *Friends* can still be seen on TV during the early evening or late night hours in syndication. Today, there are more than 100 daily or weekly shows offering several hundred hours of content. Exhibit 4.5 shows the top programs in syndication among adults aged 25 to 54 years.

Exhibit 4.5 Top 10 Syndicated TV Programs

	Show	Rating (%)
1	Big Bang Theory	3.8
2	Modern Family	2.8
3	Judge Judy	2.5
4	Family Feud	2.1
5	Wheel of Fortune	2.0
6	Jeopardy	1.9
7	Two and a Half Men	1.8
8	Family Guy	1.7
9	Law & Order: CI	1.7
10	Law & Order: SVU	1.7

Source: Nielsen, 8/2013–8/2014.

Spot Television

Spot television is another way to purchase television time. Here, instead of contracting with the network to distribute a commercial to all of that network's affiliate stations across the country, an advertiser can pick and choose which programs and stations to use, placing the message in various "spots" across the country. As noted previously, very few commercial TV stations are not affiliated at least part of the time with a network, a number that continues to diminish as networks (and their multimedia conglomerate owners) buy up independents as regulation is relaxed on station ownership. The spot TV buy could be as small as a single station in one market to a couple hundred stations across a region. While the actual cost of placing spots on local stations is lower than a total network buy, once you start including a large number of markets, it can become quite expensive.

Spot TV time is sold either by the individual station and/or by station representative firms, or *rep firms*. These firms put together packages of stations known as *unwired networks* (because they are not physically linked together, or wired). Rep firms can usually customize buys, allowing the buyers to pick only those stations in which they are interested in a given number of markets.

Cable Television

Cable television is sometimes thought of as a newer way to distribute programs and commercials, but in fact it has existed as a means of conveying television signals since 1948. Because it does not depend on over-the-air signals but comes into the home via wires laid underground (or sometimes on poles on the street), reception is much clearer in many areas. That was the original reason behind its growth—so that people in Eugene, Oregon, or Lancaster, Pennsylvania, could receive the signals of the broadcast networks more clearly. While the broadcast networks distribute their programs from a central location to each of their affiliates, cable programs are sent via satellite from the cable network to individual cable operators (franchises) within each market, who then distribute the signals to the subscribers' homes. There are 5,208 separate cable systems operating today, although the majority belong to one of the large multiple system operators (MSOs) that have cable systems in numerous markets. In 2015, the top two players were Comcast and Time Warner. Together, these two operators serve 60 percent of all cable viewers in the country.

Another difference between broadcast TV and cable TV, from the consumers' standpoint, is that they must pay a monthly subscription fee to receive cable service. The average monthly cost of cable in 2015 was about $75. For an additional monthly fee, consumers can receive one or more of the pay cable networks, such as Home Box Office (HBO), Showtime, or Cinemax, which do not show any advertising at all.

Cable TV is made up of a wide variety of different networks, many of which specialize in certain kinds of programs or appeal to certain types of people. So, for example, ESPN airs sports all the time and Comedy Central has 24 hours of comedy programming. There are several cable networks, such as USA Network and TBS, which are more similar to the broadcast networks in their programming, airing a variety of different types of shows, from adventures to situation comedies to movies and dramas. In recent years, most cable networks also produce their own original programming, and it is not uncommon for some of these to garner audiences that are not that much smaller than those for broadcast shows and, at times, the highest-rated cable programs are larger than many on broadcast TV. The original AMC series *The Walking* Dead, for example, enjoyed a household rating in 2014 of 8.2, which was far higher than the average broadcast network prime-time rating, which was less than a 5.0.

Exhibit 4.6 shows the biggest cable networks currently available, together with the number of subscribers to each one. The number of networks available varies by system. Despite having hundreds of channels to watch, the average U.S. household tunes in to about 16, as shown in Exhibit 4.7.

The development of cable TV as an advertising medium began in the early 1980s and has grown steadily ever since. Today, more than $27 billion of total TV advertising dollars go to cable television, representing about one-third of the total amount advertisers spend in television. Most of cable's ad dollars are purchased on a national basis, although the medium continues to grow at the local level, too, accounting for $4.7 billion in advertiser spending in 2014. If you manage a local restaurant or a bank,

Exhibit 4.6 Top 15 Cable Networks and Subscribers

Rank	Network	Subscribers (in thousands)
1	TBS	100,200,000
2	TNT (Turner Network Television)	100,900,000
3	Food Network	100,558,000
4	C-SPAN	100,000,000
4	Adult Swim	99,828,000
6	CNN	99,700,000
7	Headline News	99,700,000
8=	A&E	99,600,000
8=	HGTV	99,507,000
8=	History	99,500,000
11	Cartoon Network	99,300,000
11=	AMC	99,100,000
11=	Nickelodeon	99,000,000
11=	Syfy	99,000,000
15	USA Network	98,600,000

Source: Video Ad Bureau, 2015.

Exhibit 4.7 Number of Channels Received and Tuned

Number of Channels	Average Number of Channels Received per Household	Average Number of Channels Tuned per Household
2008	129.3	17.3
2009	136.4	17.7
2010	151.4	17.8
2011	168.5	17.5
2012	179.1	17.8
2013	189.1	17.5
2014	194.1	16.8
2015	200.7	15.9

Source: Nielsen Average Channels Tuned, December 2015.

you can run your commercials throughout the area, or you can confine your messages to a particular cable system's area. Both national and local advertisers use cable TV to buy certain zones within the coverage area of the operator.

Advertisers can also purchase time on several systems at once by going through a central sales office, known as an *interconnect*. This is similar to a rep firm: You select the cable systems on which your ad will appear. Most interconnects operate on a metropolitan or regional basis, such as Greater Chicago or the Bay Area.

As noted in Chapter 3, advertisers are now able to send different ads to individual households, depending on the characteristics of each home. This practice, known as *addressable advertising*, allows companies selling home furnishings to send ads to new homeowners, while makers of diapers can deliver ads just to the households with infants and toddlers. As the technology has been deployed in larger numbers, across more than 40 million cable and satellite TV homes, it is now possible for advertisers to pay only to send ads to homes they care about, rather than having to bear the cost of sending ads to all households. In this way, television can become a far more targeted, less "mass" medium, and its impact can be accurately measured on consumer response or product sales.

Satellite Television

Although listed here as a type of television, satellite TV is more of a means of distribution. From being a way for rural inhabitants to receive any kind of signal via large C-band dishes, today's far smaller satellite dishes can be seen perched on the outsides of houses all across the country, and they are as common in urban markets as in rural or suburban ones. By delivering TV signals directly from the satellite and eliminating the cables that have to be laid under the ground or above ground on poles, satellite services are able to offer a far larger number of channels to viewers. There are two major satellite providers: Dish Network and AT&T. According to Nielsen, about 30 percent of the country now receives television via satellite.[1] There is an ongoing battle for subscribers with cable operators. Without much of the high cost of transmission incurred by cable, satellite providers have been quicker in offering new or high technology services to customers, such as the ability to watch TV anywhere via mobile apps or PCs or the feature of skipping some commercials altogether.

IPTV

Newer forms of TV distribution rely on the Internet instead of wires or satellites. This so-called IPTV is being offered by several companies whose backgrounds are in telephony. Both AT&T's U-verse TV service and Verizon's FiOS offer clearer, more reliable service than their competitors. Each has subscribers in more than 5 million homes across the U.S.

In 2012, Google launched its first-ever TV distribution service in Kansas City. Called Google Fiber, the high speed Internet-delivered offering includes Internet access and TV channels. It is now in three cities, with plans to expand to another six. It remains to be seen how large a competitor Google will be in the video distribution marketplace.

TELEVISION ON DEMAND AND EVERYWHERE

The development of new forms of television began in the early 1990s, but it was not until the latter part of that decade that technology began to catch up with the pipe dreams of the inventors. One of the first to be available was video on demand (VOD). Here, several channels are allocated to special programs, such as movies or sporting events, purchased by the cable subscriber on an individual basis. They may cost as little as a few dollars or as much as $100 for a special boxing match, for example. In order to be able to send this video content to individual households, the cable linking the television to the cable system operator must be two-way, allowing the operator to deliver the programs on demand. At present, six in ten households (60 percent) are VOD enabled, allowing viewers to order up any program that they want to watch, at any time. About four in ten (42 percent) of all homes are paying for a subscription on-demand service, such as Netflix or Hulu. Those that have VOD access spend about 8 hours a month using it.[2] From a paid media standpoint, one of the issues used to be that the ads were hardwired to the program, but today, most VOD offers *dynamic ad insertion* where ads are inserted right before the program content plays, so those ads are not only more timely but can be targeted to the household viewing.

VOD's expansion has occurred largely due to the growth of digital cable, which is now in about 59 million homes. When all of the major cable system operators upgraded their systems, they could not only offer more channels to viewers, but they could also offer additional services, whether Internet access through the TV set or overlays on the screen showing statistics during a football or baseball game.

Another way that television was significantly altered is through the video recorder. The introduction of DVRs at the tail end of the 1990s promised to revolutionize the way people watched TV and, as a result, the advertising business for that medium. DVRs, now in about half (49 percent) of all U.S. households, allow people to program the device to find programs to record on a regular basis either by title (all new episodes of *CSI*, for example) or by actor/director (find anything with Brad Pitt). What happens as a result is the official program schedule evaporates and every consumer becomes his or her own program scheduler, time shifting to watch whatever programs they want, whenever they choose. More importantly for advertisers, DVRs let viewers fast forward through most, if not all, commercials. Statistics show that during prime-time programming on the broadcast networks, viewers are skipping about 60 percent of the commercials when they watch in this time-shifted mode. Dish Network's DVR-based service called the Hopper enables consumers to skip ads altogether when watching prime-time programs recorded from the four largest broadcast networks.

Cable operators can control some of the time shifting capabilities, offering a start-over option that allows viewers to restart a program that is airing, but prohibiting them from fast forwarding through ads or content.

The implications for advertising are potentially huge. As we will see in Chapter 9, television has traditionally been planned by program day-parts. What happens when there is no such thing as prime-time television anymore? And what if the viewership of a program no longer occurs simultaneously because large numbers of people are recording the program for viewing at a later date? What should the program rating be based upon? There has been much deliberation in the industry over this question, resulting in the "official" national rating now being based on "commercial + three days" or C3—that is, the audience for those watching the average commercial in the program as it airs plus any viewership of that program in the 72 hours following the original telecast. As viewers consume video content across multiple screens and watch less live TV, the industry is starting to look at the C7 rating, extending the viewing over seven days.

In recent years, TV has no longer been confined to the television set. It has become video that is watched on multiple screens and in myriad locations. The most common of these are the computer, tablet, and smart-phone. All of the major TV networks now offer TV everywhere, enabling cable or satellite customers to pay to get access to selected programs on one of these other devices. As of 2015, it was estimated that about one in eight households that subscribed to cable or satellite were using this service.

Overall, video viewing via the computer or mobile device is increasing. In 2011, about 6 percent of Internet users said they had watched video via computer. According to Nielsen, however, in first quarter of 2015, people spent about one and a half hours per week in this activity on the computer and another 15 minutes doing so via mobile devices (a figure that is twice as high among younger adults ages 18 to 24). When consumers choose to watch video on other screens, it is often to catch up on missed episodes or prior seasons or to take advantage of the convenience of the "anytime, any-where" viewing. For advertisers, the online video experience is almost wholly positive, with results from studies undertaken on these programs showing upwards of 80 percent ad recall among consumers watching TV shows on the Web. In addition to watching TV programs on these digital devices, viewers are also consuming large quantities of short-form programming, whether on sites such as YouTube or on social media platforms like Buzzfeed. This form of online video, whether professionally produced or created by individuals and then posted online, is especially popular with teens and young adults. More is covered on this in the digital section later in this chapter.

At the same time that TV is being consumed on the Internet, TV manufacturers are heavily promoting their "smart TV" sets that have built-in

Internet connections. About half of all households now own this kind of set, while about one in five (18 percent) have enabled the set to connect to the Internet. This kind of functionality, along with external devices consumers can purchase and connect to the set (wirelessly or physically) have created TV viewing that goes "over the top," or OTT. That is, instead of buying cable or satellite subscriptions, more households are paying to view through other services such as Netflix, Hulu, or Amazon Prime, thereby going over the top of the traditional TV access methods.

Another device for TV everywhere is the tablet, such as the iPad. Since Apple introduced its first iPad in 2010, about half of the U.S. population owns at least one device. One of the most popular uses for it is to watch video content.

BENEFITS OF TELEVISION TO ADVERTISERS

Whichever type of television advertising you choose, you will enjoy a number of benefits unavailable from any other medium. Among these benefits, television's ability to imitate real-life situations, its pervasiveness, and its broad reach are most noteworthy.

True to Life

The most obvious advantage of television advertising is the opportunity to use sight, sound, color, and motion in commercials. This form of advertising is generally considered the most lifelike, re-creating scenes and showing people in situations with which we can all identify. That does not mean we don't see cartoons or animated commercials or fantasies on the screen; today's electronic wizardry lets TV ads show us everything imaginable. But of all the media available, TV comes closest to showing us products in our everyday lives. This is not only important for packaged-goods advertisers— firms such as Kellogg's, Anheuser-Busch, or Unilever, who are able to show us what their products look like and how they are used or enjoyed—but also for service companies such as Marriott Hotels or American Express, which can offer us ways to use their amenities. Today, many advertisers take their 15- or 30-second TV ads and use them as *pre-roll* ads in online videos or in social media.

The Most Pervasive Medium

Television advertising is the most pervasive media form available, given that the average American is watching about five hours or so of TV every day and spending more time with TV than all other major paid media. Several slogans from TV commercials have entered the mainstream of conversation, such as Bud Light's "Whassup?" or Wisk detergent's infamous "ring around the collar" line. Characters in commercials have also become part of our lives, such as Flo for Progressive Insurance or Tony the Tiger for Kellogg's Frosted Flakes.

Reaching the Masses

Another important advantage of television from an advertising perspective is the wide *reach* of people it offers at any one time. Even in programs with ratings of eight or ten, you are reaching about nine million individuals! While there is generally a smaller audience for the commercials than for the programs themselves, nevertheless, television remains a truly mass medium. The Opening Ceremony of the 2012 London Olympics, for example, was watched by 40.7 million people in the U.S. (and an estimated 4 billion globally). On average, TV reaches 87 percent of people ages 18 and older each week.[3] Furthermore, by buying time on several different programs shown at different times and/or on different days, it is possible to reach a wide *variety* of individuals. And although each ad appears for a short time (usually 15 or 30 seconds), if it is repeated on several occasions, more people are likely to be exposed to it, often more than once. This helps build brand awareness, which in turn may lead to the formation of favorable attitudes or intentions to purchase that brand.

DRAWBACKS OF TELEVISION ADVERTISING

Unfortunately, television advertising has particular drawbacks as well as the unique benefits just discussed. Four of the most commonly encountered drawbacks are high cost, limited exposure time, cluttered airwaves, and poor placement of ads within or between programs.

Dollars and Sense

Perhaps the biggest disadvantage for advertising on TV, particularly at the national level, is the high cost. The average 30-second commercial during prime time on the six main broadcast networks in fall 2014 cost about $128,300, with a wide range from about $24,000 at the low end to $627,000 at the top.[4]

Even that cost pales in comparison to television's most expensive ad opportunity. A single ad in the 2016 Super Bowl cost close to $5 million. For many advertisers this is far beyond their budget, leading them to cable or spot TV as cheaper alternatives or, increasingly, to shifting dollars into online video.

Quick Cuts

Another drawback to this medium is its brief exposure time. Although many ads are seen several times within a short period of time, unless the commercial is particularly inventive or unusual, it is likely the viewer will ignore it or be irritated by seeing it after the first few occasions and will deliberately try to avoid the message.[5] Controversy remains over just how many times people can be exposed to spots without getting bored or annoyed, a phenomenon referred to as *commercial wearout*. This drawback may be mitigated somewhat through addressable or interactive TV, where viewers receive ads considered more relevant to their needs and/or they select the kinds of messages they are more interested in, finding out more about a specific brand or product in detail. The key here is that this self-selected audience is more interested and involved in the message.

Cluttering the Airwaves

A related factor that is a major concern for advertisers is the sheer number of ads appearing on TV. This leads to clutter of spots, again believed to reduce the effectiveness of individual commercials.[6] There is evidence to support this fear. From 1990 to 2013, the number of spots shown on prime-time network TV has tripled. Part of the explanation for this is the increase in the number of TV networks. But another major reason is the growth in the number of shorter-length commercials. For many years, the standard television spot lasted a full minute. Then, in the mid-1960s, more and more advertisers started using 30-second commercials, finding them more cost efficient and no less effective. As costs continued to increase during the 1970s and early 1980s, advertisers tried the same tactic, shifting to even shorter commercial lengths. Today, the 15-second spot accounts for 44 percent of all prime-time network TV commercials. The total number of spots aired on English-language broadcast TV in a given month is over 14,000.[7] Exhibit 4.8 shows the trend in TV ad clutter in prime time, while Exhibit 4.9 displays the expansion of 15-second commercials. The result of clutter on consumers is questionable, but research suggests that it hinders the communication, sometimes considerably.[8]

Placing Spots

Another area that has provoked a good deal of discussion is where commercials should be placed for optimal effectiveness. For network TV, you can buy time either within the program (*in-program*) or between two shows (*break*). While some believe there is no difference in viewer attention between these two options, others feel that you are likely to lose more

Exhibit 4.8 Commercial Clutter Trend: Prime Time

Year	Number of Commercials	Percentage Change	Number of Minutes	Percentage Change
1990	4,990	—	2,059	—
1995	7,609	52.5%	3,177	54.3%
2000	11,202	47.2%	4,751	49.5%
2005	11,742	4.8%	5,300	11.6%
2010	13,129	11.8%	5,615	5.9%
2013	14,466	10.2%	5,822	3.7%

Source: Nielsen, 2006, 2011, 2014.

Exhibit 4.9 Growth of 15-Second Commercials in Prime Time

Length (seconds)	1990	1995	2000	2005	2010	2013
15	36%	34%	35%	35%	40%	44%
30	62%	64%	62%	58%	55%	53%
60	1%	1%	2%	5%	3%	2%
Other	1%	1%	1%	2%	2%	2%

Source: Nielsen, 2011, 2015.

viewers during the breaks than within the program itself. On spot TV, the break position used to be the only timeslot available, though those old rules have been relaxed, as commercial breaks have slid a few minutes into the program rather than only at the top or bottom of each hour.

Related to this placement issue is where to position your commercial within the series, or *pod* of spots being shown. Evidence suggests that the first ad to appear will receive the most attention, followed by the last one; those in the middle are likely to suffer from viewers switching channels, not looking at the screen, or leaving the room. The advertiser, however, does not routinely get the choice of where in the pod to air their ad. Some advertisers will pay a premium to ensure their ads appear first, but this is not always permitted.

RESEARCH ON TELEVISION

Much of the research literature on television has focused on two key issues: the impact of a life-like message and the effects of program environment. Buchholz and Smith found that the more "involved" consumers are in the medium, the stronger their cognitive responses to ad messages.[9] Kamins and colleagues examined how TV ads are evaluated depending on the mood created by the program in which the ads appear.[10] Several other research articles are also available.[11]

RADIO: THE "EVERYWHERE" MEDIUM

Radio is the oldest electronic advertising medium. It first became popular in America in the early 1920s, and since that time it has managed to hold its own against all other media forms. Although families no longer sit around their radios as they once did to listen to the most popular programs of the day, they still rely on this medium for both information and entertainment. Indeed, almost every home in America has at least one radio, and most have several of them. People listen to the radio, on average, for 2 hours 42 minutes every day, and the medium reaches about 93 percent of adults 18 and older each week, more than any other medium. Radio listening is highest during the 7:00 a.m. hour and is nearly as high around lunchtime, with around 15 percent of people ages 12 and older listening to the radio on an average weekday. It gets higher as the week progresses, peaking on Thursdays and Fridays. On average, people listen to about seven stations per month. More and more, that listening occurs outside of the home. Almost all cars (95 percent) are fitted with radios, and six in ten adults (those aged 18 years and older) say they listen to the radio when in their vehicles on a typical weekday. Depending on the time of day, anywhere from one-half to three-quarters of radio listening occurs outside the home, which is higher than the level of mobile usage out of the house. Radio accounts for about one-fifth (22 percent) of the estimated time consumers spend each day with major media.[12]

There are 11,300 commercial radio stations across the country. Of those, about one in four operate on the AM (amplitude modulation) wavelength, while the remainder are FM (frequency modulation) stations. The primary differences between them are in reception area and audience. AM stations can broadcast over a wider distance, but because the soundwaves are impeded by any kind of obstruction (hills, tall buildings), the sound quality is inferior to FM stations, which broadcast in a narrower listening area, but AM tends to be listened to more by older adults, reflecting the fact that more AM stations offer news and talk programs rather than the music formats that dominate the FM wavelength. The average listener tunes in to about seven different stations per week. Radio stations are either commercial, accepting advertising as their chief source of revenue, or noncommercial, funded by public monies and/or audience sponsorships. Commercial stations will air, on average, about ten minutes of advertising per hour, in blocks of about three and a half minutes.

Exhibit 4.10 Radio Dayparts

Day of Week	Time Period
Monday–Friday	6:00 a.m.–10:00 a.m.
Monday–Friday	10:00 a.m.– 3:00 p.m.
Monday–Friday	3:00 p.m.– 7:00 p.m.
Monday–Friday	7:00 p.m.–midnight
Saturday–Sunday	6:00 a.m.–midnight
Monday–Sunday	6:00 a.m.–midnight

Exhibit 4.11 Top Ten Radio Formats

	Format	Share of Total Listening
1	Country/new country	15.2%
2	News/talk	10.6%
3	Pop contemporary hit radio	8.0%
4	Adult contemporary	7.6%
5	Classic rock	5.6%
6	Classic hits	5.5%
7	Hot adult contemporary	5.3%
8	Urban adult contemporary	4.3%
9	Contemporary Christian	3.5%
10	All sports	3.3%
	Share of all radio listening in U.S.	69%

Source: Nielsen, Audio Today Q1 2015.

As with television, radio is classified by both daypart and format. The different formats that are available for the advertiser are not defined the same way by the listener. Radio dayparts and formats are shown in Exhibits 4.10 and 4.11.

Today, radio represents about 5 percent of all advertising expenditures, with about $6.7 billion spent on the medium in 2014. The two main types of radio advertising are network (national) and spot (local). The way programs and ads are distributed is similar to that of network and spot broadcast TV.

Network Radio

Unlike television, network radio is less important to advertisers than is local radio. It currently receives about 6 percent of all radio dollars and reaches about two-thirds of people 12 and older each week. Like TV, however, a

Exhibit 4.12 Radio Networks

American Urban
Crystal Media
Cumulus
Premiere
United Stations
Westwood One

Source: Nielsen, 2013.

message placed on network radio is distributed via satellite to each network's affiliate stations. These stations are paid an annual sum to take, or "clear," the network's programs. Almost two-thirds of all radio stations (11,000) are affiliated with one network or another. The kinds of programs they receive from the network may be aired every day, such as the Westwood One newscast, or periodically, such as Bob Kingsley's Country Top 40 show. There are presently six major radio networks, each of which offers subnetworks based on the programming and the demographic makeup of their listeners. Altogether, there are about 40 different networks. Westwood One Radio News is aimed primarily at listeners from 25 to 54 years old through news radio, while the stations that are part of Crystal Media's Smooth Jazz Network include stations playing that format across the country. Exhibit 4.12 lists the major networks.

From an advertiser's perspective, one key benefit of using network radio is that you can go through a single source to place your ads across a region or across the country. The downside of this form of radio, however, is that you have less flexibility in choosing the stations you wish to be in. If you buy the Westwood One News Network, you may get the number-one station in Biloxi, Mississippi, but a distant fourth station in Little Rock, Arkansas.

Spot Radio

Nearly 80 percent of radio's advertising dollars are spent in spot markets, where you buy time on individual stations on a market-by-market basis. Here, if you were placing the advertising for Coldwell Banker realtors, you could buy time on individual stations in a market, regardless of which network they belong to, and choose which markets you wished to target. The advantage of purchasing radio in this way is that you can select the exact stations and/or markets in which you wish to advertise your product. This also allows you to customize the message to each location, so that Home Depot stores can mention the address or phone number of different locations in each market's ad.

Some stations are linked together only for the purpose of selling advertising time. They constitute an "unwired" network, allowing you to select which stations within the group you wish to use based on your demographic or geographic preferences. Typically, an advertiser buys time through a representative, or rep firm, rather than dealing with every station individually. So if you are trying to target teens with the Xbox One, you could go to a rep firm that offers you stations that do well against that group. Examples of unwired networks include the Wall Street Journal Radio Network, which offers business news and performs well against adults over 25. For the advertiser, using a network of this kind provides efficiency. But, as with wired network radio, you may end up buying time on less-attractive stations as part of the package deal.

Satellite Radio

In 2001, satellite radio services were introduced to the U.S. marketplace. Two companies, XM Radio and Sirius Radio, each delivered about 100 different channels via national satellites. In 2008, they merged to form Sirius XM, which today has 29 million subscribers in the U.S. Consumers need special receivers in order to tune in to these services, and they must also pay a monthly subscription (about $15/month) for the service. One incentive for them to pay is that about half of the stations air without commercials. Even on those channels that include advertising, the amount will be far less than on regular radio stations—6 minutes per hour, compared to 15 to 20 minutes on terrestrial stations.

The content offered by satellite radio ranges from niche forms of music, to college radio stations that let alumni keep up with their favorite college sports teams, to syndicated talk shows such as Howard Stern, Rush Limbaugh, or Oprah Winfrey. This type of radio resembles cable TV, in that there are so many channels, they can afford to be highly specialized (e.g., a NASCAR channel, several baseball channels, or a channel offering bluegrass music). The satellite radio company has deals with the major U.S. auto manufacturers, who have built satellite radio capability into more and more of their models and offer it as a standard piece of equipment in many vehicles.

Digital Audio

Another competitor to satellite and terrestrial radio is streaming or online radio, where radio signals are digitized, then sent via Internet to computers or mobile devices. Many traditional, land-based stations offer simultaneous signals on the Web, while other stations have been created solely online. Today, there are more than 7,000 streaming stations, and one-fourth of persons 12 years of age and older (44 percent) listen to radio online in an average week. The growth is due to two factors: more online listening in the workplace and greater usage of audio via mobile devices (phones and tablets). The online usage varies by format. The highest proportion of online listening is seen with pop contemporary hit radio, adult contemporary, news/talk, and country, where one-quarter or more of the listening audience is listening online. One problem for the sector is that advertisers typically think of radio as a local medium, but streaming audio is currently sold nationally.

In addition to local stations that stream digitally, there are several important—and growing—"pure play" digital audio offerings. The largest is Pandora, which has more than 80,000 different visitors per month who spend about 38 minutes per day with the service. Others in this space include Spotify, Apple Music, and iHeartRadio, all of whom are seeing continued growth in audiences and, as a result, ad dollars. Together, digital audio accounts for about 6 percent of radio ad dollars.

One less commercialized form of digital audio is the podcast. These are audio programs or series that people can download and listen to whenever they want. They may be developed as podcasts or be rebroadcasts of content that has already aired. While most do not come with traditional radio commercials, advertisers can sponsor them. A very popular original podcast, the 12-episode "Serial," received 100 million unique downloads in its first year.

BENEFITS OF RADIO TO ADVERTISERS

As an advertiser, you cannot afford to ignore the many benefits of radio advertising. Although it does not offer the visual power of television advertising, it does provide the opportunity to reach targeted audiences frequently and at a reasonable cost. These and other benefits of this medium are discussed next.

Local Appeal

As mentioned earlier, most advertising dollars in radio are spent at the local or regional level rather than on the networks. Radio is therefore listened to primarily as a local medium, allowing you the opportunity to tie in to local events, news, or celebrities.

Reaching the Right Audience

Because of the way radio stations are formatted, the medium provides you with targeted, specific audiences. If you run a local health club, you can reach women ages 25 to 54 by placing your message on light rock stations. Or, as the owner of a religious bookstore, you can promote your store by advertising on the local religious radio station. Radio also offers good opportunities for reaching diverse ethnic groups. In areas with sizable Black or Hispanic populations, you are likely to find at least one station that appeals to each of these minorities. It will generally have a very loyal following. For a baby-clothing manufacturer, for example, advertising to Hispanics may turn out to be very profitable because they tend to have larger families than non-Hispanic households. And with digital audio, the opportunities to reach even more defined targets based on the type of content is even greater. Those who are listening to classical music on Pandora, for example, could be assumed to be older and hence targeted with more ads for life insurance or over-the-counter medications than the people who are listening to rap music, who one would expect to be younger and more urban. For them, ads for electronics or fashion retailers might be more appropriate.

Imagery Transfer

For many advertisers, radio is seen as a secondary medium, used in conjunction with a major print or television campaign. The good news here is that research has shown the power of radio ads to create a visual image in listeners' minds from the TV commercials they have seen for that same brand.[13] This process, known as imagery transfer, gives radio ads far more impact than the auditory stimulus alone and, therefore, greater potential influence on consumer response.

Keeping Costs Down

Compared with television, radio is an extremely inexpensive ad medium. A 30-second spot in prime time on a broadcast TV network may cost more than $600,000, while the price for that same length commercial on a local radio station could be as low as a few hundred dollars or less. Of course, these costs are linked to the number of people you will be reaching. For digital audio, the costs are based on the number of digital impressions, or "thousands reached," but still do so affordably compared to other types of digital.

Building Frequency

With a TV buy, you are usually looking for high reach numbers. In order to gain frequency, you need either a very large budget or inexpensive dayparts. On radio, however, because the costs are so low, it makes sense to buy a lot of time and build up frequency against your target audience. It also makes sense to do this for strategic reasons; people tend to listen to a particular station for a fairly brief period of time, so you want to ensure you reach them while they are listening. You should keep in mind that listening habits are not seasonal, so frequency can be built up year round.

Radio and Purchasing

Research shows that the time between media exposure and purchase is shorter for radio than for any other traditional medium, as shown in Exhibit 4.13. This means that your potential consumers may well be listening while they are making their purchase decisions. According to a 2012 study, 19 percent of shoppers listened to radio within the half hour before purchase, a proportion that was much higher than for any other medium.

A study undertaken by the Radio Advertising Lab (RAL) on behalf of the Radio Advertising Bureau found that in a controlled test, consumers exposed to one radio ad and one TV ad were 34 percent more likely to recall the advertised product unaided than those who were exposed to two TV ads. Similarly, one radio with one newspaper ad generated nearly three times the unaided recall compared to two newspaper ads, and four and a half times greater when radio was similarly combined with Internet ads.[14]

Flexible Messages

Compared to the high production costs and long lead times of television, radio is extremely flexible. If your ad is read live on the air, as is often the case, you can change the message at very short notice without much difficulty. You can vary the message for different dayparts or station formats, perhaps using different music backgrounds depending on the type of music

Exhibit 4.13 Radio and Retail

Medium	Percentage Exposed to Medium within Half Hour of Purchase
Radio	19%
Mobile/web app	7%
Internet	5%
Print	2%
Live TV	2%

Source: "Where Radio Fits: Radio's Strength in the Media Landscape," Arbitron and Media Behavior Institute, 2012.

played on that station. With digital audio, as noted previously, ads can be distributed dynamically in the same way as other digital formats. For all types of radio, there is the flexibility of tie-ins to local retailers or other promotional opportunities, such as local contests or events.

DRAWBACKS OF RADIO ADVERTISING

In addition to the numerous benefits of radio advertising, there are a few drawbacks to keep in mind as well. Each of these can be seen as a challenge; most can be overcome with some planning and creativity.

In the Background

When we listen to the radio, we are usually doing something else at the same time, making it a background medium. Ads on radio must therefore work a lot harder to grab—and keep—our attention.

Sound Only

Radio can only offer sound, rather than the sight and motion of television. However, the medium can still be used to great effect because it offers the possibility of inspiring the listener's imagination. You can hear the waves crashing against rocks, or breaking glass, or party chatter, and conjure up images in your mind of what the scene looks like. Radio advertisements also tend to feature humor fairly often both as a way to get attention and because the audience is less likely to be distracted by any visuals and can listen to the words. And as noted previously, if used in conjunction with similar TV commercials, listeners will often transfer the TV images to the radio spot.

Short Message Life

Because we listen to radio in the background, for the most part, ads on this medium have a very short message life. Like TV, and unlike newspapers and magazines, once the ad has aired, the opportunity for exposure has disappeared. This makes it all the more critical to grab the audience's attention right away with a message that is relevant, involving, and interesting.

Fragmentation

One of the drawbacks for radio is the fragmentation of the medium. We no longer just have rock stations, we have active rock, classic rock, and album-oriented rock formats, among others. Each one appeals to slightly different kinds of people, so if you wanted to reach them all, you would have to buy each type of rock station in a market. Audience shares, particularly in major markets, may be very small, which makes it harder to use the medium as a reach vehicle. With pure-play digital audio such as Pandora, each listener is effectively creating their own station that plays the specific artists or type of music that he or she prefers. Advertisers then need to rely on digital targeting approaches to effectively reach the right listeners.

RESEARCH ON RADIO

Although radio is considered a "second cousin" to television in the realm of electronic ad media, research has been done to compare the two forms. In addition, the power of sound, and of music in particular, has been studied to see how that impacts radio ad effectiveness.[15]

In 2003, the radio industry started to fund significant research studies under the umbrella of the Radio Advertising Lab, or RAL. This consortium of advertisers, agencies and radio station groups helped fund and design several major studies that examined the impact of radio advertising on consumers. Its first work looked at radio's psychological role in consumers' lives. Its study, "Personal Relevance, Personal Connections," found that radio listening is considered by people to be a personal and emotion-driven experience. They listen for personal gratification more so than for entertainment or pure information. As noted earlier in this section, another study looked at the benefits of synergistically mixing radio ads with newspaper or TV ads. It exposed consumers to two radio ads or one TV and two radio ads, and did the same substituting newspaper for TV. What they found was radio ads alone performed better than either the single exposure to TV or newspapers (in terms of brand recall). When radio was used together with TV, brand awareness and brand recall were higher than either medium alone.[16]

In an online research study that compared two Internet ads with one Internet and one radio spot for the same brand, the Radio Ad Lab program found that combining the two media produced far more effect on consumers than simply using two web ads. Unaided brand recall was four times greater for the Internet–radio combination, while most brands saw greater impact also for purchase intent and emotional connection.

Another study looked at the emotional power of radio ads compared to those on TV. This project used electromyography—the measurement of facial muscles—while consumers were exposed to program content that included either radio or TV ads for the same brands. Negative and positive emotions were measured and found to be equivalent across media, in contrast to conventional wisdom that would suggest TV is a far more powerful emotional indicator.

To measure the sales impact of radio, Westwood One undertook a study with Ipsos to examine what types of advertising drove sales for Amazon on its first-ever "Prime Day" in July 2015. While 74 percent of those surveyed were aware of this event and 81 percent of those people said they had been exposed to some kind of advertising for it, radio was the most likely to drive sales, with 52 percent of those who heard radio ads then buying something on Amazon, compared to 39 percent for TV and 48 percent for digital.[17]

ALL THE NEWS THAT'S FIT TO PRINT: NEWSPAPERS

Newspapers are one of the oldest media forms in this country and perhaps one of the most troubled in the early part of the 21st century. They were also one of the earliest media to accept advertising. In fact, the first advertising agencies were established to handle the purchase of space in this medium. Some of the earliest ads were for "medicinal" remedies, such as Lydia Pinkham's Compound.

In contrast to many other countries that have national newspapers, in the U.S., the majority of newspapers are written for and distributed to a primarily local audience. As a result, most of the advertising is placed on a market-by-market basis. You can also choose which section of the paper the ad will appear in, such as news (local, national or international), sports, entertainment, business, fashion, food, home, and travel, among others.

There are currently 2,254 newspapers published in the U.S. This figure includes both weekday and Sunday editions (1,331 and 923, respectively). That number has remained relatively stable over time. In 1970, for example, there were 2,334 papers published. Newspaper audiences are measured in terms of *circulation*, or the number of people who subscribe to or purchase the newspaper. Exhibit 4.14 shows the top five daily papers across the country based on their circulation.

Exhibit 4.14 Top Five Weekday Newspapers by Circulation

Rank	Newspaper	Circulation
1	USA Today	4,139,400
2	Wall Street Journal	2,276,200
3	New York Times	2,134,200
4	Los Angeles Times	690,900
5	New York Post	497,900

Source: Alliance for Audited Media (data is for the six-month period ended September 2014 and is subject to audit).

The past decade has witnessed a decline in the percentage of the adult population that says they read a paper daily. Currently, about 24 percent claim they do so, in contrast to the 78 percent who read a paper back in 1970. What is perhaps more worrying for the newspaper industry is that the readership figure is lower among younger people, who constitute the medium's future readers (among 18- to 34-year-olds, only 12 percent read a daily paper, although that is higher for an average week). It also varies by city, with 50 percent of those in Pittsburgh reading a paper each day, compared to just 23 percent in Atlanta. Several papers have introduced daily low-priced or free tabloid papers to entice younger people to develop a newspaper reading habit. The *Chicago Tribune*'s *RedEye*, for example, reaches 840,000 readers each week for its weekday tabloid, half of whom are under 45. Another way to capture readership of younger audiences is digitally; four in ten (40 percent) of 18- to 34-year-olds have read or looked into an electronic version of a newspaper in the past month, while one-third of all adults (34 percent) have done so.[18]

Circulation, especially at large newspapers, continues to decline. From 2012 to 2014, the total number of readers for the country's weekday papers fell about 7 percent, on top of a 3 percent decline in the three years prior to that. What is keeping circulation from falling further are the digital editions of the paper. Among the top five papers, they generate about one-quarter of their total circulation from the digital paper.

Another problem the industry faces is the demise of the two-newspaper town. Most large cities used to have at least two competing newspapers; today, due to the high costs of running a newspaper, that is the exception rather than the rule. Only in the largest cities (New York, Los Angeles, Chicago) are there still two or more daily papers. This not only harms the newspaper industry, but it is not particularly good news for advertisers either. Without competition, the paper can set its advertising rates wherever it wants them, as long as it can still compete with other media alternatives.

As major cities dropped competing papers, some of the readership moved to suburban or weekly newspapers. The growth here is not too surprising, given population shifts from city to suburb in the past few decades. The focus of these titles is far more local, writing about high school sports scores or local ordinances rather than national or regional news. For advertisers, it offers the opportunity to bring the message down to the truly local level. National advertisers such as Gap stores can announce the opening of a new store in Arlington Heights, Illinois, in the *Arlington Heights Post* instead of in a zoned or regional edition of the *Chicago Tribune*.

As noted earlier, the one bright spot for newspapers is growth in their digital readership. In August 2015, there were an estimated 179 million unique visitors to a digital version of a newspaper in the past month. This included PC-only, mobile-only, and those who access via both devices. The problem remains how to make money from that audience, since most papers do not charge readers anything for the online content but cannot generate sufficient ad revenue to make up the lost subscription money. Some, such as the *Wall Street Journal* and the *New York Times*, now charge for everything but the most cursory access to the online edition. They are growing their digital audiences rapidly. Forty percent of the *Journal*'s total circulation is digital, while for the *New York Times*, nearly half of it comes from that source.

Newspaper Advertising Revenue

Total newspaper ad revenue continues to fall (in line with the drop in overall readership). In 2013, it was about $38 billion, down 3 percent from the prior year. The largest part of newspaper advertising revenue (45 percent) comes from retailers. This includes large companies, such as major national department stores like JC Penney and Nordstrom, to regional banks such as Fifth Third or First National, to local retailers like Joe's shoe repair shop. Second in importance as far as newspaper ad revenues are concerned is classified advertising (40 percent). The most important classified sections are for real estate and automotive, which together account for the majority of classified ad dollars.

The third type of newspaper advertising is that which is placed on a national basis so that it appears in all (or most) papers across the country. This type of advertising represents only 17 percent of total advertising revenues for the medium, despite the efforts of many newspapers to position themselves as valuable national vehicles in the face of increased competition with other local media, such as spot TV and radio, regional magazines, or billboards. The main problem that advertisers have with using newspapers on a national basis is the considerable premium that it costs to run their ads in all markets. Most are reluctant to pay that premium, which can cost up to 75 percent more than a local or regional ad.

Digital advertising revenues are growing. They now account for about one-sixth (15 percent) of the total, with one-quarter of that portion appearing only in digital format (sometimes referred to as *pure-play digital,* similar to audio services that are digital only, such as Pandora and Spotify).

Newspapers also offer a medium within a medium, in the form of *freestanding inserts,* or FSIs. These are preprinted sheets that are usually distributed within the Sunday paper. Most of them have coupons. In the first six months of 2015, 156 billion FSI coupons were distributed, with an average face value of $1.80. On Sunday, too, most newspapers carry a special magazine supplement, either produced by the paper itself or coming from one of the nationally syndicated Sunday supplements, *Parade* and *USA Weekend*.

Not only are newspapers competing with the Web for readers, they are also losing their premier position as the carrier of coupons. In addition to FSIs, many papers carry coupons in the ads that they print, but consumers can now seek out coupons on specific websites (e.g., coupons.com or fatwallet.com), while others receive coupons via their mobile phones. In each case, they can specify or request the categories or brands for which they wish to receive coupons.

At one point it seemed that newspaper classified advertising would be greatly diminished by the Internet. Automotive and real estate classified ad sites were very popular at first, and they threatened to take revenues from the printed newspapers. It did not take long for newspapers to set up their own Internet-based advertising sites, either as part of their own individual newspaper sites (bostonglobe.com) or in concert with other newspapers (Careerbuilder.com, FrontDoor.com). Today, all American newspapers have websites.

Another issue that newspaper advertisers must deal with is the "sacred" line between the advertising and editorial departments. It does not happen often, but occasionally advertisers will pull their ads out of newspapers that print unfavorable editorial content. General Motors, for example, removed its ads from the *Los Angeles Times* newspaper after a journalist for the paper wrote a critical review about the automaker's Pontiac G6 vehicle.[19] This is a slippery slope, potentially leading to a blurring of the "church and state" separation of editorial and advertising departments.

BENEFITS OF NEWSPAPERS TO ADVERTISERS

Although newspapers have struggled in the past several years, they continue to offer several attractive benefits to advertisers, including wide reach, timeliness, desirable audiences, editorial impact, and local or regional possibilities.

Wide Reach

As Exhibit 4.14 illustrated, the top five weekday newspapers in the U.S. reach nearly ten million consumers every day. Digital content in newspapers reaches over 80 percent of adults each month. Then, add to that the circulations of the other, smaller newspapers in the country, and you'll begin to see just what kind of exposure is possible with newspaper advertisements.

Timeliness

During the stock market crash of 2008, ads appeared in many newspapers each day reassuring consumers and stockholders that everything was still all right at financial institutions. Financial services companies reacted similarly after the terrorist attack on the World Trade Center in 2001. In 2015, after Chipotle restaurants experienced a large number of E. coli outbreaks among customers in several states, its founder placed a full-page ad in national newspapers to apologize and to emphasize its comprehensive food safety plan.

Unlike magazines or even television, newspapers are by their very nature filled with news. People turn to them for the latest information on products, prices, and availability. The role that newspaper advertisements play in purchase decisions may be critical. A Canadian study conducted on behalf of that country's newspapers found that newspapers play a critical role throughout the purchase process and more so when the actual item is bought.[20]

In addition, electronic scanner devices in most supermarkets and retail stores can assess the link between advertising and sales more directly and rapidly. Data suggest that newspaper ads can triple the sales volume for items that are advertised at reduced prices.

Desirable Audience

In the battle to attract advertisers, newspapers can offer highly desirable audiences. A newspaper reader is more likely to be better educated, have a higher income, and be more involved in upscale activities than nonreaders. People with higher household incomes are more likely to be newspaper readers. Exhibit 4.15 gives a profile of the newspaper audience, comparing print and digital editions.

Exhibit 4.15 Profile of the Newspaper Reader

Read Printed Copy Only	Read Digital Version Only
Graduated college/post graduate	Graduated college/post graduate
Aged 55 and older	Aged 18–49 years
Household income $150,000+	Household income $50,000+
Married	Young children
Own home	Work full time
County size C/D	Professional or managerial
Live in east central or west central U.S.	
Retired/not employed	

Source: GfK MRI Doublebase 2015.

In contrast to other media, readers spend a considerable amount of time with the newspaper, with readers of the daily *New York Times* taking, on average, about 42 minutes with each issue and more than an hour (69 minutes) with the Sunday edition.[21]

Another consequence of the time readers spend with the paper is that it offers the media specialist more opportunity to provide detailed information. If you are trying to sell a new home equity loan program, you need the space to provide details on the terms of the deal, as well as on bank locations so interested consumers can find you. While you might worry that so much fine print will be boring or encourage page-turning, those people who are in your target audience will probably be interested enough to read through the entire ad (assuming the copy is inviting and attention-getting).

Impact of Editorial Context

An obvious advantage of newspaper advertising is that you can choose which section of the paper your ad is placed in, putting food ads in the food section or offering investment advice in the business pages, for example. This effectively narrows your reach to those consumers most likely to be interested in your product or service.

Local and Regional Possibilities

Although advertisers are reluctant to use newspapers on a national basis, they rely on them heavily for local or regional marketing. If Unilever wishes to test a new shampoo in Peoria, Illinois, it can advertise in the *Peoria Journal Star* and feel confident that the message will only reach those people able to buy the product, thereby creating awareness for the new item. They might also test the effects of advertising on sales this way. For regional operators, such as Friendly Restaurants—located only in the northeastern part of the country—ads can be placed in newspapers in the selected markets where the restaurant is found.

Even within a market, an advertiser can buy space in only those papers being sold in a certain area. The *Chicago Tribune*, for example, offers eight different zones to advertisers within the Chicago area.

DRAWBACKS OF NEWSPAPER ADVERTISING

As with every medium, newspapers have several drawbacks. The three most critical are short issue life, the challenge of grabbing the reader's attention, and the constraints of using a largely black and white medium.

Today or Never

While magazines can often prolong their issue life and reach more people by being passed around or picked up on several occasions, at the end of each day, the printed newspaper is usually discarded. If the reader misses your ad that day, you are not given a second chance. Even for digital editions, readers will likely want the latest news, rather than returning to articles they already read. So, although newspapers are available every day, their issue life is very short.

Active Readers

The issue life of the newspaper is closely linked to how people read it. Although more than half of all pages are likely to be opened, it is up to the reader to actively choose what to look at. If your headline doesn't attract the readers' attention, they won't look at it at all; if the copy isn't intriguing and relevant, readers can simply turn to another article or piece of content. It is therefore crucial that newspaper advertisements get the reader's attention. When people sit in front of the television or listen to the radio, they are generally a passive audience with no choice but to attend to the ad (even if fleetingly) or turn off the radio or TV set. Exhibit 4.16 shows how the newspaper advertiser must fight for attention.

Black and White

In the 1980s, it was rare to find a color ad in a newspaper. Then along came the Gannett Corporation with its national newspaper, *USA Today*, which offered full-color capabilities. The quality of newspaper color reproduction has been improving ever since, although it is still a long way from looking as sharp as magazine pages (due primarily to the poorer quality of the paper it is printed on). Even so, newspapers charge a premium for use of color, generally about 17 percent extra for a one-page four-color ad. For many advertisers, particularly those who wish to show "life-like" qualities, such as food manufacturers, it remains more effective to use magazine, television,

Exhibit 4.16 Elements That Get Newspaper Readers' Attention

Color
Full page
Photography and illustrations
Product in use
Sale price

Source: Roper Starch Study conducted on behalf of Newspaper Association of America, 2001.

or digital ads. Newspapers have become increasingly creative, however, in order to attract advertisers, offering "glow in the dark" or scented ad pages within the paper or attention-getting features surrounding the paper when it is delivered. For the digital editions, the color is prominent and of the same quality as all online ads.

RESEARCH ON NEWSPAPERS

While the newspaper industry, through its trade association, the Newspaper Association of America, conducts annual research on the size and strength of the industry and periodic studies on the medium's effectiveness, academic research has been more limited in recent years. Some studies have been done on the impact of ad size on consumer responses, including work on different promotional formats for the ads.[22]

MAGAZINES: AN EXPLOSION OF CHOICE

Although magazines have a long history in the U.S., with the earliest publications appearing in the middle of the 18th century, they are also a medium that may be said to have had two very distinct life stages. Originally, most magazines catered to a very general audience, offering a mixture of news, stories, and features aimed either at the total population or, in the case of titles such as *Ladies' Home Journal* and *Good Housekeeping*, at women. The strength of publications such as *Life*, *Look*, and the *Saturday Evening Post* is reflected in the fact that an ad placed in those magazines in the 1950s would be likely to reach about 60 percent of the total population.

But with the rise of television in the 1950s, general interest magazines found they could not compete effectively either for advertising dollars or for readers. Rather than simply disappearing, magazines began to move toward greater specialization in their targeting and their editorial content. This trend continues today, with extremely narrowly focused magazines devoted to topics such as tropical fish (*Tropical Fish Hobbyist*), cross stitching (*Simply Cross Stitch!*), or aircraft (*Plane & Pilot Magazine*). And while there are still some general offerings, such as *Atlantic Monthly* or the *New Yorker*, their readership is considerably lower than the audience of their general interest forebears. Because of this increased specialization, there are today 7,240 different consumer magazines available, most of which also have digital editions. In 2014, 231 new titles were introduced.

Magazines Today

Despite this specialization, magazines as a medium reach a broad range of the population. Indeed, 91 percent of all adults read magazines in the previous six months, reading on average about nine issues in a month. The places they purchase them include supermarkets (accounting for 35 percent of all magazines sold individually), discount stores, book stores, and drug stores. Each magazine copy is looked at for an average of 38 minutes.

There are three main types of magazines available: consumer, farm, and business-to-business. Consumer magazines are usually categorized according to their editorial content, such as business, men's, women's, sports, news, and entertainment. This category includes titles enjoyed by all segments of the population, from *Time* to *Sports Illustrated* to *Cosmopolitan*. Farm magazines are geared toward that particular industry. Some may be crop-specific, such as *Corn & Soybean Digest*, while others deal with the technical aspects of agriculture. The third type, business-to-business, cover all titles aimed at the industrial user, everything from *Chemical Age* to *Hotel Business* to *Information Week*.

Taken together, magazines account for 16 percent of all ad dollars spent in the U.S. Most magazines are considered as national vehicles for advertising, although city or regional publications are also classified within the consumer segment, such as *Milwaukee* or *Southern Living*. Many national magazines offer geographic breakouts of their circulation, allowing an advertiser to place a message that will, for example, only reach southerners or people who live in the northeastern states or in the Los Angeles metropolitan area. They also offer demographic "splits," so that Fidelity Investments can advertise its mutual funds in the edition of *Bloomberg's Business Week* that is read by people earning $75,000 or more per year.

Magazines are sold in one of two ways—at the newsstand or by subscription. For most titles, it is the latter that generates the most sales, accounting for 90 percent of total magazine copies sold. Among consumer magazines with circulations of 1 million or more, paid subscriptions account for 85 percent of the average magazine's revenue. The average cost of a single issue of a magazine in 2015 was $4.69, while the average annual magazine subscription was $28.33.[23] As with newspapers, magazines are assessed in terms of their circulation (number of copies distributed) and audience (number of people who read the circulated copies). Today's top ten audience read magazines are shown in Exhibit 4.17.

Digital is perhaps the brightest spot for magazine companies. The percent of adults who have read a digital version of a magazine continues to increase. As of 2014, it was up to 32 percent in total, but nearly half (48 percent) of those aged 18 to 34 years had read a digital magazine. Many magazines have apps available that dominate many categories in the Apple App Store, accounting for 9 of the top 15 in the health and fitness category and 11 of the top 15 in the food and drink category. About 5 percent of the population has read an app version (8 percent of younger adults). There is clearly an audience for digital magazines, although currently digital versions

Exhibit 4.17 Top Ten Magazines by Audience

Rank	Title	Audience
1	People	42,089,000
2	Better Homes and Gardens	38,293,000
3	AARP The Magazine	34,942,000
4	National Geographic	30,414,000
5	Reader's Digest	20,528,000
6	Sports Illustrated	18,329,000
7	Woman's Day	17,722,000
8	Time	16,811,000
9	Good Housekeeping	16,805,000
10	Family Circle	16,690,000

Source: GfK MRI Doublebase, 2015.

of magazines account for about 2 percent of total circulation. Compared to the print version, readers of the digital edition spend about the same time with the latter, on average (54 minutes versus 53 minutes).[24]

BENEFITS OF MAGAZINES TO ADVERTISERS

To an advertiser, three of the most attractive qualities of magazines are their high-end audiences, the enthusiasm of those audiences, and the long issue life of the medium.

Upscale and Niche Audiences

One of the incentives to using magazines for your advertising message is the favorable demographic profile of magazine readers. Similar to newspaper readers, the heaviest user of this medium is in the age range of 18 to 44 years, has a college education and a household income over $75,000, and is employed in a professional or managerial job. At the same time, given the fragmented and targeted nature of magazine titles, they are able to reach a variety of audiences, from youth to multicultural segments to people at different life stages (parents, seniors, etc.).

Getting Attention

Another benefit of placing your ads in magazines is reader involvement. While this concept is rather difficult to define (and even harder to measure), it generally refers to the interest that the reader has in the material, both editorial and advertising. Since most magazines today focus on a particular subject or interest, they can tie in more readily with the personal needs and lifestyles of the audience, enabling advertisers to do so as well. In this way, automakers can target car enthusiasts or prospective buyers in *Car and Driver* or *Road and Track*; detergent manufacturers can promote their new or improved products in magazines aimed at homemakers (*Better Homes and Gardens, Good Housekeeping, Real Simple*); while financial services companies can offer their mutual funds to interested investors in *Fortune* or *Money*.

Consumers also seem less resistant to seeing ads in magazines. One study conducted in 2013 found that respondents were more likely to pay attention to the magazine ads relative to websites or TV, and similarly said they had greater trust in magazine advertising compared to those other media. These findings are in part due to the fact that, as a reader, you get to select what ads you read, whereas television ads are in the programming. Digital advertising is seen, by most users, as mere "clutter" on the screen.

Hanging Around

Another important and unique feature of magazines is their *long issue life*. While the television program is over in half an hour and the newspaper is thrown out after one day, you will probably keep a monthly magazine in your home for four weeks or longer. This not only helps to reach more of your audience, with opportunities for additional or repeat exposures to the advertising, but it is also likely that other people, known as the *secondary audience,* may see the issue, too. The importance of this *pass-along readership* is shown by the fact that the average magazine is seen by seven different readers, with each one spending about 39 minutes with the issue.[25]

DRAWBACKS OF MAGAZINE ADVERTISING

Magazines do have their drawbacks. Among the most significant obstacles to keep in mind are the considerable lead time necessary and the relatively high cost of reaching your targeted audience.

Long Planning Cycle

For most printed publications, ads have to be completed and at the printer well in advance of their publishing date, a factor known as the *lead time*. This makes it difficult for advertisers to create particularly timely or newsworthy ads such as those seen in newspapers. Moreover, despite the generally excellent color reproduction quality, the magazine remains two-dimensional (aside from pop-up displays or inserts, discussed further

later). This prevents the magazine ad from offering the truly life-like qualities of a television spot. With digital editions, these drawbacks are partially
overcome because the ads can change very quickly and there are numerous
types of ad units available, including video.

Reaching Readers

The increasingly targeted nature of magazines means that the cost of reaching 1,000 members of the audience (the CPM, explained in greater detail in
Chapter 7) is higher than that of a broader mass medium such as television.
Even some of a magazine's benefits can be viewed as potential disadvantages for you as a media specialist. The notion of readers' involvement with
the magazine also means that if they are not very interested in a particular
product or ad, they can very easily ignore it by simply turning their attention to the next page or screen.

RESEARCH ON MAGAZINES

Studies on magazines as a medium have focused on similar areas as broadcast research. The value of the context in which an ad is seen was found,
by Norris and Colman, to impact consumer recall and recognition of the
ad. The same topic was explored further by Yi to see what happened when
readers were given additional information prior to seeing the magazine ad
in its context.[26] Meanwhile, the magazine industry has itself sponsored several studies showing the impact of magazines on sales.[27]

YELLOW PAGES: FROM PRINT TO LOCAL SEARCH

Yellow pages advertising, while historically thought of as paid print media,
is today primarily a digital form of paid advertising known as *directory
advertising* or *local search*. Its roots go back as far as the telephone. Offering
advertisers (and consumers) another type of classified advertising, the yellow pages generated nearly $5 billion in advertising revenues in 2015. There
are thousands of different yellow pages directories in the U.S., distinguished
not just by location (Chicago versus New York) but also by target (the silver
pages that target senior citizens or the gay/lesbian directory for that consumer group). This can sometimes make it harder for advertisers because
of the lack of standardization in terms of ad sizes or guidelines.

People use the yellow pages to look for information and services. More than
one-fifth of the time, the search is related to business needs. The top three
categories that people turn to are food, dining out and entertainment, and
automotive. The top three headings in yellow pages directories in terms of the
number of listings are restaurants, physicians and surgeons, and auto parts.

Exhibit 4.18 Top Categories Searched in Yellow Pages in Print or Online (Past 12 Months)

Rank	Category	Adults (Aged 18+) in Millions
1	Doctors, dentists, and other medical services	26.2
2	Pizza	24.8
3	Restaurants	23.4
4	Theaters	14.4
5	Department stores	12.5

Source: GfK MRI, Doublebase 2015.

According to GfK MRI, 12 percent of the adult population has used the yellow pages in the past seven days, while more than one quarter (27 percent) have done so within the past 12 months. Of the 4 percent of the country who used a moving van in the past year, 61 percent used the yellow pages to look up information about moving and storage, and 24.8 million (4.5 percent) adults in the U.S. used the yellow pages (online or in print) in the last 12 months for ordering pizza. The "average" profile is someone who is between the ages of 25 and 49, has been to college, and has an annual household income of $78,100 per year.[28] The most popular categories looked up in print or online are given in Exhibit 4.18.

BENEFITS OF YELLOW PAGES TO ADVERTISERS

The two key benefits for advertisers of the yellow pages are consumer selection and measurable response.

Consumer Selection

Unlike many media, especially traditional forms, consumers are almost always *choosing* to look at ads in the yellow pages. Whether it is simply an alphabetical listing of plumbers' names and addresses or the display ads that appear on the pages, the person whose drain is blocked is seeking out the ad in order to solve a problem or find information; therefore, that message is desired by the consumer, leading to greater impact.

Measurable Response

The fastest way to determine if your yellow pages ad is working is to measure the response. Whether in print or online, the use of distinct phone numbers or web addresses allows the advertiser to know precisely how many calls or emails they received directly as a result of placing that ad. That makes it a lot easier to calculate the return on this investment.

DRAWBACKS OF YELLOW PAGES ADVERTISING

Drawbacks for yellow pages advertising include clutter and infrequent usage.

Clutter

When you open almost any page in the yellow pages or search within a yellow pages website such as 411.com or yellowpages.com, you are likely to be rapidly overwhelmed. You want to order a pizza? Which of the 50 listings should you choose? How do you find the best auto body shop when your car's bumper gets damaged? Online, you are either looking for a specific company (in which case you will really just be looking for a phone number to call or website to go to), or, if you are in need of a particular type of business, you'll search within a category and likely face the same kind of dilemma as on the printed page.

Infrequent Usage

The downside of the yellow pages medium always being there is that you generally only turn to it at a time of need. Unless your carpets need cleaning, you won't turn to that page or screen filled with carpet cleaning companies. So while it is a very measurable medium, the measures may show such infrequent usage that it is questionable whether the investment is worthwhile. However, it is typically a low-cost medium, so even the few calls or sales generated may be cost-effective advertising.

OUTDOOR BILLBOARDS AND OUT-OF-HOME ADVERTISING: FROM CAIRO, EGYPT, TO CAIRO, ILLINOIS

There are some in the outdoor industry who like to claim that billboards are the oldest medium in existence. They date it back to Egyptian times, when hieroglyphics were written on roadside stones to give people directions to the nearest town or village. Whether you agree with that or not, outdoor billboards are certainly well established, having been in the U.S. since the 1800s. At that time, companies began leasing space on boards for bills to be pasted (hence the term *billboard*). There are two main types of billboard: posters and bulletins. Posters come in several sizes, such as regular or junior. Posters are found mostly in populated areas in or near cities and towns. Bulletins are larger boards situated along highways and major roads.

Putting messages on outdoor boards used to be extremely labor intensive. The sheets for posters were pasted onto the board, and bulletins were hand-painted. Both were created either at the board site or at a central location within the market or region. Since this had to be done in each market, differences resulted in the look of the message from one market to another (and even one site to another within the market). Today, thanks to technology, poster messages are created electronically and then shipped either in one piece or in sections to the board site. Bulletins may occasionally be hand-painted, but computers are now used to make sure that the finished product looks identical across boards. Today, bulletins are often created using other materials, such as lithography or special stretch vinyl. Increasingly, the message is delivered digitally and in rotation with several ads on one board.

In the past 50 years, the industry has come under increased criticism from environmentalists who claim that the boards are a blight on the scenery. Many cities and several states have introduced bans on putting up new boards and, in certain cases, demanded the removal of existing structures. You won't see any billboards in Hawaii or Vermont, for example.

Unlike other media that have editorial material too, outdoor billboards exist solely for advertising messages. They are primarily a local medium, bought on a market-by-market basis, but they are used by both national and local advertisers. The type of business using the medium has changed considerably in the past 20 years. For many years, the biggest category of advertiser was the tobacco industry, but in 1999, legislation banned advertising tobacco messages on any outdoor billboards. This not only had a significant impact on the tobacco industry, but it freed up many high-profile and well-positioned billboards across the country for other advertisers who had never been able to buy that space because the tobacco companies had long-term deals with the billboard companies. Today, you are far more likely to see billboards from local retailers, the travel industry, or healthcare providers than you would have even five years ago. Exhibit 4.19 shows the top categories that spend on outdoor advertising.

The outdoor industry has moved far beyond billboards and become an out-of-home industry instead. The reason for that is simple. Ads are now prevalent in many places outside, from bus shelters and subways to "street furniture" such as newsstands or benches or kiosks.

For many years, outdoor billboard audiences were calculated from manual traffic counts conducted by each system operator of how many cars passed by a given billboard, multiplied by government statistics that are updated periodically on how many people are present in the average car.

Exhibit 4.19 Top Outdoor Advertising Categories in 2014

Rank	Category	Dollars
1	Retail stores	$407,556,781
2	Restaurants, hotel dining, and night clubs	$329,032,625
3	Physical culture	$303,764,656
4	Engineering and professional services	$265,439,344
5	Hotels and resorts	$265,061,688
6	Communications and public utilities	$198,654,031
7	Television and cable television stations	$193,017,125
8	Amusements, events, and entertainment	$160,715,438
9	Financial services	$160,147,500
10	Schools and camps	$157,043,906

Source: Nielsen Ad Intel 2014.

That became the estimated audience viewing a billboard. In 2007, the Traffic Audit Bureau (TAB) announced a major new measurement initiative to update and improve outdoor audience measurement, moving from estimates of "opportunities to see" a billboard to a system to get closer to "eyes on" ratings. The measurement combines the broad "impressions" an out-of-home sign can deliver based on traffic, with an adjustment for how visible the sign is, and an eyes on impression factor for the number of people who in fact saw it, by age, gender, household income, and race or ethnicity. The TAB also commissioned travel surveys in 15 markets to collect information on how people travel and why they are traveling, in order to calculate the reach and frequency metrics for the medium. The TAB employs statistical modeling techniques to combine all the data into sources into a system that can provide estimated audiences to the ads on every outdoor board across the country.[29]

As noted previously, outdoor billboards are increasingly electronic. Digital billboards offer advertisers the opportunity to create messages that can change by the touch of a button from a central location, altering the ad based on conditions outside, for example, or simply to create a more engaging environment. These boards also allow the outdoor company to sell ads to multiple marketers at one time, with different messages appearing on different days or times, at a higher cost. The digital element even allows marketers to send personalized messages. Mini Cooper, for example, created a promotion that involved sending owners of the vehicle a special key fob. After the recipients answered a few questions on a special website, when they drove by specially enhanced outdoor billboards, individual messages would appear on the sign, such as "Motor on Jim!"[30]

In Shanghai, China, digital billboards were used to provide ongoing social media updates from some of the athletes competing in the 2012 London Olympics, with the comments changing several times each day.[31] Indeed, the outdoor industry is far more expansive than it used to be. For example, outdoor messages are now quite commonly seen painted on the sides of buildings, on telephone kiosks and bus shelters, or in sports stadiums.

BENEFITS OF OUT-OF-HOME ADVERTISING

The advantages of billboards and other forms of outdoor advertising have contributed to the medium's popularity over the past two centuries. Four of the most consistent and important benefits are size, mobility, effective reach, and cost. Each of these advantages is discussed next.

Big Is Better

The size of the poster panel or painted bulletin means that outdoor advertising gets noticed. In fact, at a typical busy location in the center of a city, more than 10,000 people are likely to pass an eight-sheet poster panel within a given month. In addition, the message is there constantly, for 12 to 24 hours (and many posters are illuminated at night).

Mobility

Outdoor messages can be placed in many locations, not just on streets and highways. The out-of-home category is extremely broad, allowing advertisers to reach their target in specific locations or during specific activities. So you could place ads for Samsonite luggage aimed at business executives at airports to catch them when they travel, or advertise Chiquita bananas near the A&P supermarket where your target audience shops.

Reaching Ethnic Groups

With out of home you can tailor your message to members of a particular ethnic group using their own language or cultural attributes, yet still reach a mass audience within a specific market. You can buy billboards or transit ads in areas with heavy concentrations of Hispanic, Chinese, or Korean people, for example, reaching them where they live, work, and shop. It is harder to reach a large portion of these groups with traditionally "Anglo" television or magazines. Furthermore, it is valuable to be able to reach non-native English speakers in their first language, whatever language that might be.

Reinforcing the Message

Out-of-home advertising is a good supplementary medium, helping to add reach and frequency to a media schedule at reasonable cost. A fairly typical outdoor billboard buy could reach over 80 percent of adults in a given area in a month. In addition, the fact that the out-of-home message can be there all the time means that frequency builds up and the message can be a constant reminder. The ability to locate out-of-home messages in shopping areas helps to reinforce the message very close to the point of purchase.

DRAWBACKS OF OUT-OF-HOME ADVERTISING

In considering what part of your advertising budget to commit to out-of-home advertising, you will need to keep in mind the two drawbacks of the medium: short exposure time and the potential for criticism from environmentalists.

Brief Message Exposure

Since the average outdoor message is only seen for between three and seven seconds, the copy needs to be extremely concise and compelling. For products that need a lot of explanation, outdoor is clearly not the right medium. One way to gauge whether there is too much copy on a billboard is to estimate how quickly people are going to pass by it. You can try the exercise yourself and see how much of the message you can take in as you drive or walk by. Because most of the viewing is done at high speed, especially for bulletins situated along the highway, the advertisement must also be eye-catching and interesting enough to attract the driver's (or passenger's) attention.

Environmental Criticism

The outdoor industry, as noted earlier, has come under criticism for cluttering up the environment. This is felt in two ways. First, there is the literal problem of boards covering up the natural landscape. But second, there is the metaphorical "clutter" of forcing people to be exposed to brand messages that, some believe, simply add to human insecurities or anxieties, making them want products and services.[32] While this is a long-standing argument against advertising as a whole, the point about outdoor advertising is that there is no escape from it. Advertisers might shy away from the medium to avoid legal or ethical disputes, especially in areas with a recent history of environmental controversies.

RESEARCH ON OUT-OF-HOME ADVERTISING

The outdoor industry is one of the least researched of any mass medium. Studies have focused mostly on proving that the medium works, as shown by Bhargava and colleagues.[33] More recently, a study in the Netherlands looked at what factors enhance recognition of outdoor ads. More information on how the medium has been researched can be found on the website of the Outdoor Advertising Association of America (www.oaaa.org).

DIGITAL DISPLAY/SEARCH/ONLINE VIDEO/SOCIAL MEDIA: MULTIPLE CHOICES

The rapid growth of the Internet as a consumer medium in the 1990s was unprecedented in the history of media. Internet penetration rose faster than any other medium (or appliance), reaching the critical mass of 50 million users in five short years (it took radio 36 years to get to that point). Today, with more than eight in ten (85 percent) of the country able to access the Internet from home, the medium's capabilities continue to expand and develop. That is due, in part, to the ability of users to access the Web through high-speed (broadband) technology. Today, nearly all (97 percent) of those accessing the Internet from home do so at high speed, allowing them easier and faster access to everything available online. From an advertiser's perspective, there are four paid forms of digital advertising: display, online video, search, and social media. These will be covered here; owned and earned types of digital offerings, such as brand websites and word of mouth, are covered in subsequent chapters.

The Internet was first devised as a means of communication for the academic community more than 30 years ago. It was a fairly arcane and complex system, relying on a lot of computer language and processing. The hypertext markup language (HTML) that formed the basis of the Web is now seamlessly (and invisibly) connected to everything we do on the computer. That was not the case originally. It was not until the late 1990s that the Internet came to be seen as a genuine medium (as opposed to computer tool) that offered users far greater control than with any other existing medium. Even more so than print media, the Internet lets you select exactly where you want to go and what you want to see. You choose where to click and how long to stay there. Although you can browse through a magazine or newspaper, you generally have to look at each page (or a table of contents) to find what you are most interested in. On the Web, you can type in a web address (www.mediahandbook.com) and be taken straight to that specific piece of information without having to wade through other pages in which you have no interest. At the same time, your digital movement is tracked at every movement, capturing each site you visit or app that you use. This information proved invaluable in the development of digital media for advertising.

Indeed, as companies began setting up websites (a fairly inexpensive proposition), they saw huge potential for advertising to help generate revenues. Analogies to the direct response industry are common. Companies were immediately able to track visits to their sites (by computer address only) and offer advertisers more information on not only who was visiting their sites but also looking at the ads—and clicking through to the advertiser's site—than any other mass medium. They did so by placing special software, known as *cookies*, on a user's computer to monitor the path that user takes as they browse different sites on the Internet. Internet ad revenues doubled each year for several years in a row in the late 1990s, surpassing total ad revenues for the outdoor and syndicated TV industries, and by 2014, display advertising alone had reached $13 billion, while all paid digital ad dollars totaled $40 billion.

Digital Display

At first, Internet ads consisted of banners—billboards on the Web—that did little more than display a brand name or teaser and a link to another site (hence the term *display*). Companies began to consider using web advertising for brand-building purposes rather than simply offering information. And before long, the ability to purchase via the Web became mainstream rather than exceptional. Today, according to eMarketer, 76 percent of the online population aged 14 years and older has made a purchase digitally in the past year. Before long, advertisers started to get more creative, changing the size of the ad messages and incorporating (as technology advanced) more sound, motion, and interactivity, a phenomenon known as *rich media*. Not surprisingly, the research findings showed that these kinds of ads had greater impact (recall, awareness) than the plain-vanilla banners. But it became more and more clear that as fast as advertisers moved to surprise consumers, those consumers became increasingly disenchanted with web ads.

One of the most important aspects of digital advertising is its targeting capabilities. In addition to placing ads where certain types of consumers are likely to go (e.g., international travel sites for affluent consumers), advertisers can target based on where you have been online, a practice known as *behavioral targeting*. While privacy advocates are against this practice, for advertisers it provides them the opportunity to send a more relevant and, therefore, likely effective message. If you have visited kayak.com or tripadvisor. com and looked into visiting Bali, then Samsonite or Travelpro could target you either on those sites, when you return, or on other sites you go to. The technology is now available to target web ads based on what was watched on television by tracking viewership through the smart TV sets mentioned earlier.

Today, when most consumers are asked about digital advertising, their responses are primarily irritation. They talk about the clutter of websites, the irrelevance of most ads that appear, and their techniques for avoiding them. In particular, annoyance with ads that pop up, or pop under, a website is considerable. More and more consumers are installing ad blockers—software that prevents ads from loading. At the same time, if an ad appears on the Web that is relevant and informative, consumers will click on it to find out more. For many, the line between the editorial material and the advertising is a narrow one on the Web, which is viewed by most people as an information cornucopia.

One of the biggest areas of growth within paid display advertising is the practice of *programmatic advertising*. This involves using the power of computers to determine where best to reach the desired target as they go online and direct ads to them on the sites they visit. It is estimated that in the U.S., this will account for 15 percent of all display spending in 2015 and nearly double to 27 percent of the total by 2018.[34]

Display ads have been standardized by the Interactive Advertising Bureau into specific sizes and shapes so that advertisers can develop creative that works across sites. Nonetheless, advertisers continue to test out new formats in an ongoing effort to communicate with their audiences without annoying them so much that they close the ad and ignore the message.

Online Video

As more marketers have embraced digital ads, they have moved to online video ads, which primarily consist of 15- or 30-second video commercials (often transferred directly from television). These mostly appear before the content and are called *pre-roll* ads. With longer content, such as 30-minute TV shows, there may also be *mid-roll* ads during the program or even *post-roll* ads afterward. For shorter clips, such as those found on YouTube, the pre-roll video message tends to be proportionately shorter. Research has been conducted to demonstrate the immediate, short-term impact of ads seen prior to or during online video, with some studies suggesting that online video ads are 38 percent more memorable than the comparable ad on TV.[35]

Online video is not simply a consumer phenomenon, however. Companies use it for other reasons. GE's website features many videos that help showcase its products and services for future employees or investors, while

Pantene posts videos on its website featuring its current celebrity sponsor talking about haircare. The hardware store Home Depot uses online videos to help people learn how to do home improvements, showing the full range of products available while also providing guidance to the DIYers who shop in their stores.

In 2014, comScore reported that 88 million Americans watched videos online every day, while in an average month, viewers spend nearly 19 hours doing so, and 59 billion content videos are consumed. According to Nielsen, time spent watching digital video is still fairly small relative to the hours spent watching TV on a regular set. In the first quarter of 2015, the average weekly time viewing video on the web was one and a half hours, compared to nearly 36 hours watching live TV.[36] But it is expected that online video viewing will grow rapidly, especially as the speed of content delivery increases and improves. Indeed, one indicator of that is that among 18- to 34-year-olds, the number of online video views per month (356) is 37 percent higher than among 35- to 54-year-olds and two times higher than those aged 55 years and older.[37] Indeed, eMarketer forecasts that by 2016, 200 million people will regularly watch online video in the U.S.

It is impossible to discuss online video without covering YouTube. This global phenomenon, which started as a way for people to share videos with each other, is estimated today to have been seen by much of the world's population. More than 800 million unique users go on YouTube every month, with 400 billion hours of video consumed in that time span. The key benefit it offers viewers is that they can search for whatever or whomever they want, whether that is Aunt Betty's New Year's Eve party, clips from last night's *Tonight Show with Jimmy Fallon* show, or live streaming sports events. It has rapidly become the destination for online video content. According to eMarketer, people in the U.S. spent 34 billion hours watching videos on YouTube during 2015.[38] Nielsen notes the prime time for this media form is between noon and 2:00 p.m., suggesting there are a lot of people taking their lunch breaks in front of a computer screen. From a research and accountability standpoint, YouTube provides a "self-service" analysis tool that gives ongoing statistics on how many people are watching a video posted to YouTube, broken out by demographics such as gender and geography.[39]

Online Search

Perhaps the Internet phenomenon with the biggest impact on both consumers' lives and on digital advertising has been the growth of search advertising. Inspired by sites such as Google, which allow users to type in any word and find out what is available throughout the Web, advertisers started to realize that they could buy keywords or links and deliver ad messages to consumers when they requested those words. So, for example, if you do a search on Google for "fruit drinks" to find out if your fruit-based carbonated drink, Fruitola, is available, at the top of the screen you might see sponsored links from websites such as wholefoods.com or competing drink brands such as Tropicana or Coca-Cola.

Today, search has become the most popular way for advertisers to reach online consumers. In 2015, advertisers spent an estimated $7.2 billion on search alone. They now spend more on search than on display or online video ads; indeed, nearly one in two digital ad dollars go toward search. In 2014, Google generated more revenue from advertising than either the magazine or newspaper industry.[40]

There were an estimated 219 billion searches in the U.S. in 2015. In just one month, there were 11 billion searches across Google, followed by 3.4 billion on Bing, and 2.2 billion on Yahoo.[41] As noted earlier, an important area within search is at the local level, estimated to account for nearly $5 billion of total U.S. spending. Advertisers can ensure that the search results will be linked to the zip code in which the consumer lives. For example, if someone lives in Urbana, Illinois, and does a search for "dog collars," PetSmart can pay to ensure that the listings that result will include information on its store in the 61801 area.

The benefit of all forms of paid digital marketing is that it is possible to measure their impact. That is, if someone clicks on the results of a search or the ad that appears before the video content, their subsequent digital behavior can be tracked to see if that action led to a sale. The primary measures for digital ads are the number of impressions delivered and, very often, the *click through rate* (CTR). In this way, digital paid ads can be assessed in terms of their return on investment, or ROI. For every $X spent on these forms of advertising, how many dollars are returned through increased sales? In one survey, when marketers were asked which metrics they tracked related to spending on searches, the most common answer, by 51 percent, was "overall volume of traffic," with qualified leads or sales used by one-third (34 percent) of the respondents and one in ten admitting they were not sure what to measure.[42]

Social Media

When social media offerings such as Facebook and Twitter were first released, advertisers were not quite sure how to use them. They knew that many consumers quickly adopted them, but they considered them primarily for owned and earned media (covered in more detail in the next two chapters). Yet today, paid social media advertising is becoming increasingly important to consider. The amount spent in the U.S. on paid social media advertising doubled from 2013 to about $9 billion in 2015. Facebook and Twitter alone account for nearly one in three digital display ad dollars. The introduction of video ads on Facebook in 2014 spurred even greater advertiser interest (and dollars). On Twitter, brands have started creating branded emojis in their hashtags that consumers comment on or share (retweet). Coca-Cola, for example, included its branded Coke bottles in the #ShareACoke hashtag and received over 170,000 mentions within the first day it appeared. Other social networks, such as Instagram and Snapchat, which both began without any paid advertising, have looked for ways to introduce some kind of promotional messaging in ways that consumers will accept. Instagram (now owned by Facebook) created a "call to action" button on their video ads so that people could see an ad for a Toyota Prius and then find the nearest dealer, for example. Snapchat lets brands sponsor filters that appear when users are swiping through.

BENEFITS OF PAID DIGITAL ADVERTISING

As the uses and forms of online advertising change over time, the benefits of this emerging medium for advertisers are still being explored. Four of the current advantages for paid digital ads are flexibility, personalization, reach, and measurability. Each is examined next.

Flexibility

There are many forms of digital advertising. Unlike other mass media, where choices come down to 15- or 30-second commercials or full-page versus half-page ads, on the Internet there really is little limit to the imagination. From traditional banner ads to online video to search or social media, paid digital ad messages can appear in numerous forms.

Targeted Message

The Internet is the first mass medium able to offer a targeted, personal advertising message. Although direct response has been doing so for many years, it was not possible for most of their history for TV, radio, newspapers, magazines, or billboards to talk to anything less than a sizable audience. With the Internet, however, advertisers can send messages to more narrowly defined groups, such as basset hound lovers (those visiting a website devoted to the topic or watching YouTube videos featuring that dog breed) or people dealing with weight management issues (those who search on words related to weight control) or those who have "liked" a brand's page on Facebook. It is assumed that such messages, by being more relevant to that individual, are more likely to be accepted and absorbed.

Reach

Although the Internet does not offer as broad a reach as television, campaigns that appear on a range of websites (particularly the gateway or portal sites many people have as their home pages, such as msn.com or yahoo.com) can indeed reach a high proportion of everyone on the Internet. In addition, the reach on the Internet can be given against specific advertising messages, not just the sites on which those messages appear (i.e., ad exposure not just opportunity to see).

Measurability

For advertisers, the Internet's ability to measure who is doing what on the Web would seem to be answering one of the Holy Grail questions of the industry. But because the measurement is computer-based rather than person-based, the measures are in fact not as precise and valuable as they might appear. Having said that, digital measurement is certainly far more detailed than for any other paid ad medium, where at best the media specialist can look at opportunities to be exposed to the ad rather than actual viewer, reader, or listener behavior. Several advertisers have undertaken cross-media studies of ad impact on the Web compared to other media (using statistical modeling) and found that the digital ads are usually more effective at enhancing brand image and consideration than other media types. Initially, paid digital advertising was sold based on *click-throughs* (users clicking on web ads to link to advertisers' sites), but it soon became clear that if digital advertising was to be comparable to other ad media, the cost metric had to be the same. Today, most sites price their advertising based on cost per thousand (CPM). Web measurement services provide data on the demographics and lifestyles of web users, as well as web traffic to individual sites and/or ads. Today, the primary measurement companies can also demonstrate whether the digital ads were "viewable" or not, leading to new industry rules that said a digital ad was only counted if at least 50 percent of the ad was viewed for at least 1 second (or 50 percent for 2 seconds in the case of video ads), and advertisers have increasingly demanded that they only pay for those *viewable impressions*.

DRAWBACKS OF PAID DIGITAL ADVERTISING

As powerful as digital advertising is, it still cannot provide advertisers with everything they would want to reach their desired targets at a cost. Following is a summary of the downside to paid digital advertising, in terms of consumer irritation, confusion, and nonstandard metrics.

Consumer Irritation

The plethora of paid digital advertising is not always appreciated by consumers. Although users have the option to click on an ad to find out more information, there are more and more messages that appear on a site that the user has to actively remove if he or she does not want to look at them. Moreover, since people tend to use digital media to look for specific information or to catch up with friends (rather than passively consuming a TV program or browsing a magazine's pages), the irritation level with the high number of paid ad messages in digital media (display banners, video pre-roll, search ads) can become overwhelming, detracting from the impact of any one particular message.

Clutter

When the Internet was first developing as a consumer medium, there were only a few display ads that appeared occasionally. Today, that is far from the case. The top ten display advertisers alone spent nearly $13 billion in 2014! And what constitutes advertising, to a consumer, has changed too. Is it a message that appears in a list of search results? Or are the pages that pop up in moving from one page to another (so-called *interstitials*) ad messages or actual sites? When brands such as American Express or Dunkin Donuts sponsor the filters on Snapchat, do the app's users consider that helpful or intrusive? While some of this may benefit advertisers (putting out messages that users see as information rather than advertising), the likely reaction is for consumers to see all of these ad messages as "clutter," which will lead them to avoid them as quickly as possible.

Changing Metrics

Despite its use as an advertising medium for well over a decade, the Internet is still developing fully standardized measurement metrics. Each measurement service uses slightly different methods (not always fully revealed) to measure a different list of websites. Some sites try to sell advertising based on audience impressions, others on site visits (clicks), and yet others on actual sales. The Interactive Advertising Bureau has worked hard, however, to standardize the ad unit sizes so that there is consistency for the consumer and for the creative developers on rectangular billboards, pop-ups, or skyscraper ads. The guidelines include not only the size (in pixels), but also recommendations on the size of the file that has to download onto the page it appears on, along with the duration of the ad. As noted, there are standards coming into place, such as the viewable impression.

RESEARCH ON THE INTERNET

An early study conducted on behalf of the Online Publishers Association (OPA) in 2005 found that when Internet users were more engaged in the content, they not only spent more time with a site, but they also were more likely to recommend it to their friends. Through both qualitative and quantitative studies and segmentation of the data, the OPA uncovered 22 distinct online user experiences, ranging from "connection with others" to "worth saving and sharing." The experiences most likely to increase online usage were that the content was entertaining and absorbing and that it was personalized ("looks out for people like me").[43]

Others have started to try to model the uses and gratifications of Internet use, finding that those looking for information tend to interact more with messages on websites, whereas those looking for social interaction turn to the Web for human-to-human communication.[44] Additional research has burgeoned in more recent years, looking at the ability of various paid digital forms to enhance both upper funnel (awareness, preference) and lower funnel (sales) measures.[45]

MOBILE: LOCATION, LOCATION

Within the past few years, the cell phone has moved from being simply a way to make phone calls to a full-blown communications and advertising medium. Today's mobile marketing, considered by some as a form of paid digital advertising, includes display ads, video, or search. With the growth of Internet access, improvements and expansions in screens, and the addition of keyboards, today's mobile phones are seen by consumers and, increasingly, by advertisers as mobile computers that deliver messages to target audiences wherever they are, with the ability to generate a direct response. Indeed, there are now more mobile devices than people in the world! In 2015, it was estimated that there are a total of 4.4 billion mobile phone subscribers worldwide, of whom 42 percent have smartphones (with Internet access). Forecasts for mobile phone growth suggest that by 2019, phone penetration will be at 67 percent worldwide, with one-half of those (52.5 percent) having a smartphone.[46]

Indeed, mobile marketing depends heavily on that Internet connection. In the U.S., three in four (74 percent) of all mobile phones are smartphones, with about one in five consumers (16 percent) saying they go online primarily from their phone, while another 14 percent cite the tablet, which is often considered an alternative mobile device. The U.S. is behind other parts of the world when it comes to smartphones, however. In Singapore, 85 percent of the phones have Internet access, and across Asia, usage of the smartphone has eclipsed the computer. The importance of mobile access during the purchase journey is critical. People not only use the phone to find a store location or search for an item, but they will check prices, research the product, or read reviews before making a purchase.

Mobile search is increasingly used by consumers, with about one-third of smartphone owners in the U.S. saying that they do so. The potential is much greater, however; in Japan, 65 percent use this application of their phone. One of the biggest growth areas in mobile advertising has been advertising on apps. Consumer mobile phone use is now dominated by this. According to comScore, nearly seven of every eight minutes of phone usage is taken up with apps. While people download many apps, their time is usually spent on just one or two of them. Indeed, nearly three in four minutes of app usage are devoted to one of the top four apps a person has downloaded.[47] The most popular app categories are social networks (such as Facebook), games (such as Angry Birds or Words with Friends), and radio (such as Spotify or Pandora). This skew toward entertainment and communication should guide advertisers as they figure out how to best deploy their brands' messages. If you are eagerly involved in looking at a Snapchat story or playing against the clock in a game of Jelly, how receptive would you be to a banner ad for McDonald's or a video promoting fall fashions at TJ Maxx? On the other hand, a location-based ad for Olive Garden that appeared in the Snapchat post from your friends or a short video for Pepsi at the end of a tense game might be relevant and appreciated.

As shown in Exhibit 4.20, in 2015, mobile advertising had reached $30 billion.

Tablets are considered another mobile device from an advertiser's perspective. First introduced to the marketplace in 2010, tablets are now owned by about half (52 percent) of the U.S. population. The category was initially dominated by Apple, with its iPad, but today, Android devices have become significant competitors, accounting for nearly half of all tablets sold. While tablet ownership was initially the domain of younger men, the profile has broadened out, with a near-even gender split and an adoption across all ages.

Tablets can be considered all-purpose devices, allowing users to download apps and enjoy print, video, and online content. For now, the advertising opportunities seem to be mimicking those same media, with static ads in print content, video ads for video, and Internet-type banners in digital content.

Exhibit 4.20 Types of Mobile Ad Spending, 2015

US Mobile Ad Spending, by Format, 2014-2020
billions

	2014	2015	2016	2017	2018	2019	2020
Display	$9.65	$16.13	$22.40	$27.20	$31.50	$35.59	$39.67
—Banners, rich media, sponsorships and other*	$8.11	$13.25	$18.16	$21.82	$25.18	$28.39	$31.61
—Video	$1.54	$2.88	$4.24	$5.39	$6.31	$7.20	$8.06
Search	$8.72	$14.13	$19.24	$23.02	$26.52	$29.83	$33.23
SMS/MMS/P2P messaging	$0.24	$0.27	$0.28	$0.27	$0.25	$0.25	$0.25
Other (classifieds, email, lead gen)	$0.55	$1.06	$1.69	$2.27	$2.93	$3.49	$3.95
Total	$19.15	$31.59	$43.60	$52.76	$61.20	$69.15	$77.10

*Note: ad spending on tablets is included; numbers may not add up to total due to rounding; *includes ads such as Facebook's News Feed Ads and Twitter's Promoted Tweets*
Source: eMarketer, March 2016

205545   www.**eMarketer**.com

Source: eMarketer 2015.

BENEFITS OF MOBILE MARKETING TO ADVERTISERS

Advertisers considering the use of mobile marketing can benefit from its location-based capability and direct response mechanism.

Location Targeting

Although mobile marketing is still developing in terms of the right formats to use, the ability to deliver messages to consumers when they are in specific locations has enormous appeal for advertisers, allowing them to reach the target audience closer to the point of purchase.

Direct Consumer Response

As a two-way communications device, the mobile phone allows advertisers to generate immediate behavioral responses from consumers. That is, Starbucks could send Ming a text message offering him $0.50 off a coffee if he goes to his nearest store in the next 48 hours. When he presents the coupon via his phone, the company can quickly tally just how effective that advertising was. Mobile phones play a significant role for television, too, particularly for reality shows, making it easy for people to text or call in their votes.

DRAWBACKS OF MOBILE MARKETING TO ADVERTISERS

When advertisers are considering mobile marketing, they must keep in mind that there are privacy concerns and that consumer irritation may be high.

Privacy

As marketers grow increasingly excited at the prospect of being able to target and reach phone owners anywhere and anytime, their ability to do so is premised on capabilities that, for many people, are deeply concerning. That is, the geo-location function of a phone, identifying where a person is at any moment, makes some consumers deeply uncomfortable that their privacy has been compromised. When that is combined with the online targeting prevalent on the Web (knowing you like dogs because you visited a dog website, for example), it makes mobile advertising seem downright creepy to some. As noted, there has to be a clear benefit for the consumer in being reached by a marketer at that location at that time (such as a coupon or other incentive/reward).

Consumer Irritation

Research has been conducted with consumers to determine how open they are to the idea of receiving advertising on their mobile phones. While published results always indicate an openness and willingness to see it (especially if it offsets any costs incurred in phone use), it remains to be seen whether that will turn out to be the case or whether the public will ignore or avoid any marketing messages that appear out of irritation at yet more commercialization in their lives. Research on mobile marketing is still in its infancy, but researchers are starting to examine it in more detail to learn how consumers might best respond to it as an advertising medium.[48]

WHICH PAID MEDIA SHOULD YOU USE?

Now that you have some basic information on each major media category, we can start to consider why you might or might not wish to include them in

Exhibit 4.21 Pros and Cons of Paid Media

Medium	Pros	Cons
Television	True to life Pervasive Reaches masses	High cost Brief exposure Clutter Poor placement
Radio	Local appeal Targeted audience Imagery transfer Lower cost Close to purchase High frequency Flexible message	Background medium Sound only Short message life Fragmentation
Newspaper	Wide reach Timeliness Desirable audience Editorial context Local/regional	Short message life Active readers Black and white
Magazines	Upscale and niche audiences Reader involvement Long issue life	Long planning cycle Higher cost
Yellow pages	Consumer selection Measurable response	Clutter Infrequent usage
Outdoor billboards/out-of-home advertisements	Large size Mobility Ethnic groups Supplementary medium	Brief exposure Environmental criticism
Digital display/search/online video/social	Flexibility Targeted message Reach Measurability	Consumer irritation Clutter Changing metrics
Mobile	Location targeting Direct response	Privacy Consumer irritation

your media plans. To make this process less cumbersome, we'll recap some of the most important advantages and disadvantages that each medium offers. These are summarized in Exhibit 4.21.

SUMMARY

Before deciding which paid media might best be suited to achieving your plan objectives, it is important to consider the advantages and disadvantages that each medium can offer. Issues to be incorporated into your analysis include the reach and/or frequency of the medium, length of message exposure, audience involvement, clutter, targetability, and cost. For each media category, an examination of the benefits and drawbacks will help determine whether—and to what extent—it should be included in the final plan.

Checklist: Exploring Paid Media

1. Do you want primarily national or local media in your plan, or a combination of both?
2. Will the benefits of television (mass reach, closeness to reality, and pervasiveness) help achieve your media objectives?
3. Have you considered the drawbacks of television (cost, brief exposure time, advertising clutter, and uncertain pod positioning)?
4. Should you consider ways to use the newer forms of TV advertising, such as addressable TV or dynamic ad insertion in VOD?
5. Will the benefits of radio (local appeal, targeted formats, low cost, high frequency, and message flexibility) help achieve your media objectives?
6. Have you considered the drawbacks of radio (its background nature, audio-only message, brief exposure time, and fragmented market)?
7. Will the benefits of newspapers (timeliness, editorial affinity, local and regional capabilities, and upscale audiences) help achieve your media objectives?
8. Have you considered the drawbacks of newspapers, such as brief exposure, poor color capabilities, and selective readers?
9. Will the benefits of magazines (upscale audiences, involved and interested readers, and long issue life) help achieve your media objectives?
10. Have you considered the drawbacks of magazines (long lead time, and higher costs per thousand)?
11. Will your plan benefit from using yellow pages (print or online) due to their ability to offer consumer selection and measurable response?
12. Do the drawbacks of yellow pages (clutter and infrequent usage) work against their use in the plan?
13. Will the benefits of outdoor billboards (large message size, rotating message, ethnic targetability) help achieve your media objectives?
14. Have you considered the drawbacks of outdoor billboards (brief message exposure and environmental impact)?
15. Will the benefits of digital advertising (flexibility, targeted message, reach, measurability) help achieve your media objectives?
16. Have you considered the drawbacks of digital advertising (irritation, confusion, and nonstandard metrics)?

17. Do the benefits of mobile marketing fit with your objectives (location-based messaging and direct consumer response)?
18. Will the drawbacks of mobile marketing detract from your success (privacy concerns, consumer irritation)?

NOTES

1. Nielsen Media Research, Total Audience Report, Q1 2015.
2. Nielsen Media Research, Total Audience Report, Q1 2015.
3. Nielsen Media Research, Total Audience Report, Q1 2015.
4. "TV Ad Pricing Chart," *Advertising Age*, September 24, 2015.
5. "Predictors of Advertising Avoidance in Print and Broadcast Media," Paul Surgi Speck and Michael T. Elliott, *Journal of Advertising*, vol. 26, no. 2, Summer 1997, 61–76.
6. "Does Advertising Clutter Have Diminishing and Negative Returns?" Louisa Ha and Barry R. Litman, *Journal of Advertising*, vol. 26, no. 1, Spring 1997, 31–42.
7. Nielsen TV Audience 2014.
8. "Consumer Perceptions of Advertising Clutter and Its Impact Across Various Media," Michael T. Elliott and Paul Surgi Speck, *Journal of Advertising Research*, vol. 35, no. 3, May/June 1995, 29–42; "The Antecedents and Consequences of Perceived Advertising Clutter," Paul Surgi Speck and Michael T. Elliott, *Journal of Current Issues and Research in Advertising*, vol. 19, no. 2, 1997, 39–54.
9. "The Role of Consumer Involvement in Determining Cognitive Response to Broadcast Advertising," Laura M. Buchholz and Robert E. Smith, *Journal of Advertising*, vol. 20, no. 1, 1991, 4–17.
10. "Television Commercial Evaluation in the Context of Program Induced Mood: Congruency Versus Consistency Effects," Michael A. Kamins, Lawrence J. Marks, and Deborah Skinner, *Journal of Advertising*, vol. 20, no. 2, June 1991, 1–14.
11. "Multiple Resource Theory and Consumer Processing of Broadcast Advertisements: An Involvement Perspective," Robert E. Smith and Laura M. Buchholz, *Journal of Advertising*, vol. 20, no. 3, September 1991, 1–8. "Attention Versus Distraction: The Interactive Effect of Program Involvement and Attentional Devices on Commercial Processing," Kenneth R. Lord and Robert E. Burnkrant, *Journal of Advertising*, vol. 22, no. 1, March 1997, 47–60. "How the Digital Video Recorder (DVR) Changes Traditional Television Advertising," Kenneth C. Wilbur, *Journal of Advertising*, vol. 37, no. 1, Spring 2008, 143–149. "Television Programming and Its Influence on Viewers' Perceptions of Commercials: The Role of Program Arousal and Pleasantness," V. Carter Broach, Jr., Thomas R. Page, Jr., and R. Dale Wilson, *Journal of Advertising*, vol. 24, no. 4, Winter 1995, 45–54. "Context Is Key: The Effect of Program-Induced Mood on Thoughts about the Ad," Andrew B. Aylesworth and Scott B. MacKenzie, *Journal of Advertising*, vol. 27, no. 2, Summer 1997, 17–32. "Hearing versus Seeing: A Comparison of Consumer Learning of Spoken and Pictorial Information in Television Advertising," Wendy J. Bryce and Richard F. Yalch, *Journal of Current Issues and Research in Advertising*, vol. 15, no. 1, Spring 1993, 1–20. "Program Involvement: Are Moderate Levels Best for Ad Memory and Attitude toward the Ad?" Nader T. Tavassoli, Clifford J. Shultz II, and Gavan J. Fitzsimons, *Journal of Advertising Research*, vol. 35, no. 5, September/October 1995, 61–72. "The Long Tail and Its Implications for Media Audience Measurement," Scott McDonald, *Journal of Advertising Research*, vol. 48, no. 3, September 2008, 313–319. "The Advertising Impact of an Interactive TV Program on the Recall of an Embedded Commercial," Verolien Cauberghe and Patrick De Pelsmacker, *Journal of Advertising*, vol. 48, no. 3,

September 2008, 352–362. "The Secret of Television's Success: Emotional Content or Rational Information? After Fifty Years the Debate Continues," Robert G. Heath; Insights from Horst Stipp, *Journal of Advertising Research*, vol. 51, no. 1, Supplement, March 2011, 112–123. "The 38-Percent Solution: Empirical Generalizations for Repeat Viewing of Television Programs," Peter J. Danaher and Tracey S. Dagger, *Journal of Advertising Research*, vol. 52, no. 2, June 2012, 225–233. "Empirical Evidence of TV Advertising Effectiveness," Joel Rubinson, *Journal of Advertising Research*, vol. 49, no. 2, June 2009, 220–226. "The Occurrence and Effects of Verbal and Visual Anchoring of Tropes on the Perceived Comprehensibility and Liking of TV Commercials," Renske van Enschot and Hans Hoeken, *Journal of Advertising*, vol. 44, no. 1, January–March 2015, 25–36. "An Episode-by-Episode Examination: What Drives Television-Viewer Behavior: Digging Down into Audience Satisfaction with Television Dramas," Donald Miller Dennis and David Michael Gray, *Journal of Advertising Research*, June 2013, vol. 53, no. 2, 166–174. "Measuring the Long-Term Effects of Television Advertising. Nielsen-CBS Study Uses Single-Source Data to Reassess the "Two-Times" Multiplier," Leslie A. Wood and David F. Poltrack, *Journal of Advertising Research*, June 2015, vol. 55, no. 2, 123–131.

12. Radio Advertising Bureau 2015.
13. Imagery Transfer Study conducted by Statistical Research, Inc., 1999.
14. Radio Advertising Lab (RAL) studies, as reported on Radio Advertising Bureau website, www.rab.com.
15. "Information Processing Differences Among Broadcast Media: Review and Suggestions for Research," James H. Leigh, *Journal of Advertising*, vol. 20, no. 2, June 1991, 71–76. "Mental Imagery and Sound Effects in Radio Commercials," Darryl W. Miller and Lawrence J. Marks, *Journal of Advertising*, vol. 21, no. 4, December 1992, 83–94. "Creating the Contrast: The Influence of Silence and Background Music on Recall and Attribute Importance," G. Douglas Olsen, *Journal of Advertising*, vol. 24, no. 4, Winter 1995, 29–44.
16. Radio Advertising Lab (RAL) studies, as reported on Radio Advertising Bureau website, www.rab.com.
17. Amazon Prime Day, Westwood One Case Study, as reported on Radio Advertising Bureau website, www.rab.com.
18. GfK MRI, Doublebase 2015.
19. "Advertiser Registers Its Objection," Stuart Elliott, *New York Times*, April 11, 2005, C5.
20. Newspapers Canada, 2013 Report: Newspapers Drive Purchase Decisions, as reported on Newspaper Association of America website, naa.org.
21. GfK MRI, Doublebase 2015.
22. "The Advertising Exposure Effect of Free Standing Inserts," Srini S. Srinivasan, Robert P. Leone, and Francis J. Mulhern, *Journal of Advertising*, vol. 24, no. 1, Spring 1995, 29–40. "Ad Size as an Indicator of Perceived Advertising Costs and Effort: The Effects on Memory and Perceptions," Pamela M. Homer, *Journal of Advertising*, vol. 24, no. 4, Winter 1995, 1–12. "Predictors of Advertising Avoidance in Print and Broadcast Media," Paul Surgi Speck and Michael T. Elliott, *Journal of Advertising*, vol. 26, no. 2, Summer 1997, 61–76. "Communicating in Print: A Comparison of Consumer Responses to Different Promotional Formats," Kenneth R. Lord and Sanjay Putrevu, *Journal of Current Issues and Research in Advertising*, vol. 20, no. 2, Fall 1998, 1–18. "The Information Content of Newspaper Advertising," Avery M. Abernathy, *Journal of Current Issues and Research in Advertising*, vol. 14, no. 2, Fall 1992, 63–68.
23. Alliance for Audited Media, Publishers' Statements as of June 30, 2015.
24. Magazine Media Factbook 2015.

25. GfK MRI, Doublebase 2015.
26. "Context Effects on Recall and Recognition of Magazine Advertisements," Claire E. Norris and Andrew M. Colman, *Journal of Advertising*, vol. 21, no. 3, September 1992, 37–46. "Contextual Priming Effects in Print Advertisements: The Moderating Role of Prior Knowledge," Youjae Yi, *Journal of Advertising*, vol. 22, no. 1, March 1993, 1–10. "Affective Responses to Images in Print Advertising," Rafi M. M.I. Chowdhury, G. Douglas Olsen, and John W. Pracejus, *Journal of Advertising*, vol. 37, no. 3, Fall 2008, 7–18. "Evaluating the Multivariate Beta Binomial Distribution for Estimating Magazine and Internet Exposure Frequency Distributions," Yunjae Cheong, John D. Leckenby, and Tim Eakin, *Journal of Advertising*, vol. 40, no. 1, Spring 2011, 7–24. "Checking the Pulse of Print Media: Fifty Years of Newspaper and Magazine Advertising Research," Gergey Nyilasy, Karen Whitehill King, and Leonard Reid. Insights from Scott C. McDonald, *Journal of Advertising*, vol. 51, no. 1, Supplement, March 2011, 167–181. "Understanding Relatives Sales Impacts and Derived Synergy from Cross-Platform Advertising," Caryn Klein, Maggie Zak, Phillip Keefe, and Leslie Wood, *Proceedings* from Print and Digital Research Forum, 2015.
27. Association for Magazine Media website, at magazine.org.
28. GfK MRI, Doublebase 2015.
29. Traffic Audit Bureau website, tab.org.
30. Buzz Awards 2008, Special Advertising section in *Mediaweek*, B10.
31. "Digital Billboards in Shanghai Feature Wei-bo Posts from Chinese Athletes," *Advertising Age*, August 9, 2012.
32. "Assaulted in Broad Daylight," Neal Lawson, *The Guardian Weekly*, April 27, 2012.
33. "Improving the Effectiveness of Outdoor Advertising: Lessons from a Study of 282 Campaigns," Mukesh Bhargava, Naveen Donthu, and Rosanne Caron, *Journal of Advertising Research*, vol. 34, no. 2, March/April 1994, 46–55. "Split-Second Recognition: What Makes Outdoor Advertising Work?" Lex Van Meurs and Mary Aristoff, *Journal of Advertising Research*, vol. 49, no. 1, March 2009, 82–92. "Use and Effectiveness of Billboards," Charles R. Taylor, George R. Franke, and Hae-Kyong Bang, *Journal of Advertising*, vol. 35, no. 4, Winter 2006, 21–34. "Use and Effectiveness of Billboards: Perspectives from Selective-Perception Theory and Retail-Gravity Models," Charles R. Taylor, George R. Franke, and Hae-Kyong Bang, *Journal of Advertising*, vol. 35, no. 4, Winter 2006, 21–34.
34. "Programmatic Digital Display Ad Spending Forecast," eMarketer, 2015.
35. "Exploring the Effectiveness of Advertising in the ABC.com Full Episode Player," Mark Loughney, Martin Eichholz, and Michelle Haggar, *Journal of Advertising Research*, vol. 48, no. 3, September 2008, 320–328.
36. comScore, February 2015; Nielsen Total Audience Report, Q1 2015.
37. "Marketing to Millennials Report," comScore, December 2014.
38. eMarketer, 2015.
39. eMarketer, April 2015; Nielsen Total Audience Report, Q1, 2015.
40. eMarketer, May 2016.
41. comScore, February 2015.
42. "Metrics Used by U.S. Marketers to Measure the Effectiveness of Their SEO Program," eMarketer, July 2012.
43. "Online User Experience Study," Online Publishers Association, 2005.
44. "Internet Uses and Gratifications," Hanjun Ko, Chang-Hoan Cho, and Marilyn S. Roberts, *Journal of Advertising*, vol. 34, no. 2, Summer 2005, 57–70.
45. "Determinants of Perceived Web Site Interactivity," Ji Hee Song and George M. Zinkhan, *Journal of Marketing*, vol. 72, March 2008, 99–113. "Displacement and Reinforcement Effects of the Internet and Other Media as Sources of Information,"

Stanley D. Sibley and James C. Tsao, *Journal of Advertising Research*, vol. 44, no. 1, March 2004, 126–142. "Changing fortunes for Internet Advertising," Chris Dobson, *Admap*, March 2004, no. 448, 32–33. "Determinants of Internet Advertising: An Empirical Study," George Baltas, *International Journal of Market Research*, vol. 45, no. 4, 505–513. "Banner Advertising-Web Site Context Congruity and Color Effects on Attention and Attitudes," Robert S. Moore, Claire Allison Stammerjohan, and Rob A. Coulter, *Journal of Advertising*, vol. 34, no. 2, Summer 2005, 71–84. "Measuring Users' Web Activity to Evaluate and Enhance Advertising Effectiveness," Subodh Bhat, Michael Bevans, and Sanjit Sengupta, *Journal of Advertising*, vol. 31, no. 3, Fall 2002, 97–106. "Advertising Repetition and Placement Issues in On-Line Environments," Idil Yaveroglu and Naveen Donthu, *Journal of Advertising*, vol. 37, no. 2, Summer 2008, 31–44. "Evaluation of Internet Advertising Research," Juran Kim and Sally J. McMillan, *Journal of Advertising*, vol. 37, no. 1, Spring 2008, 99–112. "Internet Uses and Gratifications: A Structural Equation Model of Interactive Advertising," Hanjun Ko, Chang-Hoan Cho, and Marilyn S. Roberts, *Journal of Advertising*, vol. 34, no. 2, Summer 2005, 57–70. "The State of Internet-Related Research in Communications, Marketing, and Advertising, 1994–2003," Chang-Hoan Cho and HyoungKoo Khang, *Journal of Advertising*, vol. 35, no. 3, Fall 2006, 143–164. "Whither the Click? How Online Advertising Works," Gian M. Fulgoni and Marie Pauline Morn, *Journal of Advertising Research*, vol. 49, no. 2, June 2009, 134–142. "Do You Recognize Its Brand? The Effectiveness of Online In-Stream Video Advertisements," Hao Li and Hui-Yi Lo, *Journal of Advertising*, vol. 44, no. 3, July-September 2015, 208–218. "Empirical Generalizations: New Laws for Digital Marketing: How Advertising Research Must Change," Yoram (Jerry) Wind, Byron Sharp, and Karen Nelson-Field, *Journal of Advertising Research*, vol. 53, no. 2, June 2013, 175–180. "More Mutter about Clutter: Extending Empirical Generalizations to Facebook," Karen Nelson-Feld, Erica Riebe, and Byron Sharp, *Journal of Advertising Research*, vol. 53, no. 2, June 2013, 186–191. "If an Advertisement Runs Online and No One Sees It, Is It Still an Ad? Empirical Generalizations in Digital Advertising," Stephanie Flosi, Gian Fulgoni, and Andrea Vollman, *Journal of Advertising Research*, vol. 53, no. 2, June 2013, 192–199. "A Model for Delivering Branding Value through High-Impact Digital Advertising: How High-Impact Digital Media Created a Stronger Connection to Kellogg's Special K," Shawn D. Baron, Caryn Brouwer, and Amaya Garbayo, *Journal of Advertising Research*, vol. 54, no. 3, September 2014, 286–291. "What Is the Cost of an Unseen Ad?" Steve Millman and Zhiwei Tan, *Proceedings* of Print and Digital Research Forum 2015.

46. eMarketer, July 2015.
47. comScore U.S. 2015 Mobile App Report.
48. "The Tactical Use of Mobile Marketing: How Adolescents' Social Networking Can Best Shape Brand Extensions," Shintaro Okazaki, *Journal of Advertising Research*, vol. 49, no. 1, March 2009, 12–26. "How Mobile Advertising Works: The Role of Trust in Improving Attitudes and Recall," Shintaro Okazaki, Akihiro Katsukura, and Mamoru Nishiyama, *Journal of Advertising Research*, vol. 47, no. 2, June 2007, 165–178. "Has the Time Finally Come for the Medium of the Future? Research on Mobile Advertising," Shintaro Okaski and Patrick Barwise, *Journal of Advertising Research*, vol. 51, no. 1, Supplement, March 2011, 59–71.

CHAPTER 5

EXPLORING THE MEDIA, PART 2
Owned

As the cost of paid media has continued to go up, regardless of the state of the overall economy, marketers have turned more to media opportunities that they can own. That is, there are ways in which a company or brand can use its name, its values, and/or its position in consumers' minds to convey advertising messages to its target audience in ways that will enhance sales or other metrics and enhance the performance of paid media, while also leading to greater success with its earned media (explained further in Chapter 6).

In this chapter, we will focus on five areas that a brand can own: product placement, brand integration, brand website, sponsorship, and custom events.

PRODUCT PLACEMENT: PUTTING THE BRAND FRONT AND CENTER

While $70 billion is spent each year in the U.S. on paid television advertising (commercials), another way for advertisers to reach consumers with their brands is through product placement. Here, advertisers pay the program producer to put their brands into the storylines or content of TV shows. This began back in 2001, when contestants on the reality show *Survivor* were shown happily consuming cans of Pepsi's Mountain Dew. Sometimes the product is overtly written into the script, such as having the characters in the FX series *Sons of Anarchy* ride Harley-Davidson motorbikes. The success of a brand placement is not guaranteed. Three brands were placed in the hugely popular show *American Idol*: Coca-Cola, Ford, and Cingular (then AT&T). While consumers readily accepted and remembered the soft drink (consumed by the judges) and the phone company (linked to the text messages they sent in), there was no clear connection with a vehicle. As a result, Ford's brand equity actually declined during its time on the program.[1]

Many advertisers today are pulling dollars out of regular national television and switching it into product placement deals that have a lower out-of-pocket cost. It was estimated that in 2014, a total of $6 billion was expected to be spent in product placement, with a forecast of doubling by 2019.[2] In the 2014–15 TV season, Nielsen counted more than 4,000 brand placements.[3]

Of course, placement is nothing new. It was how commercial TV got started, with the product sponsorship of the Texaco Star Theater or daytime dramas brought to you by Tide and Dreft (i.e., soap operas). It grew to greater prominence thanks to James Bond movies, where the hero drove specific brands of cars and drank certain kinds of alcohol. In the latest film, *Spectre,* Belvedere Vodka paid millions of dollars to be the exclusive vodka used in the movie. Unlike content integration (discussed later), with product placement, the product appears more or less as a prop, such as a character opening a box of General Mills' Wheaties cereal rather than Brand X.

One of the more prominent efforts at paid product integration occurred in September 2004, when GM gave away its newly launched Pontiac G6 vehicles to every member of the studio audience in Oprah Winfrey's daytime talk show. In keeping with the theme of the program to fulfill people's "wildest dreams," Oprah gave away 276 vehicles, each of which had an estimated value of $28,400. The event generated enormous publicity for the company, most of it favorable, and Pontiac registered a record number of visits to its website in the days following the show.[4] A report by the Federal Communications Commission in 2008 noted that the popular Fox program *American Idol* had a stunning 3,291 product placements during just the first three months of that year! While there is no legislation aimed specifically at this type of owned advertising, questions are raised from time to time about whether the public should be explicitly informed when a company has paid to place their product directly in a program.

BENEFITS OF PRODUCT PLACEMENT TO ADVERTISERS

The two main benefits of placing a product directly in media content are indirect impact and lower cost.

Indirect Impact

For brands that are placed in a high-performing media vehicle and endorsed by or referred to by the vehicle or celebrity, the effect on consumers can be very positive. When Oprah Winfrey hosted her daytime talk show, a mere mention of a product would boost sales, and the overt placement of the Pontiac car mentioned earlier created strong positive consumer sentiment about the vehicle.

Lower Cost

Advertisers look at product placement as a potentially cheaper way to promote their brand, compared to national TV advertising. This could be somewhat misleading, however, because a placement alone, without other types of paid media promotion, may receive an initial favorable reaction, but in isolation, that impact is likely to be short term and brief.

DRAWBACKS OF PRODUCT PLACEMENT TO ADVERTISERS

The most common concerns mentioned for product placement are appropriateness and isolation.

Appropriateness

From a marketer's perspective, it may make all the sense in the world to pay for placement of an airline in a sitcom when the character talks about taking a trip, but if the viewer is sitting there scratching her head wondering why that particular airline was mentioned several times (or worse, ignoring it), then the impact on the brand could be completely negative. When the product is misplaced, or fits badly, consumers are less likely to remember it or associate it correctly.

Brand in Isolation

If all an advertiser does is place the product in a magazine or TV program or online content, without any supporting media activity, that will limit the effect on consumers, whether or not the fit is deemed appropriate. These types of deals often include surrounding paid media to reinforce the brand's presence in consumers' minds (and hearts).

Research on product placement is starting to examine it from all angles, including how it impacts consumer responses to the TV show, how to explain individual differences in reactions to it, and what happens when it doesn't work. A selection of articles are suggested.[5]

BRAND INTEGRATION: EXPANDING THE FIT

This type of owned media is an extension of product placement. The major difference is that with brand integration (sometimes called *content integration*) a more holistic experience is created with the brand that involves the creation of unique content specifically for that brand. This can be done across media, from customized magazines (Kraft Foods' *Real Foods* magazine) to original TV programs (Samsung's World Championship of Gaming) to digital content (Healthy Choice online videos or the Nike YouTube channel).

To successfully integrate a brand into existing content, the key consideration is fit. That is, does it make sense to put your brand in that context? This can be done figuratively, in terms of shared values, or literally. When upscale automaker Lexus was used as the "inspiration" for would-be fashion designers on Lifetime's reality TV program *Project Runway*, the challenge given the designers was to create evening wear suitable for the Emmys award show. The fit here was conceptual and symbolic rather than concrete. That is, it was about the high style of both the fashion challenge and the vehicles Lexus makes. For Wrigley's Extra Dessert Delights gum, an integration into Bravo's *Top Chef: Just Desserts* program went one step closer. Here, the competing chefs were charged with creating a dessert that would inspire the next flavor of gum for the brand. They did not use the gum in their recipes, but the linkage of flavors and desserts made the brand fit within the program context.

For some brands, no existing content seems an appropriate fit for them. In such a case, some advertisers create content. This is not the same as making an *infomercial*, a long-form commercial that lasts several minutes or more. Rather, a full-length (30 minutes or longer) program is developed in which the brand is integrated. As mentioned earlier, this was the path taken by Samsung. They wanted to reach gamers, so they created a reality program together with the World Cyber Games called *WCG Ultimate Gamer* in which gamers competed with one another while surrounded by and using Samsung technology. The program aired on Syfy network, popular with that same desired target audience. It was considered very successful for Samsung in terms of consumer response.

One of the challenges for brand integration is how to measure it. Since it is, by definition, unique, it is unlikely to get captured in traditional syndicated measures of viewership or readership, for example. Today, however, there are a variety of ways to do so. The viewership of a TV program can be captured through set-top box TV tuning data from companies such as comScore. The social impact of the integration is readily captured by looking at the trending of brand mentions on sources such as Twitter or Facebook. Or for any integrated digital content, consumer visits to a unique site or branded page can be assessed through digital audience measurement companies such as comScore or Nielsen.

To focus specifically on consumer reactions to a particular integration, in terms of shifts in their attitudes or feelings about the brand, advertisers can undertake custom research such as an online survey among those who have visited the integrated content website or Facebook page. In the Extra Desserts gum integration, for example, viewers were invited to go to the program website and vote on the potential new gum flavor, which allowed the brand to quantify the impact of the idea in a meaningful way.

A variation of brand integration is direct response TV (DRTV). Here, advertisers purchase time on local TV stations or, more often, on cable networks. This time could be anywhere from a 2-minute infomercial to a 30-minute program. What the consumer sees is an informational message with an immediate opportunity to purchase (usually via telephone). The direct-to-consumer approach works well for certain types of marketers and has typically been used by smaller or independent companies offering unusual products, such as the Snuggie blanket or NordicTrack fitness equipment. The media rates can be up to 75 percent lower than the cost of buying regular commercial time. Bigger companies occasionally use DRTV, to good effect. Johnson & Johnson's Neutrogena skincare line launched SkinID products via DRTV. One of the biggest benefits of this approach is that it is instantly measurable, whether through phone calls logged and products sold or visits to the website.[6]

BENEFITS OF BRAND INTEGRATION FOR ADVERTISERS

Advertisers considering brand integration should consider its key benefits of customization and relevance.

Keeping It Relevant

Because brand integrations are all done as ad-hoc events or activities, they can be selected to ensure that the brand's message is aligned with that of the content in which it appears and therefore, it is hoped, more relevant to the consumer of that content. The integration of a cosmetics brand in a fashion show brings the brand to life in a way that may be more meaningful to the viewer than a straightforward 30-second commercial.

Customizing for the Brand

Because brand integrations are nonstandard, they can be customized and, potentially, offer more varied and creative ways of showcasing the brand.

Red Bull created its own video channel, Red Bull TV, where it features sports, music, and events sponsored by the brand.

DRAWBACKS OF BRAND INTEGRATION FOR ADVERTISERS

Irritation and measurement challenges are the two biggest drawbacks to integrating brands.

Consumer Irritation

The notion of creating a media property that has a brand in its title may seem ideal to a marketer, but from the consumer's perspective, it could lead to intense annoyance. If they already feel bombarded by ads during a program or throughout a magazine or all over a website, then the exposure to the brand in the name of the content could just irritate them further, harming the brand's equity rather than helping it.

Measurement Challenges

Integrated brand efforts can sometimes be difficult to measure in terms of their impact. A specially created TV program or digital program or print title may have such a small audience that standard methods cannot detect it and more customized approaches may be required.

BRAND WEBSITE: BEYOND THE BRAND NAME

The strongest and perhaps most obvious earned media available is the brand's own website. In our fictional example of Fruitola, the creation of a website with original content related to the brand's values and positioning can be important ways to communicate with the desired customers. It can link to all areas of marketing. Site visitors could explore the *package* and get nutritional information. They could find which stores in their area stock the brand (*place*) as well as see where Fruitola is sponsoring events in their local community. Online coupons or other discounts could be placed on the site (*promotion*). Product users could be encouraged to submit their own experiences with the brand or suggest drink recipes.

Today, just about every brand has its own website. Type a brand or company name into a web browser, and you will arrive at the website. Increasingly, the site is used to develop a relationship with the customer that goes beyond the function of the brand. At Dove.com, for example, the consumer can find out more about the various skincare and beauty products the company sells. But she can also learn more about Dove's mission to bolster girls' self-esteem, nominate the Caring Coach of the year, or print out coupon offers for the different brands. Taking that one step further, Dove, like many brands, encourages visitors to its website to register their information (becoming a "Dove Insider") in order to receive special offers or to like the brand's Facebook page for similar benefits. The Container Store website also has the more obvious elements to it of promoting what is going on in the store, but it lets the user get expert tips and watch videos about home improvement or read blog posts about the company and its employees, thereby providing a sense of community for its workers.

BENEFITS OF BRAND WEBSITE FOR ADVERTISERS

Brand websites offer the following advantages to advertisers: expanded communication and low cost.

Expanded Communication

When brands first created their own websites, they did little more than share information and repurpose other types of advertising (TV commercials, etc.). Today, websites are an opportunity for much more expansive communication with customers and prospects. They can provide a comprehensive view of everything the brand stands for, both metaphorically and literally, and do so through both information and entertainment. In addition, the opportunity for two-way communication with brand users via social media can be hugely beneficial to the brand.

Low Cost

Because a brand owns its website, the main cost involved is primarily in its creation. After that, it needs to be maintained, but the relative cost of doing so compared to paid media is almost insignificant. It also provides an inexpensive means of communication with the company's employees.

DRAWBACKS OF BRAND WEBSITE FOR ADVERTISERS

As helpful as a brand's website can be, the two disadvantages it poses are a limited audience and weak link to goals.

Limited Audience

Although most marketers include their website in their other forms of media, the majority of people who end up visiting the site are, to some degree, already sold on the brand. That is, you would likely not spend time on Nissan's website if you are a loyal Honda car owner. So to some extent, brand websites are "preaching to the choir" of their users and loyalists. While other media forms are targeted to those likely to be interested in a brand, a website has to be actively visited by a consumer for any impact to occur.

Weak Linkage to Goals

When marketers set their goals of trying to sell a certain number of widgets or increasing awareness or recall by X percent, the brand website is rarely included as a means to accomplish this. Unless a product sells a lot directly from its website (such as Amazon), then determining how the site will be used to directly impact the goals becomes a challenge.

The research on how to make brand websites most impactful has focused on how to encourage consumer interaction with them and how they work with other media forms.[7]

SPONSORSHIP: MAKING YOUR MARK IN THE MIND

As advertisers have had to work harder to reach their target consumers, one of the owned forms of communication they have turned to is sponsorship. This involves paying an organization a fee to put a company or brand name at the head of an event or as the key sponsor of that event. Examples include State Farm Insurance's sponsorship of an ice skating competition, Citibank's sponsorship of the U.S. Olympic team, and the renaming of sports stadiums after companies (e.g., Pepsi Center in Denver, Philips Arena in Atlanta, and the Staples Center in Los Angeles). The practice of sponsorship in North America is now estimated to be worth about $24 billion, while globally it is close to $58 billion.

The majority of sponsorship spending (70 percent) goes toward sports-related events, followed by entertainment tours (10 percent), causes (9 percent), arts (4 percent), festivals (5 percent), and associations (3 percent). The growth of cause-related marketing, where companies link up with nonprofit groups and become sponsors of their causes, continues to expand. Examples include Avon's support of an annual three-day walk to raise funds for breast cancer research and Gap's support for the Red campaign to end AIDS. Even though sponsorship is generally considered to be undertaken to reach a national audience, there are often significant local opportunities, too. Sponsorship of local sports teams can enhance a business' reputation in those particular markets, while companies that choose to sponsor a local annual festival often receive positive coverage in the local media. There are also benefits to be gained by sponsoring grassroots or community festivals and fairs, especially among multicultural audiences.

The reasons companies choose sponsorship in addition to paid advertising are many. They include the opportunity for heightened visibility for their brand name, thereby increasing the chances of shaping positive consumer attitudes ("I like ice skating, therefore since State Farm sponsors a skating competition, I like State Farm more, too"). Sometimes, sponsorship works well for smaller companies. While they may have smaller ad budgets compared to bigger competitors, their sponsorship of a key event or attraction can make them seem an equal in consumers' eyes. Asics spends much less than competitors like Nike or Reebok, but through its sponsorship of the New York City Marathon, the runners or viewers of the race do not see one company as a "better" or necessarily bigger sponsor than another.

Consumer research suggests that people are indeed more likely to have positive feelings toward a sponsoring brand and are more likely to consider buying it in the future. One study, conducted by the GroupM Next agency, found that one-third or more of consumers indicated these positive feelings toward brands that sponsor award shows, TV shows, sports events, or musical acts.[8] The Olympics is often considered the apotheosis of the sponsorship world. The International Olympic Committee places restrictions on any form of advertising that does not come from one of the official sponsors of the games, companies that have paid up to $100 million for that privilege.

Nonetheless, one of the risks for sponsorship is *ambush marketing*. This occurs when another marketer (frequently a competitor) uses other media (paid and earned) around the sponsored event so that consumers end up believing that the ambusher is in fact the sponsor. This is a tactic that Nike has been known to do, especially during the quadrennial Olympics. During the 2012 Olympics, Nike created and then used its own product to make an impact on the audience for the games without spending a dollar as an official sponsor. It did so by creating a special bright green shoe, the Volt, which was worn by the athletes and made them all seem like they were part of "Team Nike." That became one of the memorable images of the Olympics.[9] For many years, Nike has purchased so much local media in whatever city the games are held in that, despite not paying for or being an official sponsor of a country or team, survey after survey would show that consumers believed them to be one. Indeed, in the 2012 London Olympic Games, a survey of consumers found that 37 percent of people thought that Nike was an Olympic sponsor, while only 24 percent correctly identified the real athletic shoe sponsor as Adidas.[10]

Even small businesses can use these tactics. A coffee brand in Hawaii that was forced out of being an official sponsor of the Ironman World

Championship found a creative solution to communicate to the participants by creating a coffee bar on the water offshore from the island of Maui where the competition was held. Not only was the bar floating in the ocean, but billboards placed 20 feet under the sea's surface could be seen by swimmers during their practice, directing them to the nonsponsoring coffee brand.

Sponsorships can be harmed by any controversy. When the world soccer organization, FIFA, was under intense scrutiny over charges that its leaders were corrupt, three major sponsors (Castrol, Continental, and Johnson & Johnson) withdrew their support in protest.

The media are getting more actively involved in creating sponsorships for advertisers. *Cooking Light* magazine created a "healthy" house filled with products of its sponsoring companies, such as Reebok (exercise equipment), Lennox Industries (air conditioning), and Whirlpool (appliances). The magazine promoted the house in its pages and digitally and attracted thousands of visitors to its Birmingham, Alabama, location. After the promotion ended, the magazine was able to sell the home privately. Sponsorships are not only aimed at adults these days. Both Macy's and Target sponsor buses that take college students from their campuses to the store. Sponsorships are, like other owned media, useful connectors between paid and earned opportunities. That is, most marketers who sponsor something (or someone) will benefit from their brand being mentioned or visible during their TV or print ads and will typically use social media to amplify the impact of the sponsorship. For example, eSurance sponsored Major League Baseball's post-season awards, which it then displayed on its Facebook page.

BENEFITS OF SPONSORSHIP TO ADVERTISERS

For advertisers, sponsorship offers the opportunity to surround consumers with a brand and enhance brand image and associations.

Surrounding the Consumer

Whether you attend the Sugar Bowl or watch it on TV, you can't help but notice that Allstate is the sponsor. From the brief "billboard" messages that appear on the TV airing, to the signage at the stadium, to the mention of the insurance company before every commercial break, Allstate's sponsorship surrounds the consumer. Promotions tied to the sponsored event can enhance the value of the sponsorship even more, such as digital or social media competitions or sweepstakes where you can win tickets to the game. All work to connect the company with the sponsorship in a way that, it is hoped, will lead the consumer to feel more positively about that brand.

Enhanced Image and Associations

When you see or hear that Bank of America has sponsored your city's annual marathon, the desired response by the advertiser is that there is a positive association made between event and brand. That is, consumers may be grateful for the corporate support of a charity race or pleased that "their" chosen brand or company has decided to associate itself with an event or sport or charity that they like. As noted previously, research has indeed demonstrated that such positive associations do in fact lead to greater purchase consideration.

DRAWBACKS OF SPONSORSHIP TO ADVERTISERS

A mismatch between sponsoring company and event and imprecise measurement are two of the drawbacks for advertisers involved with sponsorships.

Sponsor Mismatch

For sponsorship to truly make a difference, it needs to change a consumer attitude or behavior or influence opinions on the brand or company. If not done right, the sponsorship can actually backfire. Having a cooking festival, for example, sponsored by an indigestion product might lead people to feel worse not only about the festival ("these recipes will give me indigestion") but also potentially about the brand ("Are they encouraging me to eat so much I feel ill?").

Imprecise Measurement

You can tell sponsorship works—when it works! Event attendance may increase, perceptions may improve, sales may even go up. But proving that it was caused by the sponsorship is a tricky proposition. Some research has been done to assess the financial fundamentals of a company employing sponsorship, but even here, it can be challenging to determine cause and effect. Did the company's fortunes change due to the sponsorship, or was the sponsorship the result of the company's situation?

The number of research papers published on sponsorship has steadily increased in recent years. Much of the research attention has been on event management and individual sponsored events.[11]

CUSTOM EVENTS: YOUR BRAND ONLY

Sometimes there are ideas for a brand that don't fit in to any marketing category. They are completely owned by the brand and designed solely for it. These are called *custom events*, and they are defined as activities or programs specifically built to promote a brand.

One version of this type of communication is to recreate a scene or an experience so that consumers can touch or feel the product. When Ikea opened a new store in Japan, the company took over a train and outfitted the cars with items that could be purchased in the new store, including price tags. In addition to the benefit of having consumers look at the products, Ikea was sticking to one of its strategic objectives of demonstrating how it can help people furnish small spaces.

A very different way to use a subway was seen in Toronto, where the tourism bureau of the province of Alberta, to encourage visitors to travel there, recreated scenes from its rocky mountain scenery, changing rail seats into ski lifts and surrounding commuters with photos of the idyllic landscape. Visits to the bureau's website more than doubled during the two months of the campaign.

Sometimes these custom event campaigns are not even real. To launch a new car model in the U.S., BMW created a pseudo-festival called Rampenfest that featured video of a BMW car driving on an enormous ramp in a tiny town in Austria. The catch was that the ramp, and the town itself, were not real, and neither was the festival. But the buzz that surrounded the campaign certainly was, with an estimated 10 million visitors to the vehicle's website.[12] Custom events can grow from one-offs to become established. American Express first created Small Business Saturday in 2010 to encourage people to shop at local businesses on the Saturday after Thanksgiving. It quickly became an annual shopping tradition, bringing in an estimated $14.3 billion on that single day in 2014. While American Express is not used for all payments, it generates considerable goodwill for supporting small and local businesses.

Custom events may also be used for charitable purposes. The shoe company, TOMS, started its "buy one, give one" program from its inception and has so far donated more than 10 million pairs of shoes to children in need. L.L. Bean worked with the National Park Foundation to help celebrate that organization's centenary. Each time people shared their "outdoor moments" either at the stores or on social media, the clothing company donated $1 for youth programs in national parks.

BENEFITS OF CUSTOM EVENTS TO ADVERTISERS

There are two main benefits custom events offer: creativity and cost flexibility.

Endless Creativity

With custom events there are few limits to what can be created. Since the event is designed to promote the brand, just about anything can be dreamed up. Magazines and newspapers are two traditional paid media types that have created these types of events to generate revenues. *Fortune* magazine brings in $15 million from hosting conferences and special seminars, where marketers are invited in as sponsors and consumers pay to attend.[13]

Cost Flexibility

Custom events, by virtue of their wide remit, allow marketers great flexibility in expenditure. It costs relatively little to hire college students to perform street theater related to your brand. Building a platform out in the middle of the Pacific Ocean is a more costly proposition. Either way, the marketer is able to manage those expenses as necessary.

DRAWBACKS OF CUSTOM EVENTS TO ADVERTISERS

The two key disadvantages of custom events are strategic weakness and cool factor overload.

Strategic Weakness

There are often lots of ideas brainstormed by client or agency teams for "cool" or "unusual" events; the danger is in executing them for those reasons rather than because they are strategically aligned with the brand's meaning and message. Ikea's takeover of Japanese subway cars would not have been nearly as impactful (although still attention-getting) if they had not been trying to show how they could furnish small spaces. So it is critical that any custom ideas are examined through a strategic lens.

Cool Factor Overload

Perhaps the biggest potential drawback for custom events is an extension of strategic weakness. That is, ideas are approved simply because they are novel and capture the imagination of the brand's decision maker. That was probably the case a few years ago when TNT Network created fake manhole covers on the streets of Boston to promote a new program. The covers were certainly cool and attention-getting, but they had large Xs on them that quickly caused a major panic that this was some kind of terrorist plot, practically shutting down the city for several hours while police were called in to investigate.

SUMMARY

There are various kinds of media that a brand can own, from product placement, to brand integration, to sponsorship. These all usually require a sizable dollar commitment. In contrast, brand websites and custom events can be incorporated into a plan at a lower cost. In all cases, these owned media forms provide useful ways of expanding a brand's presence and enhancing its image with consumers. They can work well as bridges between paid media activity and earned media consumer response and reactions.

In order to consider the best options for your brand, consider the various benefits and drawbacks of each owned media type.

CHECKLIST: EXPLORING OWNED MEDIA

1. For product placement, are you taking advantage of its benefits of indirect impact and lower cost?
2. Do the drawbacks of product placement appropriateness and isolation outweigh its benefits?
3. Have you considered the benefits of brand integration, relevance, and customization?
4. How important are the drawbacks of brand integration, consumer irritation, and measurement challenges?
5. Can you take advantage of the brand website's benefits of expanded communication and low cost?
6. Do the drawbacks of a brand website's limited audience and weak links to goals impede its use?
7. Would the advantages of sponsorship (surrounding the consumer and enhanced image and associations) be significant contributors to your brand's success?
8. Do the disadvantages of sponsorship (risk of sponsor mismatch and imprecise measurement) lead you to not recommend sponsorship for your brand?
9. What potential events or causes could your brand sponsor?
10. How can you take advantage of the benefits of custom events, such as creativity and cost flexibility?
11. Have you considered the disadvantages of custom events, such as strategic weakness and trying too hard to be cool?

NOTES

1. "Why 'Idol' Works for Coke—But Not for Ford," Martin Lindstrom, *Advertising Age*, November 17, 2008, 18.
2. Media Daily News, June 16, 2015.
3. Reported in MediaPost, October 2015.
4. "Pontiac Gets Major Mileage Out of $8 Million 'Oprah' Deal," Jean Halliday and Claire Atkinson, *Advertising Age*, September 20, 2004, 12.
5. "I See What You Don't See: The Role of Individual Differences in Field Dependence—Independence as a Predictor of Product Placement Recall and Brand Liking," Jorg

Marches, Werner Wirth, Christian Schemer, and Anna-Katerina Kissling, *Journal of Advertising*, vol. 40, no. 4, Winter 2011, 85–99. "When Intrusive Can Be Likable: Product Placement Effects on Multitasking Consumers," Sukki Yoon, Yung Kyun Choi, and Sujin Song, *Journal of Advertising*, vol. 40, no. 2, Summer 2011, 63–76. "Audience Response to Product Placements: An Integrative Framework, and Future Research Agenda," Siva K. Balasubramanian, James A. Karrh, and Hemant Patwardham, *Journal of Advertising*, vol. 35, no. 3, Fall 2006, 115–142. "Product Placement: How Brands Appear on Television," Carrie La Ferle and Steven M. Edwards, *Journal of Advertising*, vol. 35, no. 4, Winter 2006, 65–86. "When Product Placement Goes Wrong," Elizabeth Crowley and Chris Barron, *Journal of Advertising*, vol. 37, no. 1, Spring 2008, 89–98. "Understanding Attitudes Toward and Behaviors in Response to Product Placement: A Consumer Socialization Framework," Federico de Gregorio and Yongjun Sung, *Journal of Advertising*, vol. 39, no. 1, Spring 2010, 83–96. "Product Placements," Pamela Miles Homer, *Journal of Advertising*, vol. 38, no. 3, Fall 2009, 21–32. "Using Eye Tracking to Understand the Effects of Brand Placement Disclosure Types in Television Programs," Sophie C. Boerman, Eva A. van Reijmersdal, and Peter C. Neijens, *Journal of Advertising*, vol. 44, no. 3, July–September 2015, 196–207. "The Relationship Between Product Placement and the Performance of Movies: Can Brand Promotion in Films Help or Hurt Moviegoers' Experience?" Reo Song, Jeffrey Meyer, and Kyoungnam Ha, *Journal of Advertising Research*, September 2015, vol. 55, no. 3, 322–338.

6. "Amid Cutbacks, ShamWow Marches On," Jack Neff, *Advertising Age*, March 23, 2009, 1/14.
7. "The Relation between Actual and Perceived Interactivity: What Makes the Web Sites of Top Global Brands Truly Interactive?" Hilde A. M. Voorveld, Peter C. Neijens, and Edith G. Smit, *Journal of Advertising*, vol. 40, no. 2, Summer 2011, 77–92. "The Branding Impact of Brand Websites: Do Newsletters and Consumer Magazines Have a Moderating Role?" Brigitte Miller, Laurent Flores, Meriem Agrebi, and Jean-Louis Chandon, *Journal of Advertising Research*, vol. 48, no. 3, September 2008, 465–472. Digging Deeper Down into the Empirical Generalization of Brand Recall: Adding Owned and Earned Media to Paid-Media Touchpoints," Frank Harrison, *Journal of Advertising Research*, June 2013, vol. 53, no. 2, 181–185.
8. "The New Music Model for Brands: How Live Events and Digital Are Changing the Sound of Things," GroupM Next, February 2015.
9. "How Nike Ambushed the Olympics with This Neon Shoe," Shareen Pathak, *Advertising Age*, August 20, 2012, 1/19.
10. "Consumers Don't Really Know Who Sponsors the Olympics," Adage.com, July 27, 2012.
11. "An International Review of Sponsorship Research," T. Bettina Cornwell and Isabelle Maignan, *Journal of Advertising*, vol. 27, no. 1, 1998, 1–21. "The Power of Numbers: Investigating the Impact of Event Roster Size in Consumer Response to Sponsorship," Julie A. Ruth, and Bernard L. Simonon, *Journal of Advertising*, vol. 35, no. 4, Winter 2006, 7–20. "Affective Intensity and Sponsor Identification," Kirk L. Wakefield and Gregg Bennett, *Journal of Advertising*, vol. 39, no. 3, Fall 2010, 99–112. "Fortuitous Brand Image Transfer: Investigating the Side Effect of Concurrent Sponsorships," Francois A. Carrillat, Eric G. Harris, and Barbara A. Lafferty, *Journal of Advertising*, vol. 39, no. 2, Summer 2009, 109–123. "Winning Ways: Immediate and Long-Term Effects of Sponsorship on Perceptions of Brand Quality and Corporate Image," Nigel Pope, Kevin E. Voges, and Mark Brown, *Journal of Advertising*, vol. 38, no. 2, Summer 2009, 5–20. "Explaining and Articulating the Fit Construct in Sponsorship," Erik L. Olson and Hans Mathias Thjomoe, *Journal of Advertising*, vol. 40, no. 1, Spring 2011, 57–70. "Visual Processing and Need for Cognition Can

Enhance Event-Sponsorship Outcomes. How Sporting Event Sponsorships Benefit from the Way Attendees Process Them," Angeline G. Close, Russell Lacey, and T. Bettina Cornwell, *Journal of Advertising Research*, June 2015, vol. 55, no. 2, 206–215. "How Corporate Sponsors Can Optimize the Impact of Their Message Content. Mastering the Message: Improving the Processability and Effectiveness of Sponsorship Activation," Francois A. Carrillat, Alain d'Astous, and Marie-Pier Charette Couture, *Journal of Advertising Research*, September 2015, vol. 55, no. 3, 255–269. "Brand Stereotyping and Image Transfer in Concurrent Sponsorships," Francois A. Carrillat, Paul J. Solomon, and Alain d'Astous, *Journal of Advertising*, vol. 44, no. 4, 2015, 300–314. "Predicting Return on Investment in Sport Sponsorship: Modeling Brand Exposure, Price, and ROI in Formula One Automotive Competition," Jonathan A. Jensen and Joe B. Cobbs, *Journal of Advertising Research*, vol. 54, no. 4, December 2014, 435–447. *Sponsorship in Marketing: Effective Communications Through Sports, Arts, and Events*, T. Bettina Cornwell, Routledge, 2014.

12. "Herd on the Street," Robert Klein, *Mediaweek*, December 8, 2008, 12–13.

13. "Events Businesses Are Paying Off for Publishers," Nat Ives, *Advertising Age*, April 2, 2012, 3/18.

CHAPTER 6

EXPLORING THE MEDIA, PART 3
Earned

The notion of a brand "earning" an impact on consumers was rarely discussed 10 or 15 years ago. The role of media was to provide the content and context in which to place brand messages. But as consumers gained ever greater control over their media usage, starting with the TV remote control and then with DVRs, computers, and mobile phones, the notion that people's everyday conversations about brands were worth paying attention to started to develop. For it is in these naturally occurring moments that advertisers can see how much their brands have "earned" consumer awareness, liking, preference, or other effects outlined in Chapter 3.

In this chapter, we will explore four of the ways that advertisers can use media to earn their way into consumers' hearts and minds: word of mouth, social networks, organic search, and public relations.

WORD OF MOUTH: WHO SAYS WHAT?

While considered by many to not be a true "medium," word of mouth is a popular way for advertisers to promote their brands. It is sometimes referred to as *viral* marketing, using the metaphor of spreading good words about a brand the way that a virus can spread among people. It is estimated that word of mouth helps drive 13 percent of sales (one-third of which are online).[1] In particular, products that are new or are targeting specific groups may lend themselves to this form of promotion. At its simplest, word of mouth involves getting the (positive) word out to people who are considered opinion leaders in a particular category so that they will then influence others to consider the brand. Some marketers take it further and plant people in key venues where the brand is being used (such as a new vodka in a bar) and have them talk to the people around them about the wonders of this product. Those consumers are unaware that the individual has been paid to promote the brand, so critics have complained that this is a deceptive or even unethical practice.

Today, word of mouth is often thought of in terms of digital media, particularly through social conversation, but most of the talk about brands (72 percent) actually occurs face to face, with digital accounting for about 12 percent.[2] Nonetheless, from an advertising perspective, it is digital media that offer the most earned brand opportunities. That could happen on blogs, where people who are passionate about a topic will create their own website filled with content that others can read and, in most cases, comment on. Some blogs are online equivalents of written diaries, while others share their knowledge on a topic (electronics, fashion, finance). Advertisers are only starting to determine how best to put paid messages on these sites, whether overtly through banner ads or clandestinely by paying the author to promote an item on their blog. Another venue for sharing opinions about brands is online reviews. In some cases, such as *Consumer Reports,* ads are deliberately excluded. But if you like a movie, you are encouraged to share your opinion on sites or apps such as Fandango, IMDB, or Rotten Tomatoes. Each time you make a purchase on Amazon, you are invited to share your feelings there, and similarly, when you travel, you can spread the word on your experiences on Trip Advisor, Expedia, or Kayak. In fact, the number of places where you can do so in today's digital landscape is almost infinite. Many of today's brands "listen" carefully to what consumers say about them, often dedicating staff to responding directly to positive or negative comments in the reviews.

BENEFITS OF WORD OF MOUTH TO ADVERTISERS

The primary benefits of word of mouth are consumer-driven communications and minimal cost.

Consumer-Driven Communications

When people are asked if they are affected at all by advertising, the majority always respond no. But when questioned on what made them choose a particular product or brand, the answer is often the recommendation of a friend or relative. This benefit, the fact that the "advertisement" was, in effect, from someone they know or trust, clearly works to the advantage of word of mouth.

Minimal Cost

Due to the viral nature of word of mouth, it is an extremely cost-efficient means of communication. If done correctly, word of mouth acts like a pebble dropped in a pond, with ripple effects that go far beyond where the brand mention started. And the marketer only has to pay for that initial mention!

DRAWBACKS OF WORD OF MOUTH TO ADVERTISERS

Two drawbacks of this type of communication are lack of control and weak measurability.

Lack of Control

It is always serendipitous for a brand to generate positive word of mouth without even trying (as happened to BlackBerry when President Barack Obama announced he could not give up the device), but there is no guarantee that the reverse will not occur, with celebrities or even regular consumers creating a negative buzz about the product. Either one is hard, if not impossible, to control, and this should be taken into consideration when implementing a WOM campaign.

Weak Measurability

There is an increasing effort on the part of research suppliers to provide measurement of word of mouth, but it remains nascent. The two main forms are panels of consumers who report on what they are talking about, and with whom, and passive data capture, which automatically monitors the digital "conversation." While the latter can track vastly more data, it cannot necessarily get to the nuances of human conversations. The former can do so, but typically with smaller samples and the unreliability of self-reported data.

Research on word of mouth is just starting to build.[3]

SOCIAL NETWORKS: WHO YOU KNOW

The notion of community is paramount to the explosive growth of Internet-based social networking. Websites such as Facebook or Wei-bo (in China) give users the ability to connect with friends and family locally and globally to exchange messages, video, music, or photos. It is estimated that about half of all Americans used a social networking site in 2015, with higher use among younger consumers.[4]

The biggest presence within social networks is Facebook. Created by Harvard undergraduate Mark Zuckerberg in 2004, Facebook began as a way for college students to communicate with each other. It blossomed and grew exponentially, ending up with a public stock offering in 2012 that valued the company at $47 billion. Other key social network offerings are Twitter, focused on brief (140-character) messages, used by an estimated one in six Americans; Pinterest, which lets its 8 million users share based on their interests; Instagram, for sharing photos and video; and Snapchat, for sharing brief content that automatically disappears after a few seconds. The biggest shift in social network usage in recent years has been from desktop to mobile. About one-quarter of the time that people spend with apps on their mobile devices is on social networks,[5] and two-thirds (68 percent) of the time people are using Facebook it is via mobile device. For Instagram it is 98 percent, and 100 percent of Snapchat time is mobile.

Globally, Facebook passed the 1 billion users in 2012. In the U.S., Facebook users spend, on average, seven hours each month on the site. That, together with the skew toward younger people, makes Facebook and other social networks extremely appealing to advertisers from an earned media perspective. How they engage with consumers is still being debated. It used to be all about capturing likes for a brand's Facebook page or counting the number of brand-related tweets. But today, advertisers work hard to ensure that their paid, owned, and earned media are coordinated and synchronized.

That is not to say there is no value in the like or tweet in terms of brand impact. According to research conducted by digital measurement company, comScore, in 2011, the addition of friends of the fans of a brand can expand its online reach by anywhere from one-third to twice as much as the fans alone.[6] And both fans and friends of fans were more likely to have visited the brands' websites than the 'regular' Internet user. More recently, social sharing measurement company, Shareablee, reported that in the first half of 2014, there were nearly 18 billion actions taken in relation to a brand, including a like, a comment, or a share.[7]

Indeed, the sharing phenomenon is what brands hope for from an earned media perspective. They may be disappointed, however. The tracking of that activity indicates that in most categories, brand-related sharing on Facebook has been going down. At the same time, the sharing of video content, including TV or other video clips, is going up. Some TV shows, especially the late night talk shows with Jimmy Fallon or Jimmy Kimmel, have focused efforts on making their program content easily shareable via smaller segments with broad appeal.

Twitter, a social network that is focused more on sharing comments, is used by about one in five of the U.S. population. The most popular activity on Twitter is to read a news story (42 percent said they did so in the past month). About one-quarter of people said they visited a product or brand's Twitter feed. That compares to four in ten (41 percent) who visited a company's or brand's Facebook page, which suggests that advertisers should continue to look for the best way to incorporate Twitter in marketing. Yet it clearly is a powerful social media force, especially for TV. In an average day, about 1 million people in the U.S. talk about television on Twitter. During the 2014 World Cup, a staggering 672 million tweets were sent related to the game, with half of the people following the World Cup on TV also doing so on Twitter. In research conducted by Twitter with ad agency Starcom, brands that used Twitter along with their TV ads registered a 6.9 percent increase in awareness among those who saw the ads, a 6 percent increase in brand favorability, and a 4 percent sales lift compared to homes that only saw the TV commercials.[8] Brands can connect to their customers through Twitter. Harley Davidson, which spends only 15 percent of its marketing on traditional media, uses social media not only to encourage customers to share their own stories, but also casts real riders in ads from among its Twitter followers.

While social networking began as a college student/young adult practice, Facebook has seen that spread to the point that nearly one-half (44 percent) of Facebook users were 50 or older by 2015. On Twitter, however, the usage still skews young (adults 18–29 accounted for about one in three of Twitter's users in 2015), while for Snapchat, two-thirds are under the age of 30. In terms of gender, only Pinterest continues to have a large majority of female users.

The power of social networks to spread impactful messages is quite profound. Much has been written of the role of Facebook in spurring the Arab Spring uprisings in the Middle East in 2011 and 2012, to the point where some dictatorial governments shut down access to the site in an attempt to clamp down on the population. In 2014, the Ice Bucket Challenge to raise money for ALS research was another example of huge "earned" impact. By asking people to pour a bucket of ice cold water on their heads or donate to the ALS charity, it generated more than $100 million in donations. That was four times the amount the organization raised the year before.[9] The success was attributed to the fact that it was easy for people to participate, they felt part of a community, and they could tell their own stories.

BENEFITS OF EARNED SOCIAL MEDIA TO ADVERTISERS

The main advantages for advertisers to turn to social media are engagement and coordination with paid and owned media.

Engaging the Masses

With millions of Americans turning to Facebook and Twitter each month, advertisers have a huge opportunity to reach large numbers of people in a less overt way than paid display or video ads. By creating content about the brand that consumers enjoy and will share through social media, advertisers are able to engage with both current and prospective buyers. The ability to track the activity (how many likes, shares, or comments) makes that earned media highly measurable, including basic information on those engaged in the practice, since social media sites require user registration (such as age and gender).

Social Coordination

As noted in Chapter 4, there are various ways for brands to use paid media in social formats. By combining that with earned activity and owned media (such as brand-related content), advertisers can create a social media plan that connects with the target audience in multiple ways. For example, Sargento Cheese could create short videos showing ways to use the product in easy-to-make recipes. This owned content could not only be posted to the brand's website, but also be included in paid ads on Facebook or Instagram, which busy moms will then share with friends and family through those or other social networks to amplify the impact.

Drawbacks of Earned Social Media to Advertisers

The main disadvantages for earned social media are questionable impact and creating valued content.

Questionable Impact

While there are many ways used to measure the impact of traditional paid media forms (TV, radio, etc.), the rapid growth and development of social media as an earned medium has outpaced the industry's understanding of how best to measure it. Certainly as a digital medium, it is possible to gather clickstream data on likes, comments, and shares, but fully connecting that to consumer impact measures, such as brand awareness or purchase intent, has been harder to do. And since consumers turn to Facebook or Twitter for reasons other than advertising, the proportion of social network users who choose to take action with brands, compared to those who are going to these sites purely for entertainment and communication, is still relatively small.

Creating Valued Content

As much as brands believe, or want to believe, that the original content they develop is appealing and interesting for consumers (and, therefore, worth liking or sharing), most of the time consumers are not going to be interested in hearing about the benefits of Brand A drain cleaner or do not have time to spend with a ten-minute video of Brand B's latest SUV showing off all its features. Even if someone has a blocked drain or is in the market for a new car, the chances that they will choose to like or share that branded content are still pretty slim. So for social media to be an effective earned medium, brands do have to give serious consideration to whether they are doing or creating things that not only gain the attention of the recipient but are worth more than a few seconds of their time.

As with word of mouth, the research on social media has been growing.[10]

ORGANIC SEARCH

Today, when consumers are looking for information about a topic, they usually go to Google (or Yahoo or another search engine). If you type in "Android phone," for example, the search will come up with various articles about different phones in the category, as well as images for them. This is known as *organic search* because it has been sought out naturally by an individual. At the top and to the right of the page, however, appear sponsored messages from LG and Samsung that are the paid search ads mentioned in Chapter 4, based on the keywords typed in.

Marketers can measure the amount of organic search activity, but since it is consumer-generated, it is harder to influence directly. But by buying keywords as paid media and comparing organic to nonorganic click-throughs, they do gain a better understanding of how effective each form of search might be. The research is unclear as to whether organic or paid searches produce greater results. One study suggests that about one-third (31 percent) of retail e-commerce spending comes from organic search compared to half of that (16 percent) from paid search.[11]

PUBLIC RELATIONS

Although this area of media and marketing is really worthy of a whole book on its own (and several are listed at the end of the chapter), it is important to mention how marketers can consider their public relations (PR) efforts as part of their earned media. That is, how consumers think about brands and companies may well be influenced (or improved upon) by the efforts of PR companies to help earn their trust or support or consensus. The use of PR as a form of earned media is not, most of the time, without any cost on the part of the brand. That is, when a marketer wants or needs to change or enhance its image, it does need to invest in deliberate campaigns (that utilize paid or owned media) to make that happen. In 2015, an estimated $4.6 billion was spent on PR in the U.S.

Marketers do recognize its importance. In one survey of marketers, more than eight in ten (83 percent) cited public relations as one of their most effective marketing tactics to influence buyer decisions, right behind advertising and content marketing. For example, when IKEA in France wanted to enhance awareness of the company's commitment to sustainable practices it launched a PR campaign that invited influential food bloggers to participate in a cooking contest in each IKEA store that was called "Zero Waste." By promoting these events, the company not only increased the number of its followers in social media, but also won an award for sustainable development.

Often, public relations efforts focus on the latter word—*relations*—with employees or potential employees. The oil company BP wanted to hire experienced people to work at one of its key processing terminals in an offshore Scottish island where it was ramping up production. Through promotions of the benefits of working in that area and by engaging with the local council and key islanders, the company saw a 40 percent increase in job applications for that location.

Public relations is often used to enhance other marketing efforts. The "Like a Girl" campaign, which personal care brand Always created to promote the idea that young teen girls should not lose their self-confidence as they hit puberty (a time when they start to need Always' products), used public relations successfully to promote the campaign itself, generating almost 50 million online video views and winning many industry awards. PR can be used in the opposite case, where brands make a misstep and need to use this type of earned media to rescue their reputation. Urban Outfitters, for example, created a hoodie sweatshirt that went on sale on its website which featured the logo of Kent State University surrounded by splattered blood. Since that campus was the site of anti-Vietnam student protests in which four students were killed by the National Guard in May 1970, the clothing was found to be offensive and quickly removed from sale, with the store using public relations to apologize and regain its customers' trust.

BENEFITS OF PUBLIC RELATIONS

The key benefits of using PR are its ability to change consumer perceptions and to enhance brand impact.

Changing Consumer Perception

Although most of the focus of this book is on using media to help advertise and promote brands, the ability of public relations campaigns to impact perceptions that people have of those brands (and the companies that make them) should not be underestimated. It is one of the key benefits that PR can provide, to make consumers feel good (or better) about the items that they purchase.

Enhancing Brand Impact

As noted in several of the previous examples, public relations at its best works seamlessly with other elements of marketing and media to amplify the impact of a campaign through carefully planned promotional and publicity efforts.

DRAWBACKS OF PUBLIC RELATIONS

Disadvantages of public relations are its indirect effects and the fact that it usually comes at a cost.

Indirect Effects

While other kinds of earned media, such as social networks or organic search, can be counted or measured in some way, it is difficult to quantify or demonstrate definitively the impact of many public relations campaigns. Consumer surveys can be used (before and after a PR campaign) to see how people say they feel about a brand, and response can sometimes be measured through digital media (clicks, views, etc.). But attributing the latter response solely to public relations may be difficult.

No Free Ride

Most of the earned media categories in this chapter rely on consumers choosing to respond to or talk about brands in their daily lives, where the brand has spent little to no money to generate that directly. But with public relations, a company is most likely paying for that effort to communicate information about the brand through media. While the results are often significant in terms of corporate reputations and consumer perceptions, it should be recognized that, even as it "earns" value for the brand, it does come at a cost.

WHICH MEDIA SHOULD YOU USE?

Now that you have some basic information on each major media category, whether paid, owned, or earned, we can start to consider why you might or might not wish to include each option in your media plans. To make this process less cumbersome, we'll need to recap some of the most important advantages and disadvantages that each medium offers. These are summarized in Exhibit 6.1, including the paid and owned media forms discussed in Chapters 4 and 5.

Exhibit 6.1 Pros and Cons of Paid, Earned, and Owned Media

Medium	Pros	Cons
Paid Media		
Television	True to life Pervasive Reaches the masses	High cost Brief exposure Clutter Poor placement
Radio	Local appeal Targeted audience Imagery transfer Lower cost Close to purchase High frequency Flexible message	Background medium Sound only Short message life Fragmentation
Newspaper	Wide reach Timeliness Desirable audience Editorial context Local/regional	Short message life Active readers Black and white
Magazines	Upscale and niche audiences Reader involvement Long issue life	Long planning cycle Higher cost
Yellow pages	Consumer selection Measurable response	Clutter Infrequent usage
Outdoor billboards/out-of-home advertisements	Large size Mobility Ethnic groups Supplementary medium	Brief exposure Environmental criticism
Digital display/search/online video/social media	Flexibility Targeted message Reach Measurability	Consumer irritation Clutter Changing metrics

Medium	Pros	Cons
Mobile	Location targeting Direct response	Privacy Consumer irritation
Owned Media		
Product placement	Indirect impact Lower cost	Appropriateness Brand in isolation
Brand integration	Relevance Customization	Irritation Measurement challenges
Brand website	Expanded communication Low cost	Limited audience Weak link to goals
Sponsorship	Surrounding consumer Enhanced image	Sponsor mismatch Imprecise measurement
Custom events	Creativity Cost flexibility	Strategic weakness Cool factor overload
Earned Media		
Word of mouth	Consumer-driven communications Minimal cost	Lack of control Weak measurability
Social networks	Reaching the masses Social coordination	Questionable ad effectiveness Value of content
Public relations	Changing consumer perception Enhanced brand impact	Indirect effects No free ride

SUMMARY

In considering earned media, the specialist must still focus on how each media type will enhance and achieve the plan's strategic objectives. Whether looking at word of mouth, social networks, organic search, or public relations, media experts need to assess the benefits and drawbacks of each and how to incorporate them seamlessly into the overall media plan.

CHECKLIST: EXPLORING EARNED MEDIA

1. Is there a need to go beyond paid media in your plan?
2. How and why could you generate word of mouth for your brand?
3. Can you justify how the benefits of word of mouth (consumer-driven communications and minimal cost) would enhance your brand's performance?
4. Do the downsides to word of mouth (lack of control and weak measurability) pose too great a risk for your brand?

5. How can you use social networks to earn impact for your brand by engaging large audiences and coordinating with paid and owned efforts?
6. Have you considered the downsides of earned social media, such as its questionable impact and the challenge of creating valued content?
7. Are there ways to boost more activity through organic search?
8. Can you take advantage of public relations to change consumer perception and enhance brand impact?
9. In what ways might the drawbacks of public relations, such as its indirect effects and the potential cost, hinder your brand's campaign?

NOTES

1. comScore and the Word of Mouth Marketing Association, 2014.
2. Keller Fay research study, 2015, as seen on website, www.kellerfay.com.
3. "Finding the Missing Link: Advertising's Impact on Word of Mouth, Web Searches, and Site Visits," Jeffrey Graham and William Havlena, *Journal of Advertising Research*, vol. 47, no. 4, December 2007, 427–435. "Unleashing the Power of Word of Mouth: Creating Brand Advocacy to Drive Growth," Ed Keller, *Journal of Advertising*, vol. 47, no. 4, December 2007, 448–452. "The Role of Advertising in Word of Mouth," Ed Keller and Brad Fay, *Journal of Advertising Research*, vol. 49, no. 2, June 2009, 154–158.
4. eMarketer, 2015.
5. comScore Mobile App Report 2014.
6. comScore, "The Power of Like," 2011.
7. Shareablee, 2015.
8. SMG Social TV Lab, 2014.
9. "Remember the Ice Bucket Challenge? Here's What Happened to the Money," Ethan Wolff-Mann, Time.com, August 21, 2015.
10. "Social Media and Mobile Internet Use among Teens and Young Adults," Amanda Lenhart, Kristen Purcell, Aaron Smith, and Kathryn Zickuhr, Pew Internet and American Life Project, 2010. "The Benefits of Facebook 'friends': Social Capital and College Students' Use of Online Social Network Sites," *Journal of Computer Mediated Communication*, vol. 12, no. 4, August 2007. "Generational Differences in Content Generation in Social Media: The Roles of the Gratifications Sought and of Narcissism," Louis Leung, *Computers in Human Behavior*, vol. 29, no. 3, May 2013, 997–1006. "Why People Use Social Media: A Uses and Gratifications Approach," Anita Whiting and David Williams, *Qualitative Market Research*, vol. 16, no. 4, 2013, 362–369. "Consumer Activity in Social Media: Managerial Approaches to Consumers' Social Media Behavior," Kristina Heinonen, *Journal of Consumer Behavior*, vol. 10, no. 6, 2011, 356–364. "Digging Deeper Down into the Empirical Generalization of Brand Recall: Adding Owned and Earned Media to Paid-Media Touchpoints," Frank Harrison, *Journal of Advertising Research*, vol. 53, no. 2, June 2013, 181–185. "How Do We Share? The Impact of Viral Videos Dramatized to Sell: How Microfilm Advertising Works," Tsai Chen and Hsiang-Ming Lee, *Journal of Advertising Research*, vol. 54, no. 3, September 2014, 292–303. "The Value of Earned Audiences—How Social Interactions Amplify TV Impact: What Programmers and Advertisers Can Gain from Earned Social Impressions," Judit Nagy and Anjali Midha, *Journal of Advertising Research*, vol. 54, no. 4, December 2014,

448–453. "How Digital Conversations Reinforce Super Bowl Advertising: The Power of Earned Media Drives Television Engagement," Harlan E. Spotts, Scott C. Purvis, and Sandeep Patnaik, *Journal of Advertising Research*, vol. 54, no. 4, December 2014, 454–468. "What Drives Advertising Success on Facebook? An Advertising-Effectiveness Model Measuring the Effects on Sales of 'Likes' and Other Social-Network Stimuli," *Journal of Advertising Research*, vol. 55, no. 2, June 2015, 162–175. "What Motivates Consumers to Re-Tweet Brand Content? The Impact of Information, Emotion, and Traceability on Pass-Along Behavior," *Journal of Advertising Research*, vol. 55, no. 3, September 2015, 284–295.

11. comScore U.S. Retail eCommerce Revenue Share by Device and Traffic Source, Q2 2014 and Q2 2015, July 30, 2015.

CHAPTER 7

TERMS, CALCULATIONS, AND CONSIDERATIONS

DEFINING KEY MEDIA TERMS

Just as computer programmers talk about bits, bytes, and RAM and car enthusiasts dwell on RPM, jerk, and lateral acceleration, so do media specialists converse in their own language. Before moving on to the actual media plan development, it will be helpful to review some of these terms and their definitions.

UNDERSTANDING RATINGS

Most of you are probably already familiar with the release of the Nielsen ratings that show which are the most popular television programs. The size of the audience is usually given in two ways: absolute terms (i.e., millions of people) and as a percentage of the population. It is this latter figure, known as the *rating*, that is used as the baseline measure for all media concepts.

Rating Point

One rating point equals 1 percent of a particular target group. That audience can be defined in various ways: by household; by geographic market; by a given demographic group, such as men 18 to 49 or women 25 to 54; or by product usage or ownership, such as people who own a dog. The television program *Empire* might receive a household rating of 11.3 in Memphis, which means that 11.3 percent of homes in that city watched the show. The magazine *Entertainment Weekly* might get a rating of 9.6 among females ages 18 to 34, meaning that 9.6 percent of all women in that age group read that particular issue of the magazine. In television, the "currency" rating on which national ads are bought and sold is called C3, which stands for the percent of the audience tuned to the average commercial in the program when it airs (live) and for the following three days (delayed or time-shifted).

Gross Rating Points

By adding up all the rating points we wish to achieve, we end up with a concept known as *gross rating points,* or GRPs. For media planning purposes, we set as our goal a given number of total, or gross, rating points to achieve and then figure out which media vehicles to use to obtain that number. We might want our plan to have a total of 100 gross rating points each week against our target of women with children. These could come from any media.

The reason these rating points are considered gross is that they do not take into account any duplication of exposure. That is, there are probably many people within our target for Fruitola who see our ad in *Fitness* and also hear the same message on the local talk radio show. So while our total number of rating points placed in the media each week is set at 100, each person will be exposed to a different number of them and in different vehicles. This is shown in Exhibit 7.1.

In today's complex media world, where our targets are more and more narrowly defined, the term GRP is often altered to TRP, or target rating point. This makes explicit the fact that we are planning our ratings against

Exhibit 7.1 Diagram of GRPs and Duplication

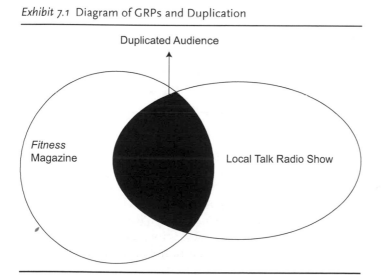

a specific *target* rather than the whole world. The concept is the same, however.

Gross Impressions

This term simply converts the gross rating points into a number by dividing the number of rating points by 100 and multiplying that figure by the size of the target audience. So if our plan calls for obtaining 200 GRPs against a target audience of 500,000 people, then we are aiming to achieve 1 million gross impressions (200/100 × 500,000).

REACH AND FREQUENCY

Although many would argue that advertising is more art than science, we still need some way to assess whether the messages we place in the media are having any impact. It is not enough to know how many impressions are made with one ad or what percentage of the target audience is exposed to a given online video or mobile ad. As media specialists, we also need an estimate of the cumulative effect of our media plan. That is provided by the concepts of reach and frequency.

Reach

Reach refers to the number or percentage of people in the target audience who will be exposed to the medium where the message appears. You should note that we mostly estimate exposure to the *media vehicle*, not to the ad itself. If you think about your own media habits, there are many intervening variables that easily prevent you from seeing or hearing an ad. You might deliberately ignore it, such as by swiping past an ad on your smartphone, fast forwarding through the TV ad when watching it in time-shifted mode, or avoiding the ad that appears at the top of your search results. You could be doing something else at the same time, such as talking to a friend on Facebook or cooking dinner, and not pay attention to the message. Or you could find the ad boring, irrelevant, or uninteresting and see or hear it but not really absorb the contents. So when we talk about the reach of a plan, we are really talking about the *opportunity for exposure* (sometimes called opportunity to see, or OTS).

And of course we should also emphasize that *reach*, like all media terms, is merely an estimate. We rarely know exactly how many people were reached or how they reacted. Even with the more precise metrics of digital media, where we can "know" how many computers clicked on an ad, we still don't know how that message was received. Perhaps they clicked by accident and just ignored the message. But if we are trying to reach women 25 to 54 to persuade them to try our new brand of body wash, then using syndicated data sources, we can find out how many women of that age watch *The View*, read *Marie Claire*, or go to Pinterest boards focused on skincare. To reach a target audience of men 18 to 49 to increase the number of inquiries for Fidelity Investment's pamphlet on investing wisely, we can learn how many men of that age go to FT Online or watch CNN.

The difference between reach and GRPs is that reach concerns the number of *different* people in the audience you are trying to communicate with through advertising. For media schedules that try to maximize reach, you would place ads in several different media vehicles to reach different people through each one. Complicated formulas are used to calculate the numbers, requiring the speed and power of computers. Here, we look at a simple example.

If the rating for *People* against our target of 18- to 49-year-olds is 15 and for *Time* magazine it is 10, then one ad placed in each magazine will deliver a total of 25 GRPs (15 + 10). However, if we know from research that 6 percent of the target audience will see both ads (the duplicated audience) then the reach, or *unduplicated* audience for this schedule, is 25 minus 6, or 19 percent. That is, 19 percent of our target of adults 18 to 49 will be exposed to our ad in *People* and/or our ad in *Time*. Even if they see both ads, they will only be counted in our audience one time. So, reach equals GRPs minus duplication. Exhibit 7.2 depicts this.

Frequency

It is not enough to know who our media plan is intended to reach. We must also set goals of *how many times* we wish to reach them with our message.

Exhibit 7.2 Example of Duplication

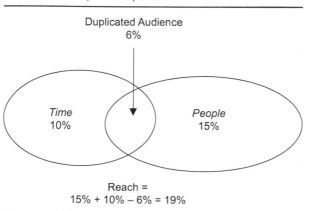

Duplicated Audience
6%

Time
10%

People
15%

Reach =
15% + 10% − 6% = 19%

As with the concept of reach, the notion of frequency, while it ultimately refers to *message* frequency, in reality is based on the frequency of exposure to the *media vehicle* rather than to the advertisement. A media plan will typically establish the desired number of times that the audience should be exposed to the message, based on past experience, judgment, or previous research into how long it takes for the audience to comprehend and remember the message. And in some media, especially digital, the number of messages delivered to each consumer can have a limit placed on it, through the practice of *frequency capping*, to ensure that one person is not bombarded with the same ad 50 times.

A simple way to back into the frequency number is from the following equation:

$$\text{Reach} \times \text{Frequency} = \text{Gross Rating Points}$$

So if you know your reach goal, and you have established the number of GRPs you will be buying, then it only requires simple mathematical division (GRPs/Reach) to figure out how many times, on average, the target will be exposed to the media vehicle(s).

Random Duplication

One of the questions that media specialists are often asked is what the reach will be of a complete media plan. The answer today is typically calculated by computers. But there is a very basic formula that can give you a rough estimate to guide you. It is known as the *random duplication formula,* and it makes the assumption that the probability of reaching the audience in one medium (or media vehicle) is independent of the likelihood of reaching them in a different one. In reality, that is not generally the case. For example, if your media plan includes food sites such as Epicurious and cooking shows on The Food Network, the odds are probably greater than average that your target is going to be exposed to both.

The random duplication formula assumes, however, that the reach of two media is the reach of one added to the reach of the other, minus the product of the two. All figures are calculated as decimals. That is:

$$\text{Combined Reach} = \text{Reach A} + \text{Reach B} - (\text{Reach A} \times \text{Reach B})$$

As an example, if your TV schedule has a total reach of 65 percent and your digital schedule has a reach of 25 percent, then the combined reach will be:

$$0.65 + 0.25 - (0.65 \times 0.25) = 0.90 - 0.1625 = 0.7375$$
$$= 73.75 \text{ percent}$$

If there are more than two media involved, then you simply take that initial product and use it as your first medium in the formula to combine with the third medium's reach number.

BEYOND REACH AND FREQUENCY

If you think about the commercials that you can remember, the ones that are most likely to come to mind are those that you have seen or heard more than once. That is, for a message to be truly *effective* in terms of communicating with the target audience, it generally has to be conveyed more than one time. Now of course this is not a hard-and-fast rule. If your bathroom drain gets blocked up, then you only need one exposure to an ad for Drano drain cleaner at the right moment in time for the message to be extremely effective. But for the most part, given the limited attention we pay to commercial messages, we need to see or hear them several times before the information is properly absorbed. And even then, it is most likely filed away somewhere in memory for use on a future occasion.

Effective Frequency

The key here is to determine *how many times* an ad has to be received for it to be deemed effective. What we mean by *effective* is that the target receives the desired communication message. A considerable amount of research was done on this topic during the 1970s and 1980s, following a landmark study by Colin MacDonald, a British researcher. After looking at the relationship between opportunities to see ads for laundry detergent and sales of the product, he concluded that the optimal number of exposure opportunities was three. This was later explained by breaking down what happens with each exposure. The first time someone sees an ad, his reaction is "What is it?" On the second exposure, he asks "What of it?" or "So what?" It is only on the third occasion that the person will start to process the information and decide if the message is relevant and interesting or not.[1]

Since those research studies were first published, there has been much controversy over their accuracy. Many have argued that it is impossible to set an arbitrary number for effective frequency. Some believe that rather than having a single figure, the most effective frequency lies within a range, typically set between three and ten. And others claim that only one exposure is needed, as long as it is placed at the right time (see the following section). The answer, probably, is "it depends." As with the drain cleaner example, sometimes a single exposure is sufficient. On the other hand, you might need to see an ad for a breakfast cereal 15 times before it has any real impact. What it ultimately depends on is the relevancy and impact of the message. There has been considerable research in this area looking to better understand the purchase process and how advertising impacts that.[2]

The key point to remember here is that when establishing your media objectives and deciding on the strategy to fulfill them, you must keep in mind that your message should probably be heard, read, or viewed several times in order for it to have an effect on the audience.

Exposure Distribution

Most media plans involve placing multiple ads in many different media vehicles, so it is important to know how many people are reached how many times (once, twice, three times, and so on). We find this by creating an *exposure distribution*, which shows the percentage of the target exposed to a given schedule at each level of frequency. The method used to calculate it is fairly complex, based on mathematical theories of probability, and today it is done by computer. At a basic level, a media model estimates the likelihood of being exposed to a given number of ads together with the number of different ways you can be exposed to those messages.

For example, if you placed one ad in *Time* and one in *People*, the reader might see anywhere from zero to two ads total—they might not see either ad, or they could see one of the two, or they might see both. Looking at Exhibit 7.2, we already know the percentage of the target exposed two times (the duplication figure) is 6 percent. In addition, we can easily figure out those not exposed at all (the total, or 100 percent, minus those exposed one or more times): $100 - 19 = 81$ percent. So to estimate what percentage is reached exactly once you subtract the duplication figure from the number reached one or more times (reach 1+): $19 - 6 = 13$. You should notice that the final exposure distribution must account for everyone in the target audience and therefore sum to 100 percent. The final exposure distribution is shown in Exhibit 7.3.

Exhibit 7.3 Exposure Distribution

Frequency (f)	Percentage reached (%)
0	81
1	13
2	6
Total	100

Frequency Planning

In the late 1990s, research evidence became available that suggested that reach was a more important determinant of media effectiveness than frequency. Based largely on the work of John Philip Jones and Erwin Ephron, the analysis of sales and TV viewing data from the same households suggested that short-term advertising sales were driven largely by exposure to a TV commercial within seven days prior to purchase. Since we as media specialists never know precisely when that sale might occur, this suggests that it is more important to maintain a lower level of media weight across more weeks than to place sporadic, albeit larger, flights of advertising throughout the year.[3] We revisit this in Chapter 10.[4]

CALCULATING COSTS

It is highly unlikely that you will be able to spend however much money you want or need. You will have to provide some kind of financial explanation of how efficiently your plan will spend your client's money. And since there are many different media types and vehicles that could, potentially, be included in the plan, it is up to the media specialist to rationalize and explain the financial reasoning behind selections.

Cost per Thousand (CPM)

Since different media are bought in different ways—a 30-second spot on radio or TV, or a banner ad on a mobile phone, or a poster for a billboard—we need some way to compare media in terms of cost. To do so, media specialists turn to the cost per thousand, or CPM. This shows the cost of reaching 1,000 of the target audience either with an individual media vehicle or the complete media schedule. It puts all media on a level playing field and is calculated as follows:

CPM = Total Schedule Cost/Gross Impressions Divided by 1,000

Let's use an example of 133,000,000 adults ages 18 to 49 and assume that an ad in *US Weekly* (5 rating) costs $150,000, while one in *People* (15 rating) costs $250,000. A total of 26,600,000 impressions would be generated (20 TRPs/100 × 133 million adults). At a total cost of $400,000, the cost per thousand would be $1.88. This means it costs $1.88 to reach 1,000 adults ages 18 to 49 with one ad in *US Weekly* and one in *People* in a given week. By using this formula, you can compare the cost efficiency of one vehicle, media category, or schedule against another.

Cost per Point (CPP)

Another useful media tool is the cost per rating point (CPP), which offers a different way of comparing media schedules. Here, you find the cost of one rating point for each media vehicle against your target by dividing the total schedule cost by gross rating points:

$$CPP = \text{Total Schedule Cost/Gross Rating Points}$$

With our total cost of $400,000 and total rating points of 20, the cost per point comes out to be $20,000. It therefore costs $20,000 to obtain one rating point against adults ages 18 to 49 using one ad in *US Weekly* and one in *People*. If you know the cost per point against a particular target group and the approximate number of rating points you wish to buy, you can then calculate an approximate total schedule cost using the same formula.

Note that the CPM and CPP are interrelated. That is, if you know the size of your target audience, you can calculate a CPP from a CPM, or vice versa.

$$CPM = (CPP/1\% \text{ of target audience}) \times 1,000$$
$$CPP = (CPM/1,000) \times 1\% \text{ of target audience}$$

Gross versus Net

One of the traditions of the media business that remains in place today is the use of gross versus net costs. This was how agencies traditionally made money—they bought the media time or space at one price and charged their advertiser clients a 15 percent margin (gross up) on the cost. Today, most agencies and advertisers have different cost structures in place. Many now have a flat fee arrangement, where the two companies set a fixed price for how much the advertiser will pay the agency for their service, or they may pay based on how well the ads perform, paying the agency more if the ads are deemed to help generate more revenue. In all these cases, the agency will pay the net costs to media companies and charge that same amount to the advertiser. So it is important as a media specialist to understand the relationship between gross and net.

Using the previous example of a one-page ad in *US Weekly* and a one-page ad in *People*, where the gross cost is $400,000, you simply multiply that gross cost by 0.85:

$$\$400,000 \times 0.85 = \$340,000$$

This would be the net amount charged to the advertiser.

CATEGORY-SPECIFIC CRITERIA

In addition to knowing the general terms that are used in media planning, it is helpful to be familiar with some of the other criteria that are used in working with each major media category. The rest of this chapter will outline these considerations.

Considerations for Television Advertising

The chief currency for a television plan is the program rating. Historically, there was no measurement of audience exposure to the actual *commercials*, relying instead on the surrogate number of how many people watched the *program* in which it ran. Starting in 2008, the industry began to look at commercial ratings averaged across a commercial break, or pod. All of the data are available from Nielsen for both national and local markets. Both types of ratings are collected on a minute-by-minute basis but are reported for programs based on the audience size at the mid-minute of the quarter hour and for commercials based on the average of all commercial minutes viewed where more than half of the minute was commercial rather than program time. Outside of the U.S., viewing data is usually collected every second and reported for each minute. The U.S. viewing data are also being gathered and reported at this level of detail by digital set-top boxes that deliver TV services (via cable, satellite, and telco). Companies such as comScore and TiVo sell TV audience data based on the more granular set-top box information they collect.

The U.S. TV marketplace operates based on the laws of supply and demand. The more people who watch a particular show, the more expensive it is to advertise within it. The ranges are enormous. You might pay $500,000 or more for a 30-second commercial on network television during prime time but only a few hundred dollars to have your ad appear on your local TV station during the night. That cost will correspond to the number of people exposed to your ad—millions versus a few hundred.

An important measure for television is the *share*. That is, of all those watching television at a given time, what percentage are tuned to the program of interest? The share can be looked at as a percentage of all households using TV (HUT) or, more commonly, as a percent of all of your desired target group (persons using TV, or PUT).

And in today's marketplace, where one-half of homes have DVRs, the issue of time-shifted viewing is significant. As noted in Chapter 4, Nielsen now provides ratings that include the Live+3 national ratings and Live+7 local market ratings, which include the audience (to commercial break for national or to program for local) at the time of airing (live), plus any audience for that same program who viewed it within 72 hours (+3) nationally or within 7 days (+7) locally. The data help account for viewers who recorded a program for later viewing and are assumed to have watched the commercials after their initial airtime.

In addition to the costs and ratings, it can be helpful to look at the viewers per viewing (or tuning) household, or VPVH, numbers (sometimes called VPTH). This figure provides you with an assessment of the concentration of a given demographic group in a program's audience, showing how many people in every thousand viewers fall into that particular category. If the VPVH among women ages 25 to 54 for *The Bachelor* is 535 and for the *Masters Golf Championship* it is 155, that indicates you will reach more than three times as many women ages 25 to 54 with an ad placed in the reality show than you will with the golf tournament.

One way that the VPVH can usefully be applied is in the conversion of household rating points to target audience ratings. This is done by creating a *conversion factor* that is then applied to the household rating. For example, if you know that there are 420 viewers per viewing household for your men ages 18 to 49 target watching *CSI*, and the total population size of that group is 66 million while the total number of households is 110 million, then your steps would be as follows:

$$(420 \times 110{,}000{,}000) / (66{,}000{,}000/1000) = 0.7 = \text{Conversion Factor (CF)}$$
$$14.3 \text{ Household Rating} \times 0.70 \text{ CF} = 10.01 \text{ M18–49 Rating}$$

What you should be most interested in, as a media specialist, is finding which programs are going to best reach your target audience. As we noted in Chapter 3, although you may have a fairly detailed description of your customer, when it comes to getting data on TV audiences, you will end up looking primarily at age and gender. Those were traditionally believed to be powerful determinants of product purchase and behavior, but the advent and expansion of newer data that combine household-level set-top box data (passively collected) with frequent shopper card or other third-party data suggest that looking at viewing behavior based on category or brand consumption may well be a better way to demonstrate how TV advertising works. The currency for TV today remains the Nielsen rating, but more advertisers are using product-usage-based (or other more detailed and targeted) ratings as secondary measures for planning and buying television advertising.

One other way to analyze TV viewing behavior in a more in-depth manner is by combining the TV ratings data with lifestyle and other media use information from another source. This process, known as *data fusion*, has been successfully used in many countries, including the U.S. What the process involves is "matching" respondents from two different databases, linking them on a number of common variables (gender, age, geographic location, ethnicity, etc.) known as *hooks,* and then "fusing" the data so that the information that is unique to one dataset can be used to describe or explain the behavior of all the respondents in both datasets. It is a complex and intricate process, however, that requires statistical expertise and understanding.

In selecting your TV programs, you should keep in mind that the list may be changed when the commercial time is bought. The plan is just that—a *plan* of which media vehicles are desired. When negotiations take place, it may be that other programs are included, or some of your recommendations are rejected, based on other considerations such as cost and availability. What you should emphasize, however, is the *daypart* that you wish your ads to appear in, because although people do tend to watch individual programs rather than time periods, there is more similarity in the kinds of programs watched within time periods than across them. Alternatively, you may wish to specify the *program type* or genre so that the buy focuses on comedies or news programming, for example, regardless of when it airs. And in a world where TV is watched anywhere, buys are now made across all video screens (TV, PC, tablet, and smartphone, for example). That is, the networks selling the ad time negotiate with the buyers to allow them to deliver the commercials on screens beyond the TV set. For now, that happens mostly when the TV ratings under-deliver.

The criteria you use to evaluate which programs to use for television do not vary whether you are planning to use network, spot, syndication, or cable. If you are planning on a local level, however, there is additional work to be done. You must select the markets to advertise in (if you have not done so already) and, more particularly, the stations within those markets that you want to use. That will depend in part on the negotiations that are done by the media buyer. That process is explained more fully in Chapter 9.

For cable TV, you may have to rely on broad network information rather than specific programs. Most individual cable shows tend to have much smaller audiences (ratings) than do shows on network or spot TV. But those audiences may be more finely targeted due to the nature of this form of television (see Chapter 4). Often, cable networks are airing programs multiple times and offering an aggregated rating to advertisers so that across all showings of an episode of *Better Call Saul* on AMC, for example, you will reach 3 percent of the viewing audience even if that audience is spread across three different airings.

Another consideration for cable is the distribution of the network. That is, some of the newer or smaller networks are not available for viewing in all U.S. households, which often leads the networks themselves to sell their audiences based on a *coverage-area rating* (a national rating that has been adjusted for the area covered by the distribution). For instance, if Cable Network X is only available in half of the country, its 2.0 nationally reported rating is really a 4.0, since only half of the population is watching it (2.0/50%). Many buyers do not like to adjust for the coverage, since it makes it harder to draw apples-to-apples comparisons.

Considerations for Radio Advertising

Radio uses the same principal term as television for planning and buying purposes. You purchase time based on audience ratings. The main difference here is that the rating is based on a time period rather than on a program. For the most part, you plan radio by dayparts (listed in Chapter 4), although it is possible, for an additional cost, to specify selected, narrower time periods. For example, if you operate a number of McDonald's franchises and only want to advertise in the hour before lunch (which technically falls in morning drive), you could request the noon to 1:00 p.m. hour, and most stations will sell that time to you, though perhaps at a premium.

Radio audiences are measured by Nielsen Audio and reported on a quarter-hour basis, so you can look at the average quarter-hour (AQH) rating for each station in a market. This is the average number of people listening to an individual station for at least five minutes within the quarter-hour period, expressed as a percentage. In many larger advertising agencies, the media planner only specifies the markets to be used, leaving it up to the media buyer to choose the actual stations based on his or her own knowledge of those markets.

The radio market can be defined (and measured) in several ways. The largest geography is called the *designated market area,* or DMA. It is defined as the viewing or listening area in which the counties that have the stations of the originating market get the largest share of household viewing or listening. Every county in the U.S. is assigned to just one DMA.

A smaller geography for radio is the *total survey area,* which consists of the metropolitan area plus outlying additional counties that listen to the major metro stations. In Chicago, the total survey area would not only include the Chicago metropolitan area but the rest of Cook, Lake, and DuPage counties, which can also receive Chicago radio station signals. The most narrowly defined measure is the *metro survey area.* This is defined by government and includes the city and surrounding counties which are closely linked economically to the central city area.

The total radio listening figure is provided in the persons using radio (PUR) measure, which is equivalent to TV's PUT number. This tells you what percentage of a given audience listens to radio at a particular time.

If you are purchasing radio time yourself, a measure that is worth considering is the *time spent listening,* or TSL. This gives an indication of how much time people are spending with an individual station in a daypart, day, or week. The calculation is as follows:

$$TSL = \frac{\text{Number of quarter-hours in daypart} \times \text{AQH}}{\text{Total Listening (Audience)}}$$

The more time people spend listening to that particular station, the greater the chance of reaching them with your message. On the other hand, if your goal is to reach as many *different* people as possible, then the TSL may be of less concern.

The media specialist should also consider the *cume rating*, which is the total number of people listening to a particular daypart, expressed as a percentage. And finally, to find out how quickly a station's audience changes, you can calculate or ask for the audience *turnover* figure, which is the ratio of total number of people listening to a particular station in a daypart to the average number listening to that station in a quarter-hour. If the turnover is high, meaning that people don't listen to the station for very long at any one time, then that would suggest you would need to air your ad fairly frequently in order to reach more people.

An important consideration for radio is merchandising and promotion, which is something the advertiser can own. Many stations are very willing to organize special contests or announcements or "added value" events if you buy time from them. If you own a Baskin-Robbins ice cream store, for instance, perhaps you could arrange for the station to hold a contest, with the prize being an ice cream party for the winner and their family. For a local Comcast cable operator, a radio station could agree to air additional announcements and public service messages in return for being mentioned on the local access cable channel. A Nissan car dealership might provide the perfect venue for the radio station to send some of its disk jockeys on the road for an afternoon, airing the program from the actual showroom. All of these "extras" can be negotiated for little or no additional cost, yet they provide valuable earned advertising for you and your company. Moreover, because they are organized on a local basis, they help to enhance your firm's place in the community, offering you some image-building public relations that can be further enhanced via earned and owned media, such as the brand's website or through Facebook or Twitter ads.

For network radio, the terms used are the same, but here you must consider which of the networks to include in the plan. At larger agencies, this is often left up to the buyer (where planning and buying are separate functions) based on demographic or format specifications.

Radio audience measurement occurs two ways. Historically, it has relied on samples of people in each market to complete a seven-day listening diary. But in the 1990s, a new methodology was developed to collect radio listening activity passively. The portable people meter, or PPM is now the currency measurement in more than 50 markets. The PPM is a pager-size device worn by a sample of people wherever they go during the day. The meter passively picks up inaudible codes that have been inserted at the radio station. These codes are used to identify which station was being listened to, by whom, and for how long. In effect, the PPM measures *listening* activity and does so with far greater accuracy for radio than the listening diary, which requires people to actively remember and write down everything they were tuned to. The technology is able to collect codes from anywhere, including television, sports arenas, or retail stores. The data collected are being used to monitor the duplication of audiences to TV, radio, and digital media by companies such as comScore, providing person-level information that can be applied to household-level set-top boxes or digital media.

For digital audio, whether the streamed version of terrestrial radio or the pure-play content from Pandora or Spotify, audiences are measured in terms of impressions served. At the time of publication, the industry was in discussion over how best to incorporate and report the digital streams into currency measurement, which has been based on the outdated average quarter hour metric that was first introduced when consumers had to fill out paper diaries and could not be expected to recall listening at a more granular level. Today, however, when radio listening is measured passively, there is increasing interest in dissecting the listenership further.

Considerations for Magazine Advertising

Some of the criteria to consider when planning for magazines include coverage, composition, circulation, subscription, rate base, readership, positioning, and discounts.

In the print world, the rating is typically referred to as *coverage*. It tells you the proportion of a given target group that saw (were "covered" by) the publication in the past month, or whatever is the relevant publication period. To determine how well a publication will reach your particular audience, in terms of how concentrated its audience is with a particular target group, the media specialist looks at a publication's *composition*. If you are advertising baby formula to new mothers, it would be important to know what proportion of the readers of *Baby Talk* and *Parents* have a newborn. While the one-page cost or the CPM may be cheaper in *Parents* than in *Baby Talk*, you may reach more new mothers in *Baby Talk*, making the cost of reaching 1,000 of *those* individuals less expensive.

A key measure for print media is how many copies of the magazine are distributed for each issue. This information, known as the *circulation*, is either provided by the magazine itself in an audit report or can be obtained from the Alliance for Audited Media, the premier source for circulation data. New or very small magazines may not be audited by this independent organization; if that is the case, one must be wary of relying on the estimates the publisher provides, as they cannot be verified. When looking at circulation, the media specialist should also find out what proportion of that figure is *controlled*—that is, distributed free of charge to potentially interested parties. They are usually not the main target audience for the publication and, therefore, would be less interested in seeing the ads that appear. In addition, you should look at the *net paid* circulation figure, which gives you the number of copies sold at no less than half of the basic newsstand or subscription price. Circulation is usually broken out by geographic area, which can be very helpful, particularly for products that have regional skews.

Another valuable measure is the percentage of copies that are sold by *subscription* versus on the newsstand (*single copies*). If people are getting their copies sent to them every month, that might suggest they are particularly keen to keep receiving and reading the magazine; on the other hand, the argument could be made that the single copy reader renews her commitment to the publication every time she purchases an issue. Whichever side you believe, it is worth finding out how the subscriptions are sold, and at what price. Publishers used to be able to discount subscriptions very heavily (up to 50 percent) and still consider them a full subscription. Today, magazines must report the net average subscription price paid by consumers and reveal the proportion of subscriptions sold at 35 percent less than that average. This is to counter the belief that, when the price is very low or there are enticing premiums offered to those who buy a year's worth of the magazine, the subscriber is more interested in receiving the low rate or the accompanying free gifts than in looking at your ads.

The growth of digital copies of magazines, first on PCs and increasingly on mobile devices, created the need for a new measure. In 2014, the Magazine Publishers of America, the industry's main trade organization, began providing Magazine 360, a measurement across all platforms. In the first quarter of 2015, for example, 40 percent of total monthly magazine readership occurred only via a digital platform (desktop or laptop, mobile, or digital video).

One last key measure of a publication's health is its *rate base.* This is the number of copies that the publisher promises the advertiser he will sell. Although the advertiser does not get anything back if that number is not reached, a magazine that consistently fails to meet its rate base is probably one to be avoided. In addition to reporting circulation, the Alliance for

Audited Media discloses how many times in the past six months or one year the publisher has not met their guaranteed audience.

For those who have access to syndicated services, there is a wealth of additional information available on reading habits for individual consumer magazines. This includes factors such as the average number of days a title is read, the average number of minutes spent with the publication, where it is read, what actions were taken after reading it, and how many readers saw each copy. These qualitative data are summarized in Exhibit 7.4. They may be provided by the individual publication.

Just as television has moved from program rating closer to a commercial rating, so do magazines now get measured in terms both of issue readership and ad exposure. GfK MRI, the company that provides the "currency" measures on which magazines are bought and sold, offers its Admeasure service that shows how many consumers remember the ads that appeared in specific publications and whether they took any action after that exposure (such as product purchase or coupon redemption).

Armed with all of this information, the media specialist can then compile a list of preferred magazines to use in the plan. Clearly, the cost of the ad page will also be a crucial factor in determining which individual titles are selected. Years ago, all magazine ads were bought off a rate card that specified exactly how much an ad would cost per issue. While discounts were given for placing ads in several issues, there was little room for any negotiation. In today's highly fragmented media world, magazines have been forced to become more competitive, both between titles and against other media. One positive result of this, for the advertiser, is that magazines are far more willing to negotiate discounts or special deals. An advertiser who places a large volume of ads (and, therefore, spends more money) in a magazine will get a special deal, as will advertisers who build up frequency or continuity with the publication.

Exhibit 7.4 Qualitative Magazine Data

Where read
Bought versus obtained
Days spent reading
Time spent reading
Actions taken (e.g. clipped coupon, called toll-free number)
Rating of publication
Interest in advertising
Attitudes toward advertising in specific publication
One of my favorites

Source: GfK MRI, 2015.

As far as where in the magazine an ad should appear, the evidence is mixed. Some studies have shown a clear advantage for being at the front of the issue or on the cover page, while others suggest there is little difference in terms of likelihood of being seen. *Positioning* will also depend on the publication. For some magazines, such as *Cosmopolitan* or *The New Yorker*, most of the feature articles appear in the first two-thirds of the book. But for more specialized magazines, such as *Discover Boating* or *Yachting World*, readers may also be extremely interested in the smaller ads at the back of the issue that feature products or services for the sailing enthusiast.

Most of today's print magazines have at least one digital version. It could include the same articles as those in print, or in more and more cases, additional content that is only available digitally. Magazines have also created app-based versions for mobile reading. In both cases, these allow the advertiser to expand into video ads in addition to the print version.

Considerations for Newspaper Advertising

If newspapers are to be included in the media plan, the first consideration is which markets are to be used. The list of markets can be developed based on population or household size, on sales data of the product, or on CDIs and BDIs. A list created according to population may be a simple ranking of the markets (top 10, top 20, and so on), or it could be a ranking based on the target audience (top 10 markets where the target is located). Market lists that are based on sales data will tend to emphasize those places where current sales are occurring, while one derived from CDI or BDI figures will also factor in potential sales opportunities. In looking at the individual markets, the media specialist needs to have a clear understanding of the product's distribution within those areas. Is it available primarily within certain parts of the market, or DMA? Is it found more in the metro area or the suburbs? Are there any major ethnic areas of the market that could play a role in product or media usage?

Once you have determined which markets to use, the media specialist will look at how many copies are being distributed, or the newspaper *circulation*. This figure is used to compare one paper with another, as well as to give some idea of how many coupons might potentially be distributed. Circulation is often broken out into counties or city zones, depending on the size of the market. While one newspaper might have a larger overall circulation, another might deliver more readers in the particular zone where your retail outlet is located and therefore be a more appropriate vehicle to use.

The *coverage* number, also called the *newspaper penetration,* is the print equivalent of a TV rating. That is, it shows the percentage of households reached by a given newspaper. As with the circulation figure, the numbers might look different depending on how the coverage is defined. Taking Boston as an example, if you only consider the overall market, or DMA household penetration, you might choose the *Boston Globe*, but if you are interested in reaching singles or African Americans, the *Boston Herald* has greater coverage.

Last but not least, newspaper *readership* figures provide more detailed information about the paper's readers according to standard demographic breaks or, where available, product usage data. This helps the media specialist find out, for example, what proportion of the readership is aged 18 to 49 years, or how many readers are working women. One newspaper may reach more men than women or more younger adults than older ones.

The media specialist can use all three criteria to compare different newspapers both within and between markets, as well as to help determine which individual papers will do the best job of reaching the given target audience. In markets where there is more than one newspaper available, it is also important to find out how much duplication there is of readers to both vehicles. It could be that one is aimed primarily at the city and the other is read mostly in the suburbs, or that Paper A reaches the northern section and Paper B is preferred in the southern section. Your selection of individual or multiple newspapers will depend to a large degree on the geographic areas that you wish to cover.

As with magazines, a critical consideration for newspaper advertisers today is to look at what proportion of readership is digital (on computer or mobile device). Newspaper circulation increasingly relies on digital distribution to maintain sales. Major newspapers, such as the *New York Times* and the *Wall Street Journal,* charge considerable amounts for in-depth online access and have had some success in boosting their subscriptions this way. In 2015, eight in ten U.S. adults said they read a digital newspaper each month.[5] The digital newspaper audience may be purchased together with the print one, but more and more advertisers are choosing to buy just the digital one. About one in four newspaper ad dollars (24 percent) are sold this way.

Considerations for Out-of-Home Advertising

As with newspapers, the main decision to be made when including out-of-home advertising in a media plan is which markets to select. Once that is known, the media specialist must determine which kind of out-of-home platform to use: poster panels, bulletins, bus shelters, video screens in elevators or health clubs, for example. The key measure for out of home is the *out-of-home rating*. As in other media, this represents the percentage of the desired target audience that will be reached by (exposed to) the out-of-home units included in the buy. Generally, the outdoor company will provide you with the information on how many boards would be needed to deliver a ratings goal. Video-based platforms are typically bought based either on the number of screens or, more commonly, the estimated number of people who will be exposed (traffic in an office building or at a gym).

Outdoor billboard measurement in the U.S. has been greatly enhanced by the Traffic Audit Bureau, which undertook the ratings measurement, including the development of "eyes on" research to calculate the visibility of each billboard. The method, discussed in Chapter 4, starts with those counts, but applies "visibility adjustments" based on ongoing research to move from very broad traffic circulation estimates to reach and add exposure measures that are more comparable to other media.

Considerations for Digital Advertising

Because digital media are considered more "measurable" than any other (except direct response), the metric used can vary. Advertisers can pay for their online display ads based on a simple cost per thousand (CPM) impressions delivered, or they can be more specific and agree to a contract that allows them to pay on a cost-per-click or even cost-per-sale basis. Indeed, although the traditional terms of ratings, reach, and frequency are employed for digital campaigns, their meaning differs from other media. Unlike TV or magazines, for example, where the number or percent of the target reached is based on the content in which an ad appears, for digital, the viewers' exposure to a web page may not necessarily be the same as their exposure to the ad on that page. The ads are served when the viewer requests a page, so the more frequently he or she does so, the more opportunities there are for ad exposure. The concept of ad *viewability* is becoming the norm for digital ads, with the requirement that half or more of a display ad is visible for at least one second, while for video there is a two-second minimum. In addition, the ad delivery can be further refined to eliminate fraudulent impressions and to verify, or validate, the proportion of ads correctly delivered to the desired target group. At the same time, the reach of some digital advertising may be more precise and accurate. With search ads on Google or other search engines, people are directly requesting information (including ads), and when they click on the ad, the publisher knows precisely how many digital devices (households) were reached and how many times.

Advertisers not only select the type of digital ad to use (display, online video, search, social media) but also when and where those ads will appear. The cheapest form is *run of site* (ROS), but most advertisers prefer to pay for a fixed *position* on a specific page within the site to have greater control over who will be exposed to that ad message, which can now be confirmed by measurement companies. The majority of display ads today are distributed through *programmatic* technology, where the advertisers specify who they wish to reach, and *data management platforms (DMPs)* collect and centralize vast quantities of data on consumers to help find the right digital targets. Then, technology known as *demand side platforms (DSPs)* use that targeting data to buy the ad inventory in real time. This explains why when you are looking at shoes or vacations or cars online, you will quickly start seeing ads in those categories in other websites or social media. More is said on this in Chapter 9.

Considerations for Owned Media

For some of the media forms that a brand can own, such as sponsorships or custom events, the key measure for a planner to consider is how many people will be in attendance or the *traffic* that will be generated. Attendance to sports stadia is easy to capture, as are the number of people at a rock concert or movie theater (e.g., if your product is the concert sponsor or is being given away as samples in the theater lobby). While not a substitute for actual impact, traffic measures at least give an indication of how many people will have the opportunity for exposure. For word-of-mouth efforts, the number to determine is how many people could potentially be influenced by the viral efforts.

Some owned media are as measurable as paid. Brand websites, for example, can be evaluated based on the number of people that clicked on them (impressions), along with information on where those users came from beforehand and where they clicked to afterward. For product placement and brand integration, the metric can be based on television audience ratings. That is, it is assumed that viewers of *The Voice* will be exposed to Starbucks drinks consumed by the judges. Additional measurement is also undertaken to confirm the percentage of people that actively remember seeing the brand in its program context, using survey research, along with any attitudinal change that can be attributed to the placement or integration.

Given that it is not enough for marketers to have their name placed in front of hundreds or thousands of happy but disinterested bodies, the planner should also try to assess the value of those expected impressions relative to the cost of obtaining them. Here, it is probably good to consider the contextual relevance of the impact. That is, it might make good sense to have Adidas be a featured sponsor at sports stadia when soccer matches are played, but less so for a prescription drug such as Viagra to be present at those same events. For digitally based owned media forms, such as brand websites or Facebook pages, the costs may be relatively low, but the impact may also be small depending on the brand. While the Expedia website is at the heart of its travel-booking business, that is less true for Charmin's website or Facebook page. The cost of developing a television program based on or incorporating a brand can be high, but the value may be worthwhile if the brand is able to reach its desired—and potentially hard to reach—target audience. This is what Samsung achieved with its *World Championship of Gaming* program, enhancing its image and reputation among the hard-core gamers that viewed the TV show, even though the size of the audience was less than 1 percent of the total population.

Considerations for Earned Media

It is ironic that although a brand's earned social media, such as its Facebook likes and Twitter mentions, are captured immediately and passively the second they occur, advertisers are still determining what the *value* is of those often-impressive numbers. It may not cost much to generate millions of followers or fans to a brand, but how that translates into increases in awareness or product sales continues to be tested.

For traditional (nondigital) word of mouth, the media specialist needs to consider value too, although it is harder to quantify. What is the benefit of placing (paid) brand advocates in a public location to subtly promote your brand of vodka or soda or eyeliner? If your local radio or TV buy includes the on-air talent talking about your brand (*added value* negotiated as part of the deal), how much can you measure the impact at the cash register or to your website?

In addition, the media specialist needs to ensure that what a brand earns through earned media is part of a holistic communications plan, rather than just used for the sake of it, and that there are clear objectives for what the earned media should achieve for the brand.

Summary

In this chapter, we covered some of the basic terms and features of media planning. In order to understand media, it is essential that the media specialist be familiar with the concepts of reach, frequency, gross rating points, and gross impressions. Beyond these, it is also helpful to understand the notion of effective frequency, which assumes that in order for an ad to be effective, the target audience has to be exposed to it more than one time. Frequency planning forces you to think about exposure within the purchase cycle. An exposure distribution lets you know the number of people who are exposed a given number of times to an individual vehicle or a complete media schedule. Media costs are accounted for by calculating the cost per thousand (CPM) and cost per rating point (CPP).

The remainder of the chapter looked at various considerations for each major media category, whether paid, owned, or earned. For television, this includes the program rating, audience composition, and viewers per viewing household (VPVH). Radio plans need to examine the time spent listening, cumulative rating, and audience turnover. When magazines or newspapers are included in a media plan, it is important to know the publication's circulation, digital audience, rate base, and actual readership. The main consideration for out-of-home advertising is planning the out-of-home rating for a given target audience, along with the "eyes on" measure of likely ad exposure. For other forms of out of home media, estimated traffic past a video screen or transit ad should be calculated. For digital advertising, the specialist should consider ad viewability and whether the buy will be programmatic. Owned media should be assessed based on the potential traffic for an event or location, as well as the cost relative to the value of the spending. Earned media considerations are the value of the social media or word of mouth efforts and how best to determine them.

CHECKLIST: TERMS, CALCULATIONS, AND CONSIDERATIONS

1. Have you figured out how many gross rating points your schedule will deliver?
2. What are the reach, effective reach, and average frequency of that schedule?
3. If you plan to include television in the schedule, have you looked at both program ratings and viewers per viewing household (VPVH)?
4. If you plan to include radio in the schedule, have you looked at the average quarter-hour (AQH) ratings, cume rating, time spent listening (TSL), and turnover for each station?
5. If you plan to include magazines in the schedule, have you looked at the coverage, composition, circulation, rate base, ad positions, and discounts?
6. If you plan to include newspapers in the schedule, have you looked at the coverage, circulation, and audience composition figures for each paper?
7. If you plan to include outdoor billboards in the schedule, have you looked at the GRPs available in each market being considered?
8. If you plan to include digital media in the schedule, have you thought about the ad type, position, and measurement metric you want?
9. If you plan to incorporate owned media in the schedule, have you thought about the traffic to be generated and the cost of the efforts relative to their impact?
10. If you plan to include earned media in the schedule, are you looking at the value of that for your brand?

NOTES

1. "Memory without Recall, Exposure without Perception," Herbert E. Krugman, *Journal of Advertising Research*, vol. 40, no. 6, November/December 2000, 49–54.
2. "Effective Frequency—Then and Now," Michael J. Naples, *Journal of Advertising Research*, vol. 37, no. 4, July/August 1997, 7–13. "If Not Effective Frequency, Then What?" Kenneth A. Longman, *Journal of Advertising Research*, vol. 37, no. 4, July/August 1997, 44–50. "What Can One Exposure Do?" Lawrence D. Gibson, *Journal of Advertising Research*, vol. 36, no. 1, March/April 1996, 9–18. *How Brands Grow*, Byron Sharp, Oxford University Press, 2010.
3. "Effective Frequency: One Exposure or Three Factors," Gerard Tellis, *Journal of Advertising Research*, vol. 37, no. 4, July/August 1997, 75–80. "Effective Reach and Frequency: Does It Really Make Sense?" Hugh M. Cannon and Edward A. Riordan, *Journal of Advertising Research*, vol. 34, no. 1, March/April 1994, 19–28. *The Ultimate Secrets of Advertising*, John Philip Jones, Sage Publications, 2002. *When Ads Work*, John Philip Jones, Lexington Books, 1995. "Recency Planning," Erwin Ephron, *Journal of Advertising Research*, vol. 37, no. 4, July/August 1997, 61–65. "Single Source Research Begins to Fulfill Its Promise," John Philip Jones, *Journal of Advertising Research*, vol. 35, no. 3, May/June 1995, 9–17.
4. "More Weeks, Less Weight: The Shelf Space Model of Advertising," Erwin Ephron, *Journal of Advertising Research*, vol. 35, no. 3, May/June 1995, 18–24.
5. NAA "20 'Tweetable truths'" about the Newspaper Industry, from Newspaper Association of America website, naa.org.

CHAPTER 8

CREATING THE PLAN

Putting together a media plan represents the culmination of all the thinking, planning, and organizing that we have discussed in earlier chapters. That is, with sound advertising and media objectives, a knowledge of who it is we wish to reach with our messages, and a clear idea of what different paid, owned, and earned media can offer us, we are now in a position to start assembling the plan. The key idea to keep in mind when doing this is your *media strategy*. What is it you are hoping to achieve by using media vehicle X as opposed to Y? How will your combination of media categories and vehicles help fulfill your advertising and media objectives? As with any process, there are several steps to the creation of the plan. These are outlined in this chapter.

TARGET AUDIENCE'S USE OF AND RELATIONSHIP TO MEDIA

The first step in building the media plan is finding out which media your target audience uses and what their relationships are with those media. There is not much point in putting your message about Allstate insurance on hundreds of radio stations across the country if the 25–54 year-olds you are trying to reach tend to be heavy television viewers. Second, you can discover the media habits of your potential customers through syndicated services such as GfK MRI or Simmons or through custom studies that you conduct or solicit on your own. The third alternative, which is the cheapest but may be less accurate, is to do some mini research on your own. You can use your own website to gather feedback, keeping in mind that if someone is on that site, they may well be biased in your favor. You could directly ask your clients or customers where they have seen your ads; if you have been sponsoring the local Little League club for years but nobody mentions it, then that might indicate the need for a different approach.

By this point, given what you now know about what each media type can offer (and what it can't), you are probably starting to see how the various media will fit in to your particular strategy. So if your goal is to increase awareness of your beauty salon's new manicure and massage treatments, you might turn to the media best suited to that awareness goal—television and out-of-home. On the other hand, if you want to increase the frequency of visits to Pizza Hut restaurant, then local radio or digital might be a better bet because you can place a large number of ads at a reasonable cost and keep repeating the message to remind people of that establishment.

Once you think you have a handle on which media should be used, you should then consider more closely the *relationship* of your target audience with their media. This notion, as explained in Chapter 2, explores the relationship of consumers to media in order to understand how and why they use the media they select.

For example, the 25–54 year-old insurance prospects might watch more television than average, according to the syndicated audience measurement data. But do they do so as an escape from their routines, because they are constantly looking for new information, or because they cannot afford other forms of entertainment? By understanding the target's motivations for media use, the planner will be better able to select the right media types and vehicles to communicate the advertiser's message.

As you start to assemble your media categories and vehicles, you also need to think about several other considerations: the timing of the plan, its scheduling, and its geographic variations. We consider each of these in turn.

TIMING OF THE PLAN

For many products, the timing of the plan is self-evident. That is, you want to advertise snow blowers in winter and sunscreen in summer. Other items are tied in to specific days or weeks of the year, such as Valentine's Day candies or Thanksgiving turkeys. But for the majority of goods and services, you would ideally want to promote them continually, getting your message out on a very regular and frequent basis to reach as many people as you can as often as possible.

There are two obvious drawbacks here. First, for most advertisers, particularly small businesses, they simply cannot afford to do this. And second, there are good reasons *not* to bombard the media constantly with your message. People are going to tire more quickly of your ads, making them tune out or ignore them sooner. They may even grow so irritated by seeing or hearing them all the time that they actually develop less favorable opinions of your brand or company. Most of all, there is no point advertising something unless you have something worth saying. Remember, an advertising message has to tell the consumer about something that they will be interested in. If all you did was place a message in the paper or online 365 days of the year saying "I'm here," you would be unlikely to see much effect, if any, on your sales.

You need to focus your efforts on particular months, weeks, or days. Deciding when to do so is not all that difficult. Most businesses have some seasonality to them, even those that are used or frequented all the time. You probably know, for example, that people stock up on office supplies at the end of the financial period (quarterly or semi-annually); they flock to health clubs at the start of the new year and when the weather begins turning warmer. Apartment leases tend to be signed in May and October, making the rental business busy just prior to those dates.

You might want to use one of two tactics here. You could focus your efforts on promoting your product right before the peak period, reminding people of your existence and trying to take additional share points away from your competitors, or you could try to build up sales at other times of the year. Or, you could try a combination of the two, maintaining a strong presence during the height of your "season," but also keeping a high profile at a couple of other times during the year, too. If you do choose to advertise when people may not be thinking about your product, then it is even more important that you tell them something new and interesting. Perhaps you lower your membership rates to the health club in March or October and announce that in local newspapers and on billboards. You need not be confined to "typical" seasonal patterns either. You can create an event for your business at any time of the year. *Cooking Light* magazine sponsored a celebrity chef tasting event in New York City in which several advertisers' products were featured. Or you can find a charitable cause to support that can enhance your image among your target audience. Conagra Foods, for example, which makes well-known brands such as Reddi Whip, Hunts tomato sauce, and Banquet frozen meals, supports many initiatives that help fight hunger, including making food donations, encouraging employees to volunteer at food banks, and conducting financial education classes to help families struggling to make ends meet. Since the key target for many of Conagra's brands is women with children, this is an approach that likely makes those moms think more highly of them when they are in the store. These kinds of special activities not only provide excellent opportunities for self-promotion in the media, but they can also generate additional coverage through public relations efforts and publicity.

It is also worthwhile to consider the seasonality of the media you are planning to use. Most media categories have seasonal variations—the fourth quarter is often very tight, for example, because of pre-holiday advertising. For media sold on a supply-and-demand basis, such as radio and television ads, this can affect prices considerably. There are only a fixed number of minutes of commercial time available. Even for those media that have rate cards, such as magazines and newspapers, heavy media demand for space during those months may mean it is especially important to place orders well in advance. Other events happen less frequently but have a predictable impact on media buys. Congressional elections every other year and presidential elections every four years mean that the spring primaries and fall elections can have a significant impact on media availability and pricing in those time periods. In the sporting world, the winter and summer Olympics, alternating with each other every two years, affect national media buys around the time of those special events.

BALANCING REACH AND FREQUENCY

As you develop your media plan, it is important to keep track of how well it will perform. That is, you need to keep calculating your reach and frequency measures to compare one potential plan against another. The goal is to find the right medium, or combination of media, that will realize your media objectives given the amount of money you have to spend. You can do so using the simple calculations shown in earlier chapters, based on the size of your target audience and the ratings of the individual media vehicles.

It may turn out that you will not be able to achieve the specific number you set as your goal for reach and/or frequency. In that event, you need to consider several possibilities. It may be that a 55 percent reach of the target is acceptable, even though you had originally planned to reach 65 percent, or that a frequency of three is all right when four was the ideal. And keep in mind, of course, that we are dealing here with plan *estimates* rather than actual reach figures. You may be restricted in the actions you can take. If your client demands that his message is seen on television, then that medium must remain in the plan. But perhaps you can opt for lower-rated networks instead of the largest, most expensive TV programs, and, by reducing the cost, be able to place the message more frequently and across more channels, thereby increasing the reach.

Alternately, you might want to rethink your timing and scheduling strategies. Maybe instead of advertising every two weeks for six months, you could place your message every week for three or four months, concentrating your efforts on the most important period and increasing your reach and frequency within that time span. Or maybe the addition of owned and earned media efforts will enhance your brand presence even when there are no paid media being used.

ROI AND MEDIA MODELS

While media planners should have a good understanding of all the media concepts outlined in Chapter 3, today's advertisers and agencies rely heavily on media models to perform the calculations. A media model is a statistical routine performed by computer software packages that goes through the data and manipulates it to project the effectiveness and efficiency of a plan. Various kinds of models are used, all with the overall goal of providing numbers to support the plan. The models are usually based on original numbers of actual audiences to a media type (magazine readership, TV viewership, etc.). They then rely on statistical techniques, such as regression, to project out from that data to other demographics, time periods, or markets (depending on the scope of the model).

Many marketers now use econometric modeling, where statistics are used to try to figure out what marketing (and media) elements are driving actual sales. In so doing, they attempt to measure the media's ROI. The key question to be answered is: For every dollar spent on television or radio or digital, how much is returned in sales? The goal is to receive at least $1 of net profit for each dollar that they invest. If they obtain much less than that, then some argue the money is being wasted. Conversely, if the ROI is much higher than $1, it can suggest they are not spending enough because if the advertising and media are having such an impact, then they should be spending more to make the most of that effect. While the techniques used are fairly complex, the idea of holding advertising media more accountable for their performance is one that has found favor among high-ranking executives at many corporations. Some find it difficult to believe that any kind of model can truly determine the proportion of sales delivered by any form of indirect and/or brand image advertising (as opposed to truly measurable direct response, promotional, or digital advertising). But as marketing budgets are increasingly scrutinized, these types of models will only gain in popularity and use.

Much of the interest in ROI has been driven by the growth in digital spending. With display or mobile advertising, for example, it became possible to look at the behavioral response to an ad. How many clicked on it? And of those, who went through to purchase the product (or take some other action)? Over the past few years, most paid media have been looking for ways to demonstrate a similar level of accountability. Some, such as radio or magazines, have relied primarily on custom research using marketing mix models to show sales driven by ads in their platforms. In television, the development of set-top box data collected at the household level has provided new ways to measure the precise impact of TV spots. The cable or satellite subscriber information can be linked to a myriad of other data, from frequent shopper loyalty cards, to auto registrations, to credit card spending, to an advertiser's own customer database, allowing them to measure directly the link between TV ad exposure and product sales.

An extension of a marketing mix model that has become popular is the multitouch attribution model. It looks at the collective impact of various media exposures not just in predicting sales but also in the way they work together over time. It helps marketers understand, for example, whether the TV ad works best if delivered before the digital ad or if an event sponsorship is most effective when promoted with TV and digital simultaneously.

Most accountability studies focus on the short-term impact of the advertising. Did it generate immediate sales of the brand? It is much harder to measure precisely the long-term impact. Let's say your ad for Fruitola fruit drink appears in a magazine in one month. Your target sees the ad but is unlikely to rush out and buy the product immediately, but when she is next at the grocery store, she sees the product, remembers the ad, and decides she will try it. Many accountability models would not be able to capture that kind of longer-term effect.

Another hard-to-measure effect is what is called the *halo effect* of advertising. You might see an ad campaign for Fantastik cleaning spray that talks about how SC Johnson, its manufacturer, cares about keeping families healthy by removing germs from their homes. Your favorable impression of the brand may be transferred to other products made by the same company, such as RAID or Pledge, even if they are in other cleaning categories. That "halo" is very hard to capture in statistical models, simply because it is difficult to measure through direct data. How much of the sales results for RAID, for example, can be attributed to consumers' reaction to the Fantastik advertising?

Indeed, advertising's impact is not always reflected solely in terms of sales. Many brands use the media to convey a message that is designed to improve awareness or enhance brand loyalty or increase brand consideration. If every ad was supposed to generate an immediate sale, companies that make cars or computers or other high-ticket items would be wasting the vast majority of their ad dollars! Despite these reservations, more and more advertisers expect answers on the ROI of their media spending. While you as a media specialist may not have simple answers, you should at least be aware of the discussions going on around the topic.

SCHEDULING YOUR ADS

You may have a good idea about when to start running your ads. The next question to think about is how to schedule them. Do you want them running each week for six weeks (continuity), or twice a month all year (bursts), or for alternating six-week periods (flighting)? The answer to this question will depend primarily on two interrelated factors: your media objective and your sales pattern. There should always be a timing component stated in your objective, which will give you some guidance for the scheduling of the plan. If you hope to reach 60 percent of your target during the next six months with the message that your hospital was rated the number-one pediatric hospital in the city by a *U.S. News* analysis, then you may want to disperse your ads throughout the period to reach as many different people in your audience as possible. For H&R Block, which wants to expose people to its message about how fast it can generate tax refunds, there would be good reason to schedule most of the ads in the three months prior to the April 15 tax deadline date, building up the frequency of the message at the time of year when it is most appropriate.

You should also think about the scheduling of different media and their combination. Perhaps you could advertise your Panera store in the local newspaper every week of the year and supplement it with local cable, display, or mobile ads around the time of each special promotion. A brand's owned or earned media presence may be continual and supplement or complement the paid media schedule.

Much of what we know about scheduling tactics comes from our general knowledge on reach and frequency. That is, if you wish to reach as many *different* people as possible in your target audience, then you want to disperse your messages across media, vehicles, or days and dayparts, for example. On the other hand, if you want to ensure that your audience hears or sees your ads several times in a given period, you would concentrate them in fewer media, vehicles, days, or dayparts.

The pattern of scheduling does not seem to make a difference, however, in terms of total reach. So whether your ads appear in two sequential weeks or alternate weeks (one week on, one week off) or are placed one week a month over four months, the final reach will be approximately the same. One thing to keep in mind, however, is that if you schedule too many ads within a short time frame, your audience is likely to ignore or tune out those messages because they are tired of seeing them, a phenomenon known as *wearout*.[1] The timing element could be critical, depending on your product. It would not make much sense to spread ads for a highly seasonal item, such as suntan lotion or Christmas decorations, across many months; but, if you are promoting your Charles Schwab office through newspaper ads and in digital media, there is something to be said for having a fairly constant presence during the year (perhaps changing the message to tie in to the financial cycle).

Two television scheduling tactics that are occasionally used among major advertisers are double-spotting and roadblocking. *Double-spotting* refers to placing two spots within the same program. The effect of this technique is to increase the likelihood of multiple exposure to your ad message (i.e., increased frequency). Often these ads appear at the beginning and end of the commercial break, a tactic known as *bookending*. Part of the expectation is that, even if you have tuned away at the start of the break, you will see the ad at the end of the break when you are returning to watch the program content. *Roadblocking* means placing the same ad across as many channels as possible at the same time, so that when Caleb is watching television at 8:06 p.m. on a Friday night, whichever channel he turns to, he'll see the same ad. That has become harder and harder for advertisers to do as the number of available channels grows higher, making it a much more expensive proposition to undertake. The impact, however, is going to be an increase in frequency, as your spot will be seen by Caleb every time he watches any of those channels at that time.

In the 1990s, considerable research was conducted on how best to schedule ad messages to impact sales. A study done by John Philip Jones examined the purchase records of households who also had their TV viewing captured via TV set meters (to record what channels were viewed). The results clearly showed that to achieve the greatest short-term advertising strength, or STAS, the best scheduling tactic was to place at least one message per week across as many weeks as possible. In this way, the plan could impact more people closer to the time of purchase. While the study had some significant limitations (it only looked at packaged goods, only dealt with television advertising, and only examined households rather than people), its impact was profound. Advertisers began switching their scheduling, moving away from trying to achieve a 3+ reach (reaching the target audience three or more times) in a month. Instead, they began looking at a 1+ reach per week, a strategy known as *frequency planning*. Here, the schedule calls for fewer GRPs per week, spread across more weeks of the year. While this doesn't make sense in many categories, especially those that require lengthy or high-involvement decisions by consumers (cars, houses, financial services), for many packaged goods manufacturers, frequency planning became the norm.

COST EFFICIENCIES

Costs are obviously very important for the media plan. So, in addition to keeping track of reach and frequency figures as you create the plan, you must also consider the costs involved. Of course, these are closely related. If you need to increase the frequency of your message, it is going to require more media time or space, which means more money. But as we noted previously, it might be possible to find a cheaper medium or vehicle to help your funds go further. Cost efficiencies can be calculated in terms of cost per thousand of the audience reached (CPM) and through cost per rating points (CPP). These were explained in Chapter 7. The more "mass" the medium, the cheaper it will be on a CPM basis, but the less targeted it will be for your situation. That is, there will be a lot of "waste" exposures of people who are probably not interested in what you have for sale. For a widely used product or service, such as car tires or a muffler shop, that might not be a bad thing. But if you are trying to reach a narrower group of people, such as Corvette car owners, to offer them a specially designed luggage rack that sits on the roof of the car, then you would be better off paying a higher CPM in a more targeted environment, such as car enthusiast websites or streaming audio focused on the classic rock music you know that target enjoys. The introduction of addressable TV advertising, noted in Chapter 4, is designed to reduce, if not eliminate completely, this waste by only sending ads to—and charging the advertiser for—the people you really want to talk to, sending different ads to different households based on the characteristics of each household.

TACTICAL CONSIDERATIONS

As you develop your plan, there are probably going to be numerous additional considerations that are specific to your product or service. These might include trade merchandising, consumer merchandising, national–local integration, and testing.

Trade Merchandising

For many goods and services, the trade plays a critical role in the brand's development and sales. Many media plans that are geared primarily to the consumer market also have some side benefits for the trade. When Frito-Lay promotes its Doritos corn chips, it is telling its distributors and retailers that it is pushing the brand and helping to increase their revenues, too. A national ad for McDonald's restaurant or the Honda Accord is also designed to help the local franchisee or dealer.

In putting the plan together, therefore, it is important to look at what trade-merchandising elements may be attached to it. Perhaps for a chain of Jiffy Lube oil-change shops, you can bring all the operators together for a kick-off party when the media campaign begins. Even something as simple as buttons with your new campaign slogan can help give the trade a sense of being part of the program. Sending them copies of the new ads and/or materials lets them know what message is being promoted to customers. The media can help here as well, particularly if you are one of their valued customers. They may be willing to co-sponsor an event for your distributors or retailers, for example.

One particular type of trade merchandising is *cooperative* (coop) advertising. With this, two groups agree to divide the cost of the advertising space or time. This may be as simple as a tag placed at the end of a retailer's commercial that mentions the address of the local store, or it can be a joint promotion of a theme park and a soft drinks company, where the latter is helping fund the ads of the former since it makes money on the drinks sold in the park. For local businesses, there are significant benefits to this type of merchandising. If you are a small health food store in Madison, Wisconsin, your ability to advertise on cable TV or in the Wisconsin tourism guide is going to be greatly enhanced if you can get supporting (coop) funds from Clif Bar & Company, whose products you sell in your store. Not only would it allow you to promote your business in more types of or more expensive media, but you will also most likely be able to afford better-looking ads! There are potential disadvantages, however. Sometimes the manufacturer will impose restrictions on the ads in terms of both their content/appearance and their distribution and scheduling. But even with those limitations, the coop approach works well in many cases.

Consumer Merchandising

Although we focus here almost exclusively on advertising media, it is important to keep in mind many of the other ways in which you can gain additional exposure for and mileage out of your media plan through owned media. There are a multitude of communications possibilities available, from coupons or sampling to press releases and exhibitions and displays. If you are promoting a line of gourmet preserves, then perhaps in addition to the magazine ads that you run, you can talk to the local grocery stores to set up sampling booths in their stores and feature the dates and locations in the ads. For a wireless phone company promoting the latest cell phones, you could go to local community festivals and let consumers see them, letting people know via local search keywords or radio ads at which events you will be present. The possibilities for these kinds of owned media events are almost endless. Whatever you do, however, should remain within the overall communications objectives of your plan—increasing awareness, obtaining customer preference, encouraging brand selection, and so on.

To gain as much advantage as possible from consumer promotions, you might also consider increasing other paid media weight when a coupon is dropped or placing more newspaper or digital ads the week that you are holding the promotion, as well as incorporating them into your earned media efforts (sending out tweets or adding information to your Facebook page).

National–Local Integration

While some products, such as new movies or product launches, are advertised solely on a national level, and others, such as the local coffeehouse, appear only in local ads, the majority of name brands include both national and local advertising in their media plans. If that is the case, you need to ensure not only that the message is consistent (something handled by the creative team), but also that the media placements are aligned. There are different ways of doing this. For some, particularly the higher spending advertisers, the local media weight is added to make an even greater impact on the national spending, such as buying spot TV on top of network TV or local newspapers in addition to national ones. For others, typically with smaller budgets, the addition of local media helps to stretch the paid media dollars further, creating the illusion (in selected markets) that the advertiser has a constant presence. Digital media are critical here too, since it is often possible to target ads down to specific geographical locations such as the zip codes in which your franchises are located. In all these situations, you should ensure that there is not unwanted duplication and that the messages do not drown out each other to the point of irritating the consumer or that they are so inconsistent with each other that the consumer is faced with competing messages.

Testing

For smaller advertisers, the notion of testing a plan may seem unnecessary. If you only have a few thousand dollars to spend, then it doesn't seem worthwhile. However, if you are about to change your entire marketing and media strategy, it is a good idea to see first—on a small scale—whether your new approach is likely to increase sales or harm them. For example, Toys "R" Us, which traditionally advertised primarily in local newspapers to announce whatever was on sale that week or month, changed its strategy in 2013 to increase awareness of the wide range of items by moving into national broadcast television. The potential impact of such a media move could be estimated by placing a few of these ads and including some kind of response mechanism, such as a unique URL or measuring traffic to the brand website. That way, the company could test how effective the TV ads are. In the case of Toys "R" Us, it appeared unsuccessful, as the company shifted dollars back to newspapers in 2015.

Testing is also a good idea for making changes in media weight (GRPs). If you are trying to persuade your client to increase annual spending from a few hundred dollars to several thousand, and you face resistance to the idea, then you might suggest a test of the proposed strategy in one or more markets to see what impact those added dollars would have to the bottom line.

PRESENTING THE PLAN

Whenever you present your completed plan, whether it is to senior management at your own company or to your client, you need to keep three points in mind. The first is to *be visual*. Most people either hate or fear media because they believe it is a morass of numbers, most of which they don't understand. So the more you can do to present the information in ways that they can *see* what is going on, the better off you will be. That means using charts, graphs, pictures, photos, or video to liven things up and bring the numbers to life. For instance, if you are presenting the demographic statistics on your target, then perhaps you can make a short video that depicts these people in real life or present charts or photos that demonstrate who they are.

The second point to remember is to *be brief.* Although you want to have all of the back-up materials and numbers to support what you are doing, when you make a presentation you should focus on the key points. Assuming you have an interested audience, they will look at the details afterward or ask you questions as you go along. Again, the common perception of media is that it is a mind-numbing experience, filled with mathematical formulas and statistics that are, quite simply, boring.

Third, and perhaps most importantly, *remember the consumer.* Ultimately, your plan is designed to help your client sell more widgets to the consumer. So if your plan simply recites a hundred different statistics and presents all of the numbers in charts, tables, and flowcharts, it may be totally accurate but will seem completely removed from the marketing reality that your client lives in.

Fortunately, there are ways around these problems. The first, keeping it visual, can be accomplished through the use of a flowchart. This can show, at a glance, when the ads will run, in which media and vehicles, at what cost, and to what effect (reach and frequency). These can be made for each target in a given plan and be broken out by medium, if desired. An example is shown later in this chapter. There are numerous ways of creating flowcharts. You can simply draw one yourself, use a spreadsheet program, or use a custom media flowchart package.

Being brief is harder to do. It usually comes down to practice. Running through your presentation with a friend or colleague and asking for their advice can be useful. It is particularly helpful to present your work to someone outside of your area; if they can understand your concise explanations of media terms, then you are doing fine! Remember, however, to include all of the pertinent information (including calculations for how you arrived at your conclusions) in the deck of materials you leave behind. In addition, you have to show how your media plan fits in with and enhances the brand's marketing and advertising objectives and strategies.

Learn as much as possible about the end user of your product, and include some of those findings in your presentation. You might want to survey some of the customers or do a couple of focus groups to find out how they currently use media and advertising in your category. Include a few of the verbatims (what consumers actually said, in their own words), or even some video of your conversations with customers, to remind your client that you know you are, in the end, dealing with people.

Last but not least, it is crucial to remind your audience that you are dealing with estimates. Some of those may be informed by years of experience, but many are based on your best judgment, syndicated data sources, or mathematical reasoning. People tend to believe that because you, as the media specialist, have placed a number on something, that turns it into "reality." If that were so, media planning would be completely automated and done by rote, a pure science, rather than the combination of art and science that it remains today.

A MEDIA PLAN EXAMPLE

Let's go through an example for a fictitious brand of breakfast cereal, Bene-Flakes. This is a nationally distributed health-oriented brand that was first introduced in 2009. The company now wishes to introduce a new line that only has natural ingredients in it. It will compete primarily with the natural cereals of Kellogg's and General Mills along with oatmeal-focused Quaker Oats.

Situation Analysis

Through the end of calendar year 2016, BeneFlakes sales are flat versus a year ago.

Marketing objectives/strategies: Introduce new BeneFlakes Natural among natural cereal eaters in two ways:

1. Year-round focus on natural benefits of new BeneFlakes cereal
2. Heavy-up during primary cold cereal months (spring/summer).

Advertising time period: January through December 2017
Media budget: $47.8 million

Marketing Background

Competitive Analysis
- Kellogg's: Total spending, $250 million; 30 percent network television, 30 percent cable TV, 5 percent Spanish-language TV, 20 percent magazines, 5 percent syndicated TV, 10 percent digital

- General Mills: Total spending, $300 million; 10 percent network television, 40 percent spot TV, 30 percent cable TV, 5 percent syndicated TV, 10 percent Spanish-language TV, 5 percent digital
- Quaker Oats: Total spending, $20 million; 20 percent network television, 30 percent cable TV, 10 percent syndicated TV, 10 percent magazines, 20 percent Spanish-language TV, 5 percent digital, 5 percent spot TV
- Category total: Total spending, $660 million; 20 percent network television, 30 percent cable TV, 15 percent magazines, 20 percent spot TV, 5 percent syndicated TV, 5 percent Spanish-language TV, 2 percent digital, 1 percent Sunday magazines, 0 percent radio, 1 percent newspapers, 1 percent outdoor.

Seasonality

Cereal usage tends to peak in spring/summer months, but the product is used throughout the year.

The following chart shows usage for each two month period compared to usage throughout the year. Where a number is 100, that means the usage in that period is the same as the annual average. If the number is above 100, usage is greater than average; if the number is below 100, usage is less than average in that time period.

BeneFlakes

J/F	M/A	M/J	J/A	S/O	N/D
74	105	126	128	100	63

Cereal Category

J/F	M/A	M/J	J/A	S/O	N/D
92	96	115	118	102	80

Advertising Objectives

Generate awareness of the natural ingredients of the new line of BeneFlakes Natural cereal among target to goal of 40 percent during calendar year 2017.

Media Objectives

1. Advertise to heavy or medium natural cereal eaters. The demographics and psychographics of this target are:
   - Women 18 to 49 years old, household income $75,000+, with children

- Well-educated, professional or managerial, nutrition-oriented, and care about natural ingredients.

  The target consists of 21.9 million women who can be defined as natural cereal users. They represent 18 percent of all women.

2. Achieve the following communication goals: Average 4-week delivery

Peak period	Rest of year
3+ reach	3+ reach
35+% of target	10% of target
reached 3+ times	reached 3+ times

3. Provide year-round media support to encourage trial and repeat usage throughout year, with additional weight during the peak summer months.
4. Schedule advertising to run Wednesday through Sunday to complement key grocery shopping days.
5. Provide national advertising support.

Media Strategies

Following the success of the master brand during the past eight years, the 2017 media plan recommends an awareness-building media strategy using television as the primary paid medium and digital media and selected magazines as the additional paid media types. BeneFlakes Natural will sponsor two programs on Food Network: *Barefoot Contessa* and *Weighing In*, with accompanying healthy eating tips on the network's website and on its Facebook and Twitter pages. It will use social media to share healthy eating tips and natural food recipes.

Television

As the primary medium, national TV provides:

- High reach/awareness builder
- Sight, sound, and motion
- Immediacy of message
- Targetability (niche networks)
- Continuity (lower cost cable networks)
- Contextual relevance
- Emotional connection to viewer/consumer.

The plan will include prime-time TV shows that appeal to the target audience. These fall into genres such as sitcoms, dramas, and reality/news.

The following cable networks are more likely to be viewed by the target:

- Bravo
- Oxygen
- Food Network
- OWN
- E!
- Lifetime.

One-half of the weight will be in daytime, with the remainder split between prime time and early morning. Daytime programming offers broad reach. Prime time helps expand that reach, and early morning will be seen by the target close to their likely time to make grocery shopping trips. The early morning weight also provides a more news-oriented context to promote the health benefits of the product.

As a smaller brand, BeneFlakes will only include a small amount of broadcast network TV during peak periods.

Digital Media

As the second medium, digital media provides:

- Additional reach
- Response-based measurement
- Contextual relevance
- Behavioral targeting.

In addition, Google will be used to drive search on natural health-related keywords.

Magazines

As the third medium, magazines provide:

- Long message life
- Repeat exposure
- Targetability—ability to provide contextually relevant and engaging message
- Editorial compatibility.

Magazine ads will include both hard copy print (one-page, four color) and the mobile/tablet version of those ads wherever possible. The latter will have links to the brand's website and social media pages and allow the reader to interact with related dietary information.

Preferred position will be:

- Health and fitness—fitness section
- Food—front of book
- General/entertainment—news section.

The recommended magazines will include the following:

Magazine	Coverage	Index
Every Day with Rachael Ray	6.6%	305
Shape	6.4%	287
Elle	6.5%	281
Self	5.0%	267
In Style	10.1%	253
US Weekly	12.8%	233

Owned Media: Brand Website

The BeneFlakes Natural website will provide diet and health information, including video clips from the TV shows it sponsors, *Barefoot Contessa* and *Weighing In*.

Sponsorship

For its connection to *Barefoot Contessa* and *Weighing In*, BeneFlakes Natural will get TV billboards before and during each show's episodes, in addition to commercial time, and a significant presence on the TV shows' websites and in the network's app. It will include sponsored program-related quizzes and games in those venues where consumers can sign up to receive weekly nutrition tips.

Earned Media: Social Networks

In addition to its Facebook page, BeneFlakes will provide diet and healthy eating tips on other social media, such as Twitter and Instagram.

The Final Plan

The total cost of this plan will be $47.8 million (including a 5 percent amount as contingency). The flowchart in Exhibit 8.1 depicts how the plan would be laid out during the year.

Exhibit 8.1 Sample Flowchart

		January					February				March				Totals
		1	8	15	22	29	5	12	19	26	5	12	19	26	TRPs/$000
BeneFlakes Natural															
PAID															
Television	Cable: prime time		15	15	15	15					10	10	10	10	
	Broadcast: daytime		5	5	5	5				10					
	Broadcast: prime time		10	10	10	10					10	10	10	10	
	Total TRPs		30	30	30	30	0	0	0	10	20	20	20	20	
	Total cost ($000)								$7,500						
Magazines	All titles														
	Total TRPs								30 TRPs/month						
	Total cost ($000)									$1,000					
Digital	Online														
	Search														
	Total impressions (imps)								150,000 imps/month						
	Total cost ($000)									$750					
OWNED															
Product Placement	*Barefoot Contessa*	5	5	5	5	5	5	5	5	5	5	5	5	5	
	Total cost ($000)									$300					
EARNED															
Social															
	Total cost ($000)								$300						
															360/$9,850

(Continued)

Exhibit 8.1 (Continued)

BeneFlakes Natural

		April					May				June				Totals
		2	9	16	23	30	7	14	21	28	4	11	18	25	TRPs/$000
PAID															
Television	Cable: prime time	15	15	15	15	15	20	20	20	20	25	25	25	25	
	Broadcast: daytime							10	10	10	10	10	10	10	
	Broadcast: early morning						10	10	10	10	10	10	10	10	
	Broadcast: prime time									15	10	10	15	10	
	Total TRPs	15	15	15	15	15	20	40	40	55	55	55	60	55	
	Total cost ($000)									$15,000					
Magazines	All titles														
	Total TRPs							35 TRPs/month							
	Total cost ($000)							$1,200							
Digital	Online														
	Search														
	Total impressions							200,000 imps/month							
	Total cost ($000)							$900							
OWNED															
Product Placement	Weighing In	5	5	5	5	5	5	5	5	5	5	5	5	5	
	Total cost ($000)							$250							
EARNED															
Social															
	Total cost ($000)							$300							625/$17,650

		July					August				September				Totals
		2	9	16	23	30	5	13	20	27	3	10	17	24	TRPs/$000
BeneFlakes Natural															
PAID															
Television	Cable: prime time	30	25	25	25	25	25	25	20	20	20	20	20	20	
	Broadcast: daytime	10	10	10	10										
	Broadcast: prime time	15	15	15	15										
	Total TRPs	55	50	50	50	25	25	25	20	20	20	20	20	20	
	Total cost ($000)						$12,000								
Magazines	All titles														
	Total TRPs						50 TRPs/month								
	Total cost ($000)						$1,350								
Digital	Online														
	Search														
	Total impressions						250,000 imps/month								
	Total cost ($000)						$1,200								
OWNED															
Product Placement	*Barefoot Contessa*	5	5	5	5	5	5	5	5	5	5	5	5	5	
	Total cost ($000)						$300								
EARNED															
Social															
	Total cost ($000)						$250								615/$15,100

(Continued)

Exhibit 8.1 (Continued)

BeneFlakes Natural

		October					November				December				Totals
		1	8	15	22	29	5	12	19	26	3	10	17	24	**TRPs/$000**
PAID															
Television	Cable: prime time					10	10	10							
	Broadcast: early morning														
	Broadcast: prime time														
	Total TRPs	o	o	o	o	10	10	10	10	10	o	o	o	o	
	Total cost ($000)							$1,500							
Magazines	All titles						20 TRPs/month								
	Total TRPs														
	Total cost ($000)							$750							
Digital	Online						150,000 imps/month								
	Search														
	Total impressions														
	Total cost ($000)							$400							
OWNED															
Product Placement	Total cost ($000)							$0							
EARNED															
Social	Total cost ($000)							$150							100/$2,800

Total TRPs	1,700
Total $000	$45,400
5% safety	$2,390
Total budget ($000)	$47,790

Although this is a very generalized and simple version of what to include in a plan, it provides the basic information that has been covered earlier in this book. You should note that all of the recommendations need to be backed up by research data, wherever possible, beyond simple tables showing indices or coverage for individual media vehicles or gross expenditures for the year. Here is a brief list of the kinds of analyses that could be included in the backup for this plan:

- Media usage
- Cable TV network comparisons
- Magazine comparisons
- Website comparisons
- Brand website traffic patterns
- Social media usage (e.g., likes, tweets for brand and competitors)
- CPM comparisons (e.g., cable versus print versus digital)
- Daypart/program rankings by target
- Detailed reach and frequencies by medium
- Media quintiles
- Purchase volume for brand and category
- Facebook page traffic patterns and analysis
- Twitter traffic and analysis
- Demographic/lifestyle analysis of natural cereal users
- Category geographic analysis (BDI versus CDI by DMA)
- Seasonality analysis
- Grocery shopping patterns.

Once you have completed your media plan, you might think your task is over. Even as you are creating the plan, you should be starting to think about various alternatives.

SPENDING MORE MONEY

The opportunity to gain a larger budget than you were originally expecting does not happen very often, and certainly not as often as a media specialist might like! However, there are several good reasons for being prepared to spend more on paid advertising media than was originally proposed. It is your job as the media specialist to prove to the client how much more effective the media plan *could* be if there were more dollars available.

To some people this might sound wasteful. But for the most part, research supports the notion that placing more dollars in advertising media to reach more people on more occasions (assuming, of course, that they are the right people for your product) will increase sales.

So, how do you best prepare to offer the alternative of spending more? In many situations, the best way is to simultaneously create a second media plan that has a larger budget. If your primary plan has an annual media budget of $2 million, then you might consider creating an additional one at the $3 million level to see how that would perform. In doing so, you should not simply throw extra media weight around randomly. Instead, you should revisit your advertising and media objectives and consider what you might set as your goals if you had that extra money to spend. If, for instance, your original goal was to boost awareness of the latest Target store to open in Atlanta, then, perhaps if your budget was to be 20 percent larger, you might think about setting your objectives higher also, proposing that with the additional funds you could increase awareness to 40 percent in that same time period.

Another option with increased funding is to increase the efforts in owned and earned media. If your paid media plan for Tropicana Orange Juice for kids consists of network television and magazine ads, then the extra dollars you are recommending could permit you to integrate the brand into youth-oriented TV shows. Or keyword searches could be purchased related to juice or children's nutrition, and Facebook and Instagram ads could promote the brand socially.

Of course, in suggesting where and how this extra money could be spent, you must always show what will be achieved in return. That is, you need to quantify, wherever possible, the positive impact those dollars will have. This can be done through reach and frequency calculations that show how many additional people in the target will be reached and how many more times they will have the opportunity to be exposed to the message. Supplementary funds may also end up *lowering* the cost of individual ads, either through volume or frequency discounts, or by reducing the cost per thousand (CPM). So although the bottom-line cost of the plan may go up, the cost efficiency may actually improve.

Another advantage to spending more media dollars is that they may allow you to reach a secondary target more readily. If you are putting a plan together for the Beef Council, where the primary target audience is women who like to cook, then perhaps expanding the plan will allow you to address more clearly a secondary target audience of restaurant chefs. You might also think about using additional dollars to reach people who can influence your primary target. For a media plan offering a college fund that is aimed at parents, you might spend the extra monies to promote your company to financial planners to whom the parents will turn for advice.

Whatever you recommend for your increased-spending scenario, you must justify it in terms of the objectives and strategies that you have stated up front (even if you propose modifying those objectives if you get additional funds).

SPENDING LESS MONEY

Unfortunately, for most media specialists, the more common case is that you will end up having to spend less than originally proposed.

Whatever the reason for the cost reductions, as you prepare an alternative plan, think carefully about how you can put together a media schedule that will come as close as possible to meeting your original objectives. There may be several ways to cut corners without decimating the plan. Perhaps you can shorten the flight times, running TV ads for two weeks at a time instead of four, or reduce the digital programmatic video buy, or rely more on owned or earned media that may cost no additional money.

Creating a reduced-spending scenario should not be a case of simply cutting spots or digital placements arbitrarily. It must be done with strategic reasoning in mind. For instance, let's say you have a media plan to get more parents in your area to consider sending their children to your client's preschool program, but instead of having $300,000 to spend, you end up having only $240,000. You had originally intended to send direct mailings to all parents of young children in the vicinity inviting them to visit the school, as well as placing newspaper ads in community papers. Now, with less money to spend, you could enhance the school's website or build a Facebook page, both at minimal cost, and promote your owned media through ads in the digital versions of the newspapers. Note that a reduction in frequency of paid media may result in the loss of some volume discounts and potentially lower your reach.

Sometimes there is no alternative but cutting one or more media forms from the plan. Before doing so, it is important to think about how important that medium is in consumers' lives. If you take out all TV from a plan, then remember that you are losing a key medium that offers sight, sound, and motion and the opportunity to deliver the message to a large audience. That might be less important for a Ford dealership, but critical for a Red Lobster restaurant where you want to showcase the food. And it also depends on how consumers interact with the media. For example, if you know that your coffee shop has generated strong response to mobile coupons, then removing that from your plan is likely to be detrimental to the plan's impact on your audience.

Another way to reduce media spending is to use briefer or less expensive ads. Instead of 30-second commercials, maybe you could switch to 15-second ones; instead of a rich media "takeover" digital ad, perhaps standard display banners will suffice. Once again, however, this must be considered not simply in numerical terms (such as reach or CPM), but also in terms of the impact on consumers seeing or hearing that commercial message.

It might seem appropriate, given a reduced media budget, to cut the size of your target audience, but that can turn out to be *more* costly; the more narrowly you try to target your media, the more expensive it becomes to try to reach them. If your original plan for a new Betty Crocker cake mix is aimed at all women 18 to 49 years old and uses a mix of magazines and TV, then by trying to narrow it further to reach only those women 18 to 49 who have household incomes of more than $75,000 and have three or more children, you will probably end up looking at more expensive media vehicles. Instead of picking a broadly popular woman's service magazine, such as *Good Housekeeping* or *Better Homes and Gardens*, you might end up with magazines that have a smaller circulation and cost more per ad page, such as *Food and Wine* or *Bon Appetit*. While they *will* reach more of your more narrowly defined target, the cost may be correspondingly higher, too.

Sometimes costs are cut by removing any secondary targets you had planned to reach through separate media. A plan that was intended to increase awareness of an environmentally friendly detergent might be aimed at both environmentally aware consumers and opinion leaders. Faced with a cutback in media dollars, you might consider targeting only one of those groups initially, rather than both of them at once.

CHANGING TARGETS

Sometimes after a complete media plan has been presented to the client they might ask, "Did you consider targeting X instead?" That simple question might at first induce panic, but instead should be considered on its own merits. For example, is the media target really in line with the brand's marketing target, so as to achieve the overall marketing objectives?

It could also be important to include different targets in a plan, or create a separate plan for those targets, when you think that there are critical secondary audiences who need to be addressed. This is highly dependent on the product category. For medicines or healthcare items, for example, it is often essential to communicate with the medical profession as well as consumers, because they are the ones who influence which brands are selected. With the removal in the late 1990s of restrictions on television advertising for prescription drugs, there was an enormous increase in the amount pharmaceutical companies are spending on that medium. Even though consumers must still ask their doctors to prescribe these specialized drugs (such as Humira, Crestor, or Advair), the advertising is aimed at influencing the consumers to ask their physicians for a specific brand-name medication, rather than simply "something to help with my depression" (or arthritis or allergies).

Another area where critical secondary audiences exist is with children's products. When they are targeted, it is frequently advisable to have a separate target of moms or parents, because they are the ones who typically make the purchases. It is estimated that children influence tens of billions of dollars of spending each year. In many countries around the world, there are strict limits on which products can be advertised directly to children and how, out of concerns that they are more easily misled by advertising.

Whoever the target is, the media specialist must determine which media are needed to reach those people. That, in turn, will depend upon the marketing and advertising objectives for that distinct audience. Are they identical to the main target's goals, or do they differ in some way? How much do the two targets overlap, both in terms of those objectives and in their media usage patterns? It could be, for example, that if you are trying to encourage both consumers and contractors to select your Grohe faucets, then using digital display ads on home decorating sites would reach both groups, but more specialized trade sites will do a better job at convincing contractors of the merits of your brand, and ads on a broader array of sites could help expand brand awareness among consumers.

Changing Media

As the media specialist, your job entails considering different media from the beginning to the end of media plan development. That means taking time to investigate alternative media options as you put the plan together.

This could include assessing different media vehicles within the same media form. If you are recommending magazines, then perhaps you might look at more specialized publications or just their digital versions to reach your target. For TV, reconsider whether you should use broadcast, spot, or cable TV to convey your messages, or perhaps switch to a brand integration instead. With a radio plan that uses spot markets, a network buy might be more efficient and appropriate. With digital buys, you can compare buying display ads programmatically or paying for premium online video. The use of different media vehicles will depend primarily on two factors: cost efficiency and targetability. Switching from smaller local papers to bigger, more regional ones may bring you a larger audience, but those people may not be close enough to your chain of Olive Garden casual Italian restaurants to be worth reaching with your message.

The bigger change when thinking about different media is a switch in media forms altogether. Instead of recommending newspapers, what happens if you use digital instead? How about using streaming audio instead of terrestrial radio? Or what would be the result of switching dollars out of product placement and into sponsorship? And how much would that change be affected by the relationship of your target with the media you are considering? The media specialist must think through these scenarios from the point of view of both strategy and cost. How would a move from newspapers to digital display affect your overall objective of boosting awareness of your health food store? Would the same number of people be reached? Would they be the same people? What is the cost difference? And how would message frequency be impacted? What are the creative implications of such a change? All of these questions need to be answered as you develop a plan using different media.

One of the tools used in helping determine alternatives for a plan is the optimizer. Developed in the U.K. in the 1980s, these computer systems were first designed to select the optimal mix of national TV dayparts or types against a specific target. They use algorithms that balance the reach of a plan against its cost to arrive at a solution that maximizes one or the other (cost or reach). Although they are models based on historical data (ratings), they are now routinely used predictively to help media planners and buyers determine what TV dayparts or specific programs to include. Following their introduction, multimedia optimizers were created that include television, digital, radio, and print.

All of these considerations about alternative plans reinforce the notion that media planning is both art and science. There are potentially hundreds of different ways that you could plan your media to obtain the designated goals. Your job as the media specialist is to come up with the one that you believe will do the most effective and efficient job, while fully understanding that there are alternatives available that might achieve the same ends.

TESTS AND TRANSLATIONS

There are two common ways to conduct tests of a media plan on a local or regional basis. They are known as *as it falls* and *little America*. Here we will consider the basic concepts for each one, rather than going through all of the mathematical calculations needed to prepare such plans. Although this procedure is really a test, it is also sometimes referred to as a "test translation," to reflect the fact that a national or bigger plan is being recreated in some fashion on a smaller scale. And even though, as media specialists, we are most concerned with testing the media plan itself (increasing GRPs, trying different scheduling strategies, and so forth), tests are also often conducted to determine the impact of new creative, or to see how a new product fares in the marketplace.

As It Falls

This type of test is most often used for brands in existing product categories, where the competitors are well known. The main premise of this method is that the rating points are allowed to occur as they normally would in each market, or as it falls. So rather than have the same GRPs across all test markets, the plan's goals would vary somewhat from location to location, depending on how well the individual vehicles perform in each place. That also means that the budgets will vary by market, too. It may cost $5,000 to buy 100 radio GRPs in Boise, Idaho, but $10,000 to get the same GRP level in Madison, Wisconsin. The main advantage to this testing system is that it provides a realistic scenario for assessing the impact of the test plan. If the plan were expanded to a national level, there would still be market-by-market differences similar to those seen in the as it falls test situation.

Little America

This test market procedure is used more often with new brands or products where there is no existing competition. What it sets out to do is recreate a national plan in one (or a few) markets, or get as close to that as is feasible. It usually involves more complex planning, first to determine how individual media categories perform in the markets you choose, and then to figure out how to adjust the test plan so that it matches the national delivery.

SUMMARY

When creating a media plan, it is crucial to consider first the target audience's use of media in terms of which categories and vehicles they use. You then must determine the plan's timing, if there are seasonal sales or other elements of the marketing mix (pricing, promotion, distribution or product changes) that will affect the plan's timing. For scheduling of your chosen vehicles, financial considerations and reach and frequency goals will help determine when and how often your ads appear. Tactical elements are important, too, particularly trade and consumer merchandising, to receive maximum support from dealers, distributors, and retailers and maximize the impact of the advertising. Then plan alternatives have to be evaluated, including having larger budgets to spend, as well as fewer dollars. Areas of focus with these alternatives are the media types used and the targets to be reached. Any potential changes can be tested by translating the plan into a local or regional test market situation and seeing what happens there first.

CHECKLIST: CREATING THE PLAN

1. Have you found out as much as possible about your target audience, either through syndicated services or primary research you conducted yourself?
2. Have you determined the appropriate timing for your messages?
3. How will your messages be scheduled—continuously, in flights, or in bursts?
4. Will your reach and frequency goals be met by your timing and scheduling strategies?
5. Are there merchandising possibilities for your brand with either the trade or with consumers?
6. Do you need to test the plan first in a smaller location before rolling it out?
7. Can you present your plan in a visually interesting and succinct fashion?
8. Do you have a flowchart or schematic that summarizes the distribution, delivery, and cost of your media plan?
9. Have you prepared a second media plan at a higher budget level?
10. Have you considered how extra funds would be spent—longer flights, wider geographies, secondary targets—and how those would impact your media (reach and frequency) goals?
11. Do you know the impact of spending fewer media dollars on your plan (fewer media categories or vehicles, reduced number of targets, reduced schedule, lower reach and frequency results)?
12. Are there other target audiences or media categories you should consider?
13. Is it necessary to test your media plan first, either as it falls (existing brands) or in a little America (new products) test?

NOTE

1. "An Empirical Investigation of Advertising Wearin and Wearout," Margaret Henderson Blair, *Journal of Advertising Research*, vol. 27, no. 6, December 1987/January 1988, 45–50.

CHAPTER 9

MAKING THE MEDIA BUYS

Even the most impressive media plan will not satisfy the client until the time and space have actually been bought. The role of the media specialist may involve none, some, or all of the media buying functions. This chapter provides a brief overview of how paid media are purchased. The subject really requires book-length treatment on its own; the goal here is to show how media buying fits in with the planning process, rather than to explain the many details and intricacies of the buys themselves.

MERCHANDISING A MAGAZINE BUY

It is fairly common in many smaller or midsize advertising agencies for media planners to be responsible for magazine buys, although at larger agencies there is usually a specialized staff of print buyers who focus solely on the negotiations. It used to be that all magazines worked off a *rate card*, listing the cost of buying various page sizes with or without color or other special features. Additional charges were also made for preferred positions, such as the inside front or back covers and the back cover itself, which are believed to be read by more people.

While the extra costs remain, today's magazine buys require negotiating. That is, the rate card is usually the starting point, but then it is up to the media specialist and the magazine's representative (or rep) to discuss the final cost for the client. Discounts may be offered for volume buys if, for example, the client purchases ads in multiple issues, buys several pages in one issue, or, increasingly, buys space in several magazines owned by the same publisher. As we learned in Chapter 4, the cost of a magazine ad will depend on the size and nature of the magazine's readership. Obviously, you will pay more to reach more people. It would cost you about $575,000 for one full-page, four-color ad in *Better Homes and Gardens*, which reaches about 16 percent of the population, whereas the same ad placed in *Cooking Light*, which reaches 5 percent, will cost only $155,000.

At the other end of the spectrum, however, you may also have to pay more to reach a highly specialized audience. Although both *Eating Well* and *Every Day with Rachael Ray* have similar sized audiences of around 5 million, the one-page ad will cost $95,000 in the former and $170,000 in the latter because it is assumed that the more practical material of articles and recipes is reaching a more interested, involved audience that is more likely to pay attention to the ads in that publication. There have been research studies both supporting and rejecting this hypothesis, with the dissenters claiming that if the reader is more involved in the subject matter, he or she is in fact *less* likely to pay attention to the ads. For the media specialist, the main focus should be on the suitability of each individual magazine to the media objectives and how efficiently and effectively each vehicle can be used.

When the magazine space is negotiated, the specialist will usually request certain positioning preferences. As noted, for some of these a premium must be paid. Aside from covers, the specialist may want a Hellman's mayonnaise ad, for example, placed near or within the food editorial or a Cover Girl cosmetics ad to appear in that section of the magazine. Sometimes it is enough to simply request that the ad is in the first third of the issue, under the assumption that those pages are more likely to be seen. The willingness and ability of the magazine to fulfill these requests will vary depending on who the client is and how many ad pages it needs to fill. One of the important things to remember about magazines is that, unlike TV or radio, which have a finite amount of airtime, printed media (including newspapers) can simply add pages if they can attract enough additional advertisers.

In addition to the practice of magazines negotiating off the rate card, many publications also offer further benefits to their advertisers. These might include special promotions, editorial features, bonus circulation, ads in their digital or app versions, or trade deals. While these are usually offered at little or no extra charge, the cost is built into the amount the specialist pays for the ad pages. These extras reflect the extremely competitive media landscape, with an increasingly fragmented marketplace not only within the magazine industry, but also across different media. *Good Housekeeping* not only competes with the other women's titles (such as *Better Homes and Gardens, Real Simple,* and *Woman's Day*), but it must also fight for dollars with television, radio, newspapers, outdoor billboards, direct mail, digital—the list is almost endless.

Once the magazine space has been agreed on, including the price of special features and positioning, it is time to make the actual buy. At larger agencies, this is accomplished through a magazine authorization, which sets out the terms of the contract to which both parties must agree. Some clients may like to see this first, to be sure they know what they are getting. If everyone accepts these terms, the media specialist can go ahead and authorize the buy.

GETTING NEWS INTO NEWSPAPERS

The purchase process for newspapers is similar to that of magazines. First, the buyer must analyze all possible newspapers available in each selected market, looking at factors such as circulation, coverage, audience composition, color possibilities, and zoning (the ability to customize ads to different areas of the paper's coverage area or only appear in selected editions). Today, most newspapers can vary the inserts by zip code.

Then, the buyer must negotiate with each newspaper to obtain the best rate. Newspapers are purchased in terms of standard ad unit sizes, or SAUs; although the size of the newspaper itself may vary, its ad sizes are standardized. Just as with magazines, the newspaper buyer will usually want to specify where in the paper the ad will appear—an ad for Hidden Valley salad dressing in the food section, an ad for Universal Studio's latest movie in the entertainment section, and an Ethan Allen furniture store ad in the home section. Sometimes, that decision is made based on what the target audience is more likely to read, so an ad for Verizon cellular phone service might appear in the business section to reach professionals who are more likely to be interested in that item.

Once the deal has been negotiated and agreed upon, an insertion order is placed with the newspaper. At the same time, the agency will issue a newspaper authorization that sets out all of the specifications for the ad, such as whether it will be black and white or color, whether it includes a coupon, and any special instructions. Then all the print details must be confirmed, including the insertion dates, closing dates, ad size, column inches, inch rate, gross cost, contract rate, and position in the newspaper. This is done for every newspaper in which the ad will appear. After that has received approval, the insertion order goes ahead and the buy is made.

THE TELEVISION TRADE

There are three ways that national television is bought, for both broadcast and cable TV and syndication—long term, short term ("scatter"), and opportunistic. The first, and most intense, is what is generally known as the *upfront marketplace*. For broadcast TV, this usually takes place in late

May after the networks present their new programming slate to advertisers, while for cable, it runs from May to July. With either television form, the media specialist negotiates time with the major networks well in advance of the actual air dates. Most typically, these fall during the following TV season that starts in September and runs through to the following May. The time purchased is usually over three to four quarters of the year.

When TV advertising was initiated in the late 1940s, all commercial time was, in effect, bought up front. That is because programs were fully sponsored by advertisers, so the negotiations for which companies would put their names in front of new programs' names occurred as those same programs were being developed (e.g., the Philco Theater Hour). After quiz show scandals in the late 1950s, where contestants were secretly fed the right answers in order to maintain viewer suspense, the networks took back control of programming from advertisers (who had sponsored those unfair quiz shows). It was in 1962 that ABC became the first TV network to air all of its new programming in one week, right after Labor Day, and the "new fall season" was created. From then on, the annual schedule was born. The network marketplace is a modified version of supply and demand, with TV ratings (viewers) acting as the supply and advertiser budgets providing the demand. However, given that the networks have certain profit goals to meet, they will only offer programs at prices that are in line with those goals, therefore diminishing the dynamics of a true supply-and-demand market. In 1967, ABC also became the first network to offer the "guaranteed" program rating to advertisers who agreed to buy up front. Although this meant the advertiser had to commit to a buy in advance, the advantage was that hit programs might be purchased at a relatively inexpensive cost. Today, upfront buys account for 80 to 85 percent of all network prime time sales. In 2015, more than $8 billion worth of network TV ad time was sold this way.[1]

When you buy *long term*, you receive a guaranteed rating, along with the opportunity to set up cancellation options. Typically, the options decelerate over the future quarters. For instance, in the first quarter you might buy all of the spots confirmed; in the second quarter, three-quarters or 75 percent might be firm, with the option to cancel the remaining 25 percent by an agreed-upon date. Then for the third or subsequent quarters, only half of the spots you negotiate are firm and half are cancellable by a certain date. One advantage of buying time this way is that more favorable rates may be offered, as the networks like to lock in the advertisers to their shows (both new and returning series). Also, advertisers are more likely to get a better mix of programs and to be ensured of spots in the time periods and/or shows they want. The disadvantage, from the buyer's standpoint, is that there may be less room for negotiation because everyone is trying to buy from a limited amount of inventory. That is, the networks can choose how much of the available airtime they wish to sell up front, manipulating the demand for that time. The buyers also don't know how well the new programs will perform, basing their judgment on brief promotional excerpts the networks release, along with their historical experience of similar shows from the past.

The commercial minutes the networks hold back or don't sell then form the bulk of the second type of national television time, which is known as the *scatter* market because it is scattered throughout the broadcast day across months. Buyers typically purchase this type of commercial time on a quarterly basis, usually two to three months in advance of the quarter, unless demand is soft. Prices in scatter will vary, depending on the supply and demand, and what happens in scatter tends to impact the long-term or upfront marketplace, too. In boom years when the economy is thriving, advertiser demand during the upfront period is high, but when a recession hits, advertisers are loathe to commit large funds in advance, so upfront deals tend to decrease while scatter buys rise.

Advertisers who purchase spots in the scatter market may or may not get guaranteed ratings, depending on the supply and demand. Those spots are usually purchased by advertisers who are unable or unwilling to commit to a schedule a year in advance. If demand for scatter time is high, the network can close a particular daypart on very short notice, pulling it out of sale and then repricing it for future buyers. Advertisers who do not move quickly enough may find themselves shut out of the daypart completely.

Finally, the third way to buy time in national television is the *opportunistic* buy. Here, the advertiser chooses to purchase at the last minute, picking up whatever remains available. The advantage here is that the rates are usually most favorable to the buyer because the network wants to sell that time. The obvious drawback, however, is that there is less choice and little or no flexibility in the deal. Spots can be purchased as late as the day before airtime. Several sports events are sold this way.

Deciding how to purchase TV time depends on many factors, not the least of which is the size of the advertising budget. The number of quarters in which the commercial is to run also plays a key role here, as does the type of programming mix desired. First and foremost, however, should be strategic considerations regarding the impact of the decision on the marketing, advertising, and media goals.

How Television Time Is Bought

The process of buying television time is as follows. The buyer requests a package of programs from the seller (broadcast, syndication, or cable). The package may be based on costs or on ratings, but it is ultimately based on the goals of the plan. The sellers submit their inventory, and the buyer chooses the package that best meets the client's needs and negotiates the price. Instead of purchasing them immediately, however, the buyer "goes to hold," which means the buyer is almost certain he or she will buy that time but has not fully committed to it yet. Both sides agree on how long that hold will last; generally, it is three to five days in the scatter market and four to eight weeks in the long-term market. After that period, the buyer will either purchase the time or drop out. Once the deal is finalized, however, the buyer effectively owns that time. If, later on, the buyer wants to get rid of the commercial time he or she bought, the network may try to sell it to a different advertiser if the marketplace demand is strong. If for some reason the spot does not run as promised, the buyer is given the option of a comparable spot on the program schedule. This is known as a *make-good*. That might mean moving with a program to another day or time, if the network decides to reschedule it, or staying in the same daypart but switching programs. When programs do not achieve the audience rating that the network had guaranteed to the advertiser, the network will then provide, over the course of a year, *audience deficiency units*, or ADUs. These no-charge units are provided in the same or comparable programs to the advertiser.

All national television time is priced based on a 30-second spot. For advertisers wishing to buy more or less time than that, the rates are adjusted accordingly. Hence, a 60-second spot costs twice as much, and a 15-second spot is half the full rate. Negotiations are conducted based on CPMs for the target, defined in terms of age and sex. For example, it could be the CPM for reaching women 18 to 49 or adults 25 to 54. As TV set-top box tuning data started to be used more for television, it enabled buys made on more granular targets because that tuning data can be matched up at the household level to many other data sources from companies such as Experian or Acxiom, so that the buyer can start to buy programs that are more likely to reach households with infants (for Huggies diapers) or high-income households (for Lexuses). In an addressable advertising environment, those are the only homes that would see the ads, while other networks or technology companies deliver ads to all homes but skew the buy to those households of greater interest.

Buying Time on Syndication and Cable

Buying national television time on syndication and cable is not that different from the broadcast network marketplace. There are long-term, scatter, and opportunistic buys available in each television form. Additional considerations need to be given, however, to the individual buys. With syndication, for example, *coverage* is critical. Because syndicated programs are sold to individual stations in each market, they may not be seen in every market across the country. The buyer therefore has to know what percent of stations in the U.S. will air a given program. It may be as low as 60 percent or as high as 99 percent. The day and/or time of airing will also vary by town or city, and although people do watch programs rather than dayparts, it may make a difference to the effectiveness of a media schedule if you are trying to reach women 25 to 54 with *Ellen* and find that it airs at 9:00 a.m. in Chattanooga, Tennessee, but at 3:00 p.m. in Gary, Indiana. The audience delivery and composition could be quite different in those markets because of that airtime variation.

Syndicated programs are guaranteed, but the syndicator will typically overstate the ratings estimate. That means the buyer then has to be given make-goods, either in the form of bonus units or cash back. While this might seem an inefficient way to operate, the syndication marketplace has been like this since its inception, and despite a decline in ratings beginning in the late 1990s, the marketplace still works this way. Many packaged goods advertisers still rely on syndication to reach their "average" American consumers.

Cable television also sells a good deal of its commercial time in advance, usually with guaranteed ratings. Cable is bought either by individual program or by daypart rotation. A few networks, such as Nick at Nite and Headline News, largely sell time this way, because there is strong enough advertiser demand for their units that they do not need to sell individual programs. While this might appear to be a big problem for advertisers, it is less critical on certain cable networks, where the programming is "vertical," and an advertiser knows that his spot will most likely air, for example, between news content on CNN or in classic sitcoms on Nick at Nite. Most others have moved to program-based buys as they have worked to create brand images for themselves based on their well-known personalities or, increasingly, their original programming. Examples here include Comedy Central's *The Daily Show* and ESPN's *Sports Center*.

MAKING IT LOCAL WITH TV AND RADIO

The purchase of time on spot television and spot radio has both similarities and differences to the network process. Local television buyers usually buy time on shorter notice than for national television. They also have to deal with individual stations in each market, rather than buying a complete network, unless they make a buy across various stations that are linked together into an ad sales network. The planner provides the buyer with the details of the specifications, which include the marketing and media objectives, a demographic and psychographic description of the target, the desired dayparts and flights, the number of ratings points per market and/or time period, the total budget, and the mix of commercial lengths (15, 30, and 60 seconds).

Armed with this information, the buyer can then start negotiating with stations in those markets. Rather than discussing the cost of an individual spot or the cost per thousand used in national television buys, both of which will vary considerably by market, buyers typically negotiate the cost per rating point, or CPP. That way, they ensure that the appropriate number of rating points are purchased at or below the amount budgeted. The negotiating process is quite subtle. The buyer does not want the seller to know how much money is available (as the station would want to get all of it), and the seller does not want the buyer to know how much inventory is available (as that would let the buyer know how low a price he or she could get). The buyer will usually talk to all of the stations in the market that have programs or formats appropriate for the target in the desired daypart and ask each of them to submit prices. For some advertisers, price is the most important criterion, so the buyer looks to purchase "tonnage"—lots of media weight at the lowest price available. For others, the program or format is key; they may be willing to pay slightly more to get a closer fit between target and vehicle. It depends on the strategy outlined in the media plan.

Once the buyer has received submissions from each station, he or she can then start negotiating to see if any of the sellers are willing to lower their price any further. Once final prices and terms are agreed to, then the buy is made, and an electronic confirmation of the order is sent from seller to buyer.

In theory, local television and radio buys are fixed; that is, the time is bought on a given daypart and/or program (unless the buyer purchases run-of-schedule, or ROS, which means that the station can air the spot at any time). In practice, however, stations may preempt a spot if another advertiser comes in who is willing to pay more for that time slot. If this happens, the first advertiser will usually request a make-good or compensation if the station airs their spot at a less favorable time. The make-good is supposed to be of equal or greater value.

While buying local radio is similar in many respects to buying television, there are two opportunities for advertisers that are commonly made available in the audio medium. The first is merchandising and promotions. This has become an extremely important consideration for many companies that use spot radio, particularly national advertisers. Local radio stations may be willing, as part of the deal, to run special contests for listeners, allow sponsorship of a commercial-free hour, or set up a remote site broadcast or hold a special event for the trade, for example. The Scion car dealership could offer a new car as the grand prize in an on-air contest; the afternoon music show could be aired from the dealer's showroom, or a cocktail reception for all new Scion owners could be held at the radio station one evening.

Such promotions need to be negotiated as part of the buy, but they may add considerably to the efficiency of the purchase.

The second difference that local radio can offer advertisers is the chance for live commercials. In the earliest days of radio, all commercials were spoken live by announcers on the air. Today, that is only possible at the local-market level. Some advertisers believe that having a local radio personality deliver the message adds greater authority and credibility to the product, giving it an implied endorsement. While this is not in fact true (the station never officially endorses any individual brand), it can be beneficial for the advertiser. In addition, because relatively few commercials are presented this way anymore, it offers another way to stand out from the crowd. The standard commercial length in local radio is 60 seconds, although 30-second commercials have become more common.

When buyers work with local rep firms in either TV or radio, they will send out an *avail* request that includes markets and dayparts, then the two sides will negotiate based on an overall cost per point, and typically go back and forth to agree on terms, often focusing on the share of the buy being given to a specific station in a market.

A Note about Buying Digital Audio

While the digital version of a magazine or newspaper is often negotiated into the print buy, for radio there is an additional option for the buyer. That is digital audio, buying ads with companies such as Pandora or Spotify. While the buys are made similarly to other digital media (see later), the audiences on which those buys are made are sometimes considered as radio and sometimes as digital. They have call letters similar to other radio stations and can be assessed in terms of quarter-hour ratings. At the same time, digital measurement companies provide impressions-based audiences for them, too.

THE GREAT OUTDOORS

Because outdoor billboards are bought on a market-by-market basis, the buying process is, in some ways, akin to local TV and radio buying. Here, instead of dealing with individual TV or radio stations (or rep firms that put stations together into a network), the media buyer must either deal with individual outdoor plant operators or with networks of plants that are available through large outdoor companies such as Clear Channel or Viacom.

Negotiations for outdoor billboards focus on several key elements: size, location, and cost or CPM. The first criterion to consider is the poster or panel size—from an eight-sheet to a painted bulletin. As explained in Chapter 4, different boards are purchased for different time frames, with posters typically being sold on a 30-day basis and bulletins sold in much longer-term deals, such as six months or one year.

Location is really the key as far as outdoor advertising is concerned. For certain products, such as a local restaurant, you might want to be on smaller posters in the city to remind people of your address; for hotels or gas stations, highways would make more sense, to reach drivers as they are passing through your area. And today, many advertisers place their billboards strategically close to their competitors' locations. CVS, for example, looks for boards that are near its key competitor, Walgreens, reminding consumers as they get close to Walgreens why they might want to reconsider that decision.

It is important, too, to know which side of the street the board is located (the right side is preferable) and whether there are any potential blockages that could get in the line of sight for the board, such as a tall building or tree. This kind of information can best be gained by actually going to the location to look at the board. The operator can provide you with a complete inventory of addresses for both bulletins and poster panels. In the case of posters, you can also find out if the poster is in an ethnic neighborhood and/or in a restricted location (no alcohol) and whether it is on a wall or a pole.

While billboards used to be bought by *showing*, or the number of daily exposures on the number of boards to generate the desired reach, today outdoor advertising is purchased purely on ratings, similar to other media, along with the cost of reaching 1,000 of the target audience (CPM). Unlike TV or radio, though, there are usually only a couple of operators to choose from in a given market, which limits the flexibility that the buyer has to negotiate. With considerable industry consolidation in recent years, many markets are now dominated by a single outdoor company that is part of a multimedia conglomerate. And even where there is more than one company to choose from, one will typically have better locations for a particular size board, while the other will have better offerings in a different size or location.

Once all of the negotiations have taken place, the media specialist will issue an outdoor authorization, laying out all of the details, or specifications, of the buy. These are then confirmed with the client and the seller, and the purchase can proceed.

DRIVING A DIGITAL BUY

As noted in Chapter 4, there are many forms of digital advertising, and the buying process continues to evolve. As with most other media forms, media specialists have the choice of working directly with individual websites, such as Epicurious.com, or placing buys with networks of aggregated sites, such as Tremor or Yume. In either case, the media buyer negotiates the ad placement (fixed position or rotation) and cost. Another type of buy is based on *behavioral* targeting, which targets users based on their prior behavior. For example, if you visit Amazon.com on a regular basis to look at the latest kitchen gadgets, then you might be sent an ad from Williams-Sonoma or crateandbarrel.com, because your behavior indicates you have an interest in those items. The benefit for advertisers is that they can find their target audience in places where they might not have expected them to be to find sites that the target considers *contextually relevant*. This may mean relevance to the campaign, such as an ad for Kellogg's Special K cereal that touts its value in a dieting plan on e-diets.com. Or it can be relevance to the target's mindset, such as ads that include JD Power award rankings appearing when a user is clicking on an automotive website searching for information.

In addition, the buyer has to determine with the seller the basis for the sale—cost per thousand impressions, cost per click, or cost per transaction, for example. Research of those who come to the site is often included as a "value added" bonus, though the drawback here is that it could be biased in favor of the site if they are conducting or hosting the survey. An alternative is to pay for "neutral" third-party research through companies such as comScore and Nielsen. In either case, the idea is to sample every *n*th person who comes to the site and offer them a survey that can include questions about advertising recognition or brand attitudes and compare those exposed to the ad to the nonexposed control group.

Much of the digital advertising marketplace is now bought *programmatically*, where both buying and selling occur automatically to reach precisely defined target audiences. Data about those potential audiences sit in a data management platform (DMP) that is accessed by ad exchanges, which aggregate the data and allow buyers to bid on the inventory. Advertisers place bids on different online inventory through their demand side platforms (DSPs), stating how much they are willing to pay to reach their desired target audiences on various sites. The publisher can then sell that space to the highest bidder. This programmatic marketplace has turned the display market into a quasi stock market.

INVESTING IN OWNED MEDIA

Although it might seem like an oxymoron to pay for media that a brand or company owns, the opportunities noted in Chapter 5 do often require investment and, sometimes, negotiation. Sponsorships, for example, are usually sold by the venue (sports stadium, concert stadium). Product placement or brand integration into TV shows and movies is typically offered by the producers of the entertainment, though TV networks have started to move into this highly profitable arena. For custom events, the cost discussions would occur with whatever company (media or otherwise) is hired to create and manage that event.

THE COST OF EARNED MEDIA

The intent of most earned media forms is for there to be little to no investment costs because word of mouth or social networks are supposed to "earn" consumer interest or action without having to spend money. When brands buy display or video ads on Facebook or Instagram, those are paid media buys that fall under the responsibility of the digital buyer. Similar to owned media opportunities, there may be some out-of-pocket costs (creation of a video news release to send to TV stations, for instance, or payment of the people who are "planted" in a social scene to promote your product). It does remain the media specialist's job to negotiate the price and determine the metrics against which the cost of the program will be evaluated (traffic, impressions, clicks, shares, tweets, etc.). The goal should be to try to make these buys as comparable as possible to the other media in the plan.

SUMMARY

Even the most impressive media plan will not achieve its goals if the buys are not made effectively. That means the time and space need to be purchased in accordance with the plan's specifications in terms of criteria such as timing, ad size, and placement or position within the media vehicle. For magazines and newspapers, editorial adjacencies may be key so the ad message is seen in an appropriate context, such as an ad for Verizon mobile phone service targeting business people in the business section of the *New York Times,* or an Olay anti-wrinkle cream targeting women in the beauty section of *Marie Claire* magazine. The costs for print media are usually negotiable, depending on the competitiveness of the magazine category.

Buying time on TV and radio is always done through negotiations, either with a network or individual stations. TV buys may be long term (purchased up front) or short term (in the scatter market). The guarantees and costs of those buys will vary accordingly. For radio, where most time is purchased locally, buyers deal with stations or rep firms that sell them a package of stations across the markets in which the buyer is interested. Deals are made based on the cost per rating point. For outdoor billboards, the key buying criterion to consider is the location of the board, whether a poster or a bulletin. Buyers negotiate the cost based on demographic ratings. The process can be handled with individual plant operators or through networks. For paid digital, the buys are made with individual sites or networks that aggregate those sites or programmatically through ad exchanges. With owned and earned media, it is the specialist's job to negotiate fair market value and determine the metrics against which to evaluate the media impact.

CHECKLIST: MAKING THE MEDIA BUYS

1. Do you have all the necessary specifications regarding the objectives, the target audience, vehicle preferences, GRP needs, and budget limitations to proceed to the buys?
2. Does the client have to approve the buys before they are finalized?
3. For magazines, is a discount available for a volume buy?
4. Do you want a preferred position for your magazine ad?
5. Are you trying to reach a more specialized or generalized audience with magazines (priced accordingly)?
6. Are any special promotions, editorial features, bonus circulation, or trade deals being offered by any of the magazines?
7. Do you want your newspaper ad to appear in a special section?
8. Are there any special instructions needed for your newspaper ad, such as a coupon or inclusion of color?
9. Do you want to buy time on network, cable, or syndicated TV?
10. Is your national television buy going to be made for the long term (up front) or short term (scatter)?
11. Can you get ratings guarantees for your national TV buy?
12. For a syndicated TV buy, what is your clearance?
13. With a cable TV buy, do you want a specific time period, or will a rotation suffice?
14. For a local TV buy, is media weight (tonnage) more important than specific program selection?
15. For local radio or local TV, do you want to deal directly with each station, or do you prefer to use a rep firm?
16. Are your outdoor billboards' locations satisfactory?
17. Have you purchased enough demographic ratings for outdoor posters in each market?
18. Have you negotiated digital ad placement and type with individual websites, search engines, or ad networks?
19. How many of your display ad buys will be auction-based and done programmatically?

20. What are the terms of negotiation for your owned and earned media?
21. What are the metrics you are using for the owned and earned media against which you will evaluate their cost efficiency and impact?

NOTE

1. "How the TV Nets Got the Upfront," Erwin Ephron, Ad Age Special Report on TV's Upfront, May 14, 2001, S2/22, *Advertising Age*, June 2005.

CHAPTER 10

EVALUATING THE MEDIA PLAN

One of the most often-repeated quotations about advertising was attributed to John Wanamaker, Philadelphia department store magnate, who said that he knew half of the money he spent on advertising was wasted; he just didn't know which half. Your job, as a media specialist, is to try to ensure that your client's dollars are not wasted. One way to achieve that is by evaluating the media plan before it is executed and then again once it is up and running.

It is no longer true that an annual plan is left unchanged for a whole year; more and more, advertisers will make changes to at least some part of the marketing plan while the campaign is running. This may be in response to changes in any part of the marketing mix. Consumer response could end up being greater or less than anticipated; product improvements could necessitate additional promotional efforts; new channels of distribution could become important; or competitive pricing strategies may require alterations to the original, approved plan. And beyond that, economic trends can affect almost all marketing efforts. For example, in recessionary times, most "experts" tend to predict that the economic hard times will be over soon, suggesting that consumer spending will improve. What often happens is that consumer confidence in the economy remains low for longer than such optimistic forecasts, leading people to continue their restrained purchasing habits. This has a marked effect on the manufacturers of high-ticket items such as cars and electronics. It also impacts overall eating habits, causing people to eat out less and stay home more.

This chapter presents four of the ways that a media plan can be evaluated, before and after it begins running. We have explained the concepts of reach and frequency. With today's sophisticated computer tools, syndicated data on past purchase and media consumption can be analyzed to give a "best guess" estimate of how well a medium, or total plan, will reach the chosen target audience. This can later be compared with actual results on reach and frequency to see how well the plan actually performed, which is crucial information for preparing next year's plan. The second type of evaluation is to check that your ads actually run as scheduled, a practice known as *post-buy analysis*. It is up to the media specialist to make sure that if, for some reason, the ad did not run as scheduled or was not positioned in the agreed-upon place, that some form of compensation is given, either monetary or in time or space. Third, it may well be worthwhile to spend additional dollars to research the consumer impact of the media (and/or marketing) plan. After you doubled the spending levels in television, are your brand's awareness levels considerably higher? How well is your commercial message being recalled now that you have switched dollars out of magazines and into digital? These kinds of questions can best be answered by talking to some of the consumers you were trying to reach. Last, but not least, in the weeks and months after your plan is executed, you can use statistical analysis to assess the return on investment, or payout, of your plan.

Pre-Plan Analysis

The first time to evaluate the impact of the media plan is before it is presented to the client. That is, in selecting the media vehicles you think will best meet the advertising and marketing objectives, the media specialist needs to figure out which combination of vehicles will do the best job of reaching the target an acceptable number of times. Data systems and tools are readily available to help make these kinds of analyses simple and fast.

For example, let's say you were considering two alternative combinations for your media plan for Pillsbury cake mix. The first combination would use monthly insertions in *Every Day with Rachael Ray* magazine, along with periodic commercials in prime time on the Lifetime cable television network. Another possibility would be to place continuous messages on cable, with occasional ads in the magazine. Here is how the two schedules might look for the year:

Schedule One	Schedule Two
10 insertions (50 GRPs) in *Rachael Ray* 400 GRPs in Lifetime	4 insertions (20 GRPs) in *Rachael Ray* 1,000 GRPs in Lifetime

And here is how the two schedules would perform against your target of women 25 to 54:

	Schedule One	Schedule Two
Total GRPs	450	1,020
Reach 1+	34.1%	32.6%
Reach 3+	25.2%	22.7%
Frequency	13.2	31.3

So, even though you are using far more cable in Schedule Two, the impact on the overall reach is actually less than if you used more magazine advertising, as in Schedule One.

POST-BUY ANALYSIS

What the media specialist must find out once the plan is running is whether the ads ran as scheduled and how well the plan actually delivered. For the first part, determining that the ads did in fact run as scheduled, you can turn to various sources, depending on the medium. For newspapers, there are *tear sheets*, which are provided by commercial services, to show you examples of the actual ad in the newspaper. Magazines will usually pro-vide copies of the issues in which your ad appears. For television and radio, you should receive affidavits confirming precisely when each spot aired. With digital ads, you will also receive affidavits confirming where your ad appeared and use a third-party service to verify that the ad was viewable. In each case, the media specialist must check that the terms of the contract were adhered to. If you requested being in the food section of the paper, or the first third of the magazine, or on the home page on a website, is that where your ad was placed?

For broadcast media, the task is usually more complicated because program schedules are far more prone to being changed. You might have arranged for your radio spot to air between 6:00 p.m. and 8:00 p.m., only to find that it came on at 5:30 p.m. or 8:20 p.m. Or, you could have bought a rotation of spots (ROS), which in theory means that your spots will run equitably in all dayparts. In analyzing the affidavits, you might discover that more than half of the messages were aired between midnight and 6:00 a.m., or at some other inappropriate time. It is then incumbent upon the station to explain what happened and, in all likelihood, offer some type of make-good, running the ad later in the correct daypart or provid-ing financial compensation for the cost differences between ROS and the overnight period.

In larger agencies or organizations, this post-analysis checking is typically done by the media buyers or business service department. It is more of an accounting than a media function but, ultimately, the media specialist should know what happened and why.

Later on, additional information becomes available to show how your ad schedule delivered. This is in the form of syndicated data, such as Nielsen for television, Nielsen Audio for radio, GfK MRI for print media, and comScore for all digital media. Each service provides the ratings and audience delivery of media vehicles to help you determine whether, in fact, you met the goals of your plan. Other companies can access this data also, acting as third-party vendors of the information.

The kinds of questions the data can help you answer include what percentage of the target was reached by the media (and vehicles) that you used (reach), and how often, on average, was the target exposed to them? It is worth emphasizing again that these terms refer only to media exposure and not to actual exposure to the ads themselves. They should therefore be thought of as *opportunities to see* your message. Many advertisers will discount or "weight" the exposure levels to account for this distinction, assuming, for example, that only half of the people reached by the media vehicle will actually see the ad. Or they may only look at the proportion of the target that is exposed a certain number of times (*effective reach*), assuming here that people will require several opportunities to see your message before they in fact will do so.

Custom Consumer Research

The importance of evaluating the plan's impact on consumers once it has gone into effect cannot be underestimated. That way you can find out, first, whether you got what you (or your client) paid for and, second, whether the plan worked as you intended. It will provide invaluable help in preparing for next year's plan, too. This may be by undertaking surveys of consumers before and after their exposure to your ads to assess their brand recall and any brand attitude shifts. Or it could be through qualitative research such as focus groups or in-depth interviews, where consumers are asked to explain their feelings about their media exposure in greater detail. Why did they pay attention to the TV ads but ignore the radio ads, for example? How were the mobile ads effective (or not) in influencing their purchase decision? Although ultimately the impact of the media plan, and the other elements of the marketing mix, are determined at the cash register, it is helpful to be able to analyze the individual parts to find out what is or is not working. Having said that, and acknowledging the truth to this chapter's opening comment by John Wanamaker, you should keep in mind that it is sometimes difficult to determine the precise effect of advertising media messages on consumers. We know *when* it is working, though we may not always know *how*.

ROI IMPACT

For more sophisticated analyses of media's impact, econometric or attribution modeling can provide the answer. Here, as noted in Chapter 7, complex statistical models analyze as many of the marketing mix variables as possible (depending on the category) to see what role advertising media play in generating sales (or other goals, such as awareness, consideration, or purchase intent). The models can look at everything from GRPs to distribution to weather patterns and attempt to isolate the part that each plays in the mix. For attribution modeling, the goal is not only to understand the role of each medium's individual contribution to the outcome, but how they worked collectively, over time. Is it more effective when consumers in the market for a sedan vehicle see your TV ad first, followed by the paid social media and print ads, with outdoor billboards, radio, and mobile ads sealing the deal close to the point of purchase?

Without evaluating how a media plan performs, we are left even more in the dark than when we began. In effect, it means that each time we create a plan, we end up recreating the wheel. This can lead you down two paths. Either the same plan is reproduced because it "seemed to work" (or at least didn't cause any disasters). Or the plan is completely changed to see if that makes a difference in sales, or awareness, or attitudes. Both of these options are flawed. To continue doing exactly the same thing as before without knowing whether it is working, or if it could possibly be improved upon, is detrimental to your product (and client), keeping them from performing at their best. Similarly, to overturn the plan without analyzing how it worked (or didn't work) means that you run the risk of losing the momentum your ads might have started to build and jeopardizes your chances for success.

So although there is a strong temptation, once the media plan is completed and the ads are running, to file it away and move on to the next task, the true media specialist will carry on through to the end. He or she is responsible for ensuring not only that the ads run as intended, but also that they delivered what was planned. If these two evaluation tasks are carried out successfully, you will not only have a more satisfied client, but will also have already taken an important step forward in preparing for next year's media plan.

SUMMARY

A completed media plan is really not final until it has been evaluated to see how it has performed. This should be done both before the plan is executed, by calculating estimates of reach and frequency that the plan should achieve, and afterward, through post-buy analyses to ensure that the ads ran as scheduled. If the messages did not air as intended and specified in the buys, it is up to the media specialist to obtain some type of compensation. Without these checks, there is no way of knowing whether this year's plan should be continued into the following year with or without modifications. And, although it is always difficult to pinpoint precisely the impact of advertising on sales, the process of evaluating the success or failure of the media plan in achieving the media, advertising, and marketing objectives will help the brand and the client know how to do better next year.

CHECKLIST: EVALUATING THE MEDIA PLAN

1. Have you performed reach and frequency analyses of the media plan before presenting it to the client?
2. Have you contacted clipping services or the print media themselves to determine that your ads ran as scheduled?
3. Are the post-buys for television and radio available to ensure that your ads ran as scheduled?
4. Do you have access to syndicated data such as Nielsen, Nielsen Audio, GfK MRI, and comScore for future analysis of how your media vehicles performed against your target?
5. Do you have ideas on how your media plan can be improved for next year?
6. Is there need, and budget, to conduct some custom consumer research to assess the impact of your media plan on consumer recall, attitudes, and opinions?
7. Can you bring together sufficient post-buy delivery data to incorporate into an econometric or attribution model that shows how each media type performed against your objectives?

KEY RESEARCH RESOURCES

Advertising Age
685 3rd Avenue, New York, NY 10017–4024
(212) 210–0100 www.adage.com
Industry trade journal, published 24 times a year

Advertising Research Foundation
432 Park Avenue South, 6th Floor, New York, NY 10016
(212) 751–5656 www.thearf.org
Primary industry research organization

Adweek
Mediabistro Holdings
825 8th Avenue, New York, NY 10019
www.adweek.com
Industry trade journal, published weekly

Alliance for Audited Media (formerly Audit Bureau of Circulations)
48 West Seegers Road, Arlington Heights, IL 60005
(224) 366–6939 www.auditedmedia.com
Circulation auditing company for magazine and newspaper industry

CEB Iconoculture
1919 North Lynn Street, Arlington, VA 22209
(571) 303–3000 www.cebglobalcom
Trends, observations, and consumer research, both qualitative and quantitative, in U.S. and global markets

comScore
11950 Democracy Drive, Suite 600, Reston, VA 20190
(703) 438–2000 www.comscore.com
Measures what people do as they use digital media (Internet, mobile, tablets, and television)

eMarketer
11 Times Square, New York, NY 10036
(800) 405–0844 www.emarketer.com
Provides statistics and information on trends in digital marketing, media, and commerce

Forrester Research
60 Acorn Park Drive, Cambridge, MA 02140
(617) 613–5730 www.forrester.com
Research and advisory firm in the technology space

The Futures Company/Yankelovich
11 Madison Avenue, 12th Floor, New York, NY 10010
(212) 896–8112 www.thefuturescompany.com
Consumer research company that offers annual trend studies on various demographic or lifestyle segments; part of Kantar Media

GfK MRI
200 Liberty Street, 4th Floor, New York, NY 10281
(212) 240–5300 www.gfk.com
Measures demographic, media, and lifestyle information among 50,000 adults per year; used for target and audience analysis

Ipsos Affluent Study
1271 Avenue of the Americas, 15th Floor, New York, NY 10020
(212) 265–3200 www.ipsos-na.com
Provides media, demographic, and lifestyle information for upper-income adults

IRI
150 N. Clinton Street Chicago, IL 60661
(312) 726–1221 www.iriworldwide.com
Collects and reports marketer and shopper information using supermarket checkout data

JD Power & Associates
3200 Park Center Drive, 13th Floor, Costa Mesa, CA 92626
(888) 477–5372 www.jdpower.com
Provides annual demographic, lifestyle, and media information linked to automotive industry

Kantar Media Audiences
11 Madison Avenue, 12th Floor, New York, NY 10010
(212) 991–6000 www.kantarmedia.com
Parent company to several audience research companies (TGI), as well as social media listening

Kantar Media Intelligence
11 Madison Avenue, 12th Floor, New York, NY 10010
(212) 991–6000 www.kantarmediana.com
Measures advertisers' media spending across 20 media types; owned by WPP

Media Ocean
45 West 18th Street, New York, NY 10011
(212) 633–8100 www.mediaocean.com
Third-party software platform and systems to process audience data for buying and selling media; also major bill payment system for advertising agencies

Mintel
333 West Wacker Drive, Suite 1100, Chicago, IL 60606
(312) 932–0400 www.mintel.com
Global market and consumer intelligence on product categories and consumer trends

Nielsen
85 Broad Street, New York, NY 10004
(800) 864–1224 www.nielsen.com
Main provider of national and local television viewing information; national service based on national panel of 40,000 households using people meters, local service based on local people meters in top 25 markets; household set meters (top 55 markets); and additional weekly viewing diaries (all remaining non-LPM markets)

Nielsen Audio
85 Broad Street, New York, NY 10004
(800) 864–1224 www.nielsen.com
Radio audience measurement using weekly listening diaries and personal portable meters (PPM)

Nielsen IMS
85 Broad Street, New York, NY 10004
(800) 864–1224 www.nielsen.com
Third-party media software that provides media planning tools to assess multimedia audiences

Nielsen Scarborough Research
85 Broad Street, New York, NY 10004
(800) 864–1224 www.scarborough.com
Measures demographic, media, and lifestyle information in 75 local markets

Simmons Market Research
800 Fairway Drive, Suite 295, Deerfield Beach, FL 33441
(800) 551–6425 www.simmonssurvey.com
Collects demographic, media, and lifestyle information on 40,000 adults each year; offers special annual studies on children, teens, and Hispanics

SRDS Media Solutions
600 North River Road, Suite 900, Rosemont, IL 60018
(800) 851–7737 www.srds.com
Provides databases of media rates and information on all major media categories; owned by Kantar Media

Telmar Information Services
711 3rd Avenue, 15th Floor, New York, NY 10017
(212) 725–3000 www.telmar.com
Third-party media software company that provides media planning tools to assess multimedia audiences

KEY MEDIA ORGANIZATIONS

Advertising Club of New York
989 Avenue of the Americas, New York, NY 10018
(212) 533–8080 www.theadvertisingclub.org
Forum for ad professionals

Advertising Council
815 2nd Avenue, 9th Floor, New York, NY 10017
(212) 922–1500 www.adcouncil.org
Organization sponsoring and promoting public service advertising

Advertising Educational Foundation
220 East 42nd Street, Suite 3300, New York, NY 10017–5806
(212) 986–8060 www.aef.com
Distributes educational content to enrich understanding of advertising

Advertising Research Foundation
432 Park Avenue South, 6th Floor, New York, NY 10016
(212) 751–5656 www.thearf.org
Industry organization focused on Advertising and Media Research

Advertising Self-Regulatory Council
112 Madison Avenue, 3rd Floor, New York, NY 10016
(866) 334–6272 www.asrcreviews.org
Fosters truth and accuracy for national advertisers through voluntary
self-regulation

Advertising Women of New York
28 West 44th Street, Suite 912, New York, NY 10036
(212) 221–7969 www.awny.org
Forum to advance women in the field of communications

American Advertising Federation (AAF)
1101 Vermont Avenue NW, Suite 500, Washington, DC 20005
(202) 898–0089 www.aaf.org
Protects and promotes advertising; sponsors annual National Student
Ad Competition (NSAC) and has 226 college chapters with nearly 8,000
undergraduate members; offers more than 1,000 internship opportunities

American Association of Advertising Agencies (AAAA)
1065 Avenue of the Americas, 16th Floor, New York, NY 10118
(212) 682–2500 www.aaaa.org
Main trade organization of advertising agencies

American Marketing Association
311 South Wacker Drive, Suite 5800, Chicago, IL 60606
(312) 542–9000 www.ama.org
Professional association for marketers with strong educational component

Art Directors Club
106 West 29th Street, New York, NY 10001
(212) 643–1440 www.adcglobal.org
International group that provides forum for creatives in advertising
communication

Association of Hispanic Advertising Agencies
8280 Willow Oaks Corporate Drive, Suite 600, Fairfax, VA 22031
(703) 610–9014 www.ahaa.org
Trade group for Hispanic advertising agencies

The Association of Magazine Media
757 3rd Avenue, 11th Floor, New York, NY 10017
(212) 872–3700 www.magazine.org
Trade group promoting consumer magazines

Association of National Advertisers (ANA)
708 3rd Avenue, 33rd Floor, New York, NY 10017
(212) 697–5950 www.ana.net
Main trade organization for national advertisers

Digital Content Next
1350 Broadway, Suite 606, New York, NY 10018
(646) 473–1000 www.digitalcontentnext.org
Trade group for digital content providers

Direct Marketing Association (DMA)
1333 Broadway, Suite 300, New York, NY 10018
(212) 768–7277 www.the-dma.org
Global trade organization for the direct marketing industry

Interactive Advertising Bureau (IAB)
116 East 27th Street, 7th Floor, New York, NY 10016
(212) 380–4700 www.iab.net
Trade group promoting interactive advertising

International Advertising Association (IAA)
747 3rd Avenue, 2nd Floor, New York, NY 10017
(646) 722–2612 www.iaaglobal.org
Professional group focused on advertising as a global industry; has chapters
in more than 50 U.S. universities

Local Search Association
820 Kirts Boulevard, Suite 100, Troy, MI 48084
(248) 224–6200 www.thelsa.org
Trade group promoting yellow pages and local search marketing in print,
digital, mobile, and social to help local businesses get found

Mobile Marketing Association
41 East 11th Street, 11th Floor, New York, NY 10003
(646) 257–4515 www.mmaglobal.com
Trade association representing all sides of mobile industry

National Association of Broadcasters (NAB)
1771 N Street NW, Washington, DC 20036
(202) 429–5300 www.nab.org
Trade group promoting the local television and radio industry

Newspaper Association of America (NAA)
4401 Wilson Boulevard, Suite 900, Arlington, VA 22203
(571) 366–1000 www.naa.org
Trade group promoting newspapers

The One Club
260 5th Avenue, 2nd Floor, New York, NY 10001
(212) 979–1900 www.oneclub.org
Organization to promote excellence in advertising through an annual creative awards show

Outdoor Advertising Association of America (OAAA)
1850 M Street NW, Suite 1040, Washington, DC 20036
(202) 833–5566 www.oaaa.org
Trade group promoting the outdoor advertising industry

Point of Purchase Advertising International (POPAI)
440 North Wells Street, Suite 740, Chicago, IL 60654
(312) 863–2900 www.popai.com
Global association for in-store marketing industry

Radio Advertising Bureau (RAB)
125 West 55th Street, 5th Floor, New York, NY 10019
(212) 681–7200 www.rab.com
Trade group promoting radio advertising

Television Bureau of Advertising (TVB)
120 Wall Street, 15th Floor, New York, NY 10005
(212) 486–1111 www.tvb.org
Trade group promoting the broadcast television industry, with particular focus on spot TV

Traffic Audit Bureau for Media Measurement
561 7th Avenue, 12th Floor, New York, NY 10018
(212) 972–8075 www.tabonline.com
Audits circulation of and provides ratings for out-of-home media and supports other out-of-home research initiatives

Video Advertising Bureau (VAB)
830 3rd Avenue, 2nd Floor, New York, NY 10022
(212) 508–1200 www.thevab.com
Trade organization for ad-supported television

Word of Mouth Marketing Association (WOMMA)
200 East Randolph, Suite 1500, Chicago, IL 60601
(312) 577–7610 www.womma.org
Trade association for the word of mouth marketing industry

World Federation of Advertisers
166 Avenue Louise, 1050 Brussels, Belgium
(011–32) 2–502–5740 www.wfanet.org
Trade group representing the global interests of marketers

INDEX

Page numbers in italic format indicate exhibits and tables.